In Black and White

Voices of Apartheid

In Black and White
Voices of Apartheid

Barbara Hutmacher

Introduction **Roger Omond**
Foreword **Donald Woods**

ALETHEIA BOOKS
University Publications of America

First published in the United States by
University Publications of America, Inc. (1982)

Frederick, Maryland

ISBN: 0-89093-465-7

Library of Congress Catalog Card Number: 82-6772

Manufactured in the United States of America

First published in Great Britain by Junction Books Ltd.

Contents

To the people of the Border and in particular to those individuals, some of them now dead or exiled, whose stories make up this book.

Acknowledgements

A very special thanks must go to Sylvia Hagerty of East London who, in her usual thorough way, gathered much of the information about people used in the Epilogue. I also wish to express my gratitude to Bob Baker, Dr Mort Vinecor and Bob Holt for their professional advice and encouragement, to Donald Woods and Roger Omond for their unique contributions, and finally and especially to Fraser for his boundless patience and support during the too many months of writing.

Abbreviations

ANC	African National Congress
BCP	Black Community Programmes
BPC	Black Peoples' Convention
CRC	Coloured Representative Council
NP	National Party
NRP	New Republic Party (formerly UP)
NUSAS	National Union of South African Students
PAC	Pan-Africanist Congress
PFP	Progressive Federal Party (formerly PP)
PP	Progressive Party
PRP	Progressive Reform Party
SAP	South African Party
SASO	South African Students' Organization
UP	United Party

Foreword

It isn't often that one has the experience of being interviewed as part of the subject of a book, then being invited to write the foreword. For me the experience is overlaid with a special sense of pleasure, because the author is one of my favourite human beings. When Barbara Hutmacher first came to work for me on the *Daily Dispatch* I soon realized that she was an unusually perceptive person. On Saturday mornings I used to drop in to a chair in her office for a chat: those chats were often one-sided because I did most of the talking and Barbara most of the listening.

Her gift of being a good listener to many people in our community resulted in this book — a rare and revealing glimpse into our microcosmic area of South Africa. Reading over all the interviews in it I am struck by how faithfully she has recorded what she experienced, and how freely she has let the people concerned speak for themselves. The result of all her work is now here in print — an accurate cross-section of a strange little community awaiting its own apocalypse.

It is both amusing and sad to read the interview with an eccentric such as H. Veen: his irrationality is one of the more extreme forms of the general irrationality of apartheid — an irrationality glimpsed here in the remarks of even such well-intentioned people as Corder Tilney. It all comes through, even when those interviewed are on their best behaviour.

Then there are people like Trudi Thomas, one of those rare individuals who have the qualities of a saint. It is in countries like South Africa, where the issues are still raw and basic, that the gut-realities of the situation produce extremes of goodness along with extremes of evil.

Somewhere in the middle are the rest of us — those of us who could perceive something of the developing tragedy of our country and felt we could do something to avert it. We, and friends like the

Belonskys, the Van Gends, the Omonds and others reflected in these pages, knew that our influence was miniscule, but we did what we felt we should do at that time and in that place, and the author has caught us as we were then.

Barbara Hutmacher's book will help to enlighten people about South Africa through this candid glimpse of a section of it. Most books on South Africa are general, dealing with the broad issues, but Barbara's book is specific, and as far as I know is the first such example of a professional journalist's cameo of a South African community.

Roger Omond's introduction is splendid. It provides the perspective for what follows, and nobody is better qualified to write it. I was often proud of the *Daily Dispatch,* and recalling the calibre of people on the staff during my editorship — Barbara Hutmacher, Fraser MacLean and Roger Omond — I have an abiding sense of privilege through my association with them.

I would like to be able to say that my commendation of Barbara Hutmacher's fine book is based on an outsider's assessment of its merits. I'm sure readers will agree that it has these merits, but I can't be objective about them. The book will have to be judged by others less partial.

I commend it nevertheless, without reservations, and with every wish for its deserved success.

Donald Woods

Introduction

The Border area of South Africa, centred around East London, is an almost perfect microcosm of the land of apartheid. It faces, in more concentrated and immediate forms, every problem of the country. It is frontier territory — in geographical, political, social and economic terms. It is an area of paradoxes, mirroring the country at large.

In this area came the first contact and conflict between black and white. At issue then was the question of who should occupy and own the land: this remains a major controversy today. The Dutch, who arrived in South Africa in 1652, were moving east from Cape Town in the late 1700s and the Africans west. The fighting over land, known as the Frontier Wars, lasted for a century leaving the blacks defeated. Today much of the area is black-owned because of the ruling white National Party's Bantustan policy. Bantustans, or 'homelands', the theory runs, are where the black man finds his place in the sun: owning the land, running his own government, working in his own economy. The practice is rather different from the theory, and there is deep-rooted controversy within both black and white communities about the entire policy.

In geographical and historical terms, the Border is on the frontier. It is midway between Cape Town (where the first white settlers landed) and Durban (where some of the last waves of immigrants arrived — Indian labourers in the latter half of the nineteenth century and whites dispossessed of their lands in Kenya, Zambia and Zimbabwe-Rhodesia).

The Border is also 700 miles from the Witwatersrand industrial complex, where the gold is mined that made this industrialization both necessary and possible. Yet little of that wealth percolates through to the Border — which adds to its many problems.

Politically, it is where the government's Bantustan policy was first tested. Today Transkei, the first 'homeland', is an independent state an hour's drive from East London. Even closer is the Ciskei, another Bantustan moving towards independence. (In February, 1980, however, the Quail Commission, appointed by the Ciskei Government to investigate whether the Bantustan should take independence, recommended against this final step, suggesting instead that a new multi-racial state, with blacks and whites sharing power, should be created in the Border and Ciskei. The Ciskei Government accepted the recommendation against independence. Whether the multi-racial state will be created remains to be seen: on balance it seems unlikely, and the Ciskei could still opt for independence in the not-too-distant future.) The area also provides the headquarters of the black consciousness movement. Those radicals (in white South African terms) demand nothing less than majority rule over the whole of South Africa, and a socialist economy — goals similar to the two other black liberation movements, the African National Congress (ANC) and the Pan-Africanist Congress (PAC), both of which have strong ties to the Border. All three now are illegal organizations according to statutes passed by the whites-only parliament.

So the conflict between black and white that started in the late eighteenth century in this region goes on today. It is not, of course, confined to the Border area, but it is present here in immediate and concentrated forms: black versus black, black versus white and (to a lesser extent) white versus white. The latter conflict began when Britain took over control of the Cape colony in 1802. The Dutch settlers, suspicious of outsiders, were almost anarchic, fearing and despising government controls.

By the time the British arrived, the Dutch had migrated from the Cape to around Grahamstown, and the clashes with the blacks moving in the opposite direction had begun. The new British colonial administration realized, somewhat reluctantly, that the best way to keep the peace between black and white was to populate the area with new settlers. In 1820 just over 5,000 British settlers were imported; in the 1850s 2,000 German peasants and troops were brought in as well. In both cases, the overriding aim was to keep the land in white hands.

So the settlers were given the best farmland (ill-suited though it may have been to British immigrants with little agricultural experience). They established rudimentary centres of what is now called Western civilization, and treated the blacks as marauders or reservoirs of cheap labour. But the settlers also brought with them what have been called 'the habits of free men' — a desire to rule themselves, not to be subject to the whim of a colonial governor, some nodding acquaintance with the tide of liberal thought that was sweeping Europe in the aftermath of the Napoleonic Wars. The Dutch, or Boers as they were now calling themselves, shared many of the English settlers' desires. But they perceived the British as conquerors, and what is more conquerors with some strange idea that the blacks were, or could one day be, equal to the whites. The Boers retreated in disgust at the English liberalism to undertake in 1836 what became known as the Great Trek to Natal, the Orange Free State and Transvaal. Unfortunately, they found that the British followed them. A man like Cecil John Rhodes wanted both the gold that was found in the Boer's Transvaal Republic and the British Empire to be extended through Africa. When the Boers ran out of land, some returned to the Border area they had abandoned at the start of the Great Trek. They are now a sizeable minority among the whites in the Border and East London.

For many years East London (first called Port Rex) was little more than a convenient harbour for supplies destined to go inland; King William's Town, 40 miles away, was the administrative and military capital of the region. It was in the late eighteenth century and early nineteenth century that the hinterland of East London grew in importance as it became the site of conflict between black and white. The placing of 5,000 British settlers to the west — around Grahamstown — in 1820 pushed the psychological white border closer to East London, and by 1835 the mouth of the Buffalo River where the city now stands was included as part of the 'conquered territory' taken from the blacks by the British colonial government and renamed the Province of Queen Adelaide.

That year, and again in the following year, the possibilities of a port to ease the supply of troops and guns and food for the whites inland at centres like Fort Beaufort and King William's Town were investigated. Until then, supplies had to be landed at Port Elizabeth, 200 miles to the south, and transported overland. The Buffalo River's harbour prospects were considered good, and in 1836 the brig *Knysna* was charted to land supplies there. The brig was owned by the Rex family — thought to be illegitimate descendants of an English monarch — and so the harbour became known as Port Rex. From King William's Town, Captain John Bailie was sent to collect the cargo, and it was he who hoisted the Union Jack on Signal Hill, close to the present-day harbour, claiming the future port for Britain.

But the British had Port Rex for less than two months: the Province of Queen Adelaide was handed back to the African tribes on 31 December 1836 in a colonial mix-up and reversal of policy caused, at least partly, by the expense of keeping the peace in the area. Ten years later, shortly after another Frontier War had broken out in the continuing conflict between black and white for land, the British returned and again made it a supply base for troops in the interior. The following year, 1847, a start was made on laying out a town on the West Bank which became the nucleus of the present city. It included the establishment of Fort Glamorgan: a name that survives as one of South Africa's grimmest prisons. In 1848 the colonial Governor of the Cape, Sir Harry Smith, annexed the Buffalo River mouth and all the land for two miles around, naming it East London. In 1857, once again trying to populate the interior with whites, Britain imported 2,315 German settlers as a buffer against the still restive blacks. Settlement then began on the East Bank of the river.

Development was slow rather than spectacular — as it has been ever since. East London, as part of one of the two Kaffraria constituencies, was given representation in the Cape Parliament with its limited powers of self-government in 1865. The biggest boost came in the 1870s with the discovery of diamonds at Kimberley and the realization that the Cape needed more efficient ports to cope with the huge increase in seaborne traffic. In 1873 work on development of the harbour, and on a railway from East London to Queenstown 120 miles away, set East London moving. The same year the three separate villages that made up the settlement were amalgamated, to be joined later by the village of Cambridge. Economically, there was steady progress: the harbour was expanded and for several years shipped more wool overseas than any other South African port. Fruit, beef and lamb all became major exports.

Politically, the mainly English-speaking whites of the city are and were conservative. But they were conservative in the mould of the opposition United Party — partly because the UP was the English-speaker's party and the National Party, which came to power in 1948, was seen as the Afrikaner's political home. It was only in the 1960s that the Nationalists managed to win a Border constituency, Queenstown. Then, in the 1977 general election, the opposition citadel that was the Border crumbled.

It was a swift Nationalist victory. The East London City seat, for example, had gone uncontested by the Nationalists only three years before, but in 1977 they won by a majority of 2,951 votes out of a total electorate of about 10,000. In the Albany constituency, centred around the almost archetypal English-speaking city of Grahamstown, the Nationalists won by 971 votes — partly because the opposition vote was split three ways. In King William's Town, the

Nationalists turned a 1974 defeat by 478 votes into a victory three years later by 2,912. Only East London North stood firm.

The string of defeats was partly because the United Party, which commanded loyal and often unthinking support in the Border as elsewhere, changed its name and lost its most precious asset — its identity and identifiability. The party that had been narrowly defeated by the Nationalists in 1948 also had fudged its policies and hedged its bets: relatively liberal one day, conservative the next. On its right was the National Party; on its left the Progressive Party — the UP shed votes to both sides. In a final, desperate effort to revive its fortunes, the UP changed its name to the New Republic Party. But the gamble failed, and throughout the Cape Province the only MP it returned to parliament came from East London North.

The Nationalists were perceived to be tough: the party that could protect South Africa against the world's condemnation of the apartheid policies it had introduced. The UP/NRP was divided, its string of election defeats had demoralized it, and nobody really knew any longer what it stood for.

In opposition to the UP/NRP was the Progressive Party (later the Progressive Federal Party), formed as a more liberal offshoot of the official Opposition which the UP had formed since 1947. It had a relatively small number of fanatically loyal supporters who had worked faithfully in the years since its formation in 1959. But it never managed to attract votes in the Border, mainly because it was too 'liberal'. In the East London North constituency — wealthy suburbs where it should have been the party that the bourgeoisie turned to — its highest ever total was 2,928 votes. In East London City it was a mere 1,287, and in Albany 3,257 — second to the Nationalists but not enough to win the seat.

Paradoxically for a city whose white population is innately conservative, the local newspaper was perhaps the most radical in the country. The *Daily Dispatch* succoured the white liberals in the PFP and to its left. It was the first newspaper to pay serious attention to the burgeoning black consciousness movement, partly because of the friendship between its editor, Donald Woods, and the movement's founder, Steve Biko. Yet the paper relied heavily on white advertising, controlled by the conservatives. The *Dispatch*'s answer to this was to expand its black readership and to point out that the black market was an important new one for advertisers. By the 1970s more blacks than whites read the *Dispatch* — the only white-run newspaper in the country to have that advantage. White conservatives might fume about the paper's editorials and news coverage, but they knew they had to use it to attract the consumers who would buy their products.

Outside the PFP and the *Dispatch* were other groups of white liberals: the Institute of Race Relations, the Black Sash and various church and charitable groups helping the black poor and needy. Their memberships were not large: the same people would reappear in different capacities in different organizations. Most felt that they were a beleaguered minority, caught in the middle between white racism and black reaction, searching somewhat desperately for a middle path.

That road has not yet been found. The white liberals have not discovered a role for themselves; East London itself is uncertain about its future. The main reason for that is the grand design of apartheid — or, as changing Nationalist government euphemisms have called it, separate development, parallel development, separate freedoms, peaceful coexistence. For it is in the eastern part of the Cape Province that apartheid is best seen. The Transkei Bantustan came first, shortly after the then Prime Minister, Dr Hendrik Verwoerd, ordained in 1959 that henceforth relations with the blacks would be regulated through self-governing Bantustans which would be led towards independence. Then came the Ciskei.

Even the dullest white supremacist who cared to look at a map realized that the patchwork quilt of small bits of land making up the Ciskei had to be consolidated — and that consolidation leading to independence was nonsensical unless East London was incorporated into the Ciskei. They were not reassured by government promises that it would never happen: time and again in the 1960s and early 1970s the same administration had pledged that the nearby small white holiday resort of Port St Johns would not, in the South African shorthand, 'go black'. But Port St Johns had been handed to the black Transkei Government.

The threat of 'going black' still faces East London, hampering, some say, its economic development and sapping its self-confidence, although others argue that settling the city's status once and for all and making it the Ciskei's port would bring new investment to the area. The argument continues in the wake of the Quail Commission recommendation of a new multiracial state in the Border-Ciskei area. In the meanwhile, East London continues as a rather embattled anachronism.

The city's street names reveal the Englishness of the place: Oxford, Cambridge, Caxton, Fleet, Gladstone, Tennyson, Longfellow, Browning, Burns and a host of others named after

English and Scottish counties. There is a suburb called Cambridge and another called Selborne after a half-remembered Earl who came to South Africa as Britain's High Commissioner in 1905 and who also lent his name to the city's premier school for boys. The *Daily Dispatch* was known for its outspoken liberalism but, paradoxically, until a few years ago defiantly flew the Union Jack more than a decade after South Africa had left the Commonwealth. To many people, at least until the 1960s, England was regarded as 'home', even if these descendants of the 1820 settlers never went there except on holiday after a leisurely trip on a Union Castle mailship.

White East London is essentially middle class, conservative and English-speaking. The older houses in the solid and select suburb of Selborne once attracted the elite who have now tended to move to newer suburbs like Bonnie Doone on the Nahoon, one of the city's three rivers, or Beacon Bay. The business centre of the city is stunted and architecturally old-fashioned in the style of the 1920s and 1930s: few shop or office blocks rise more than four storeys and there are only a couple of skyscrapers. The city has a depressed, and depressing, air about it: to local fury some years ago South Africa's leading financial magazine ran a cover story on East London headlined: 'Quiet: City sleeping'. It is both provincial and insular. Partly it is because East London is physically small and has a population to match: 60,000 whites, 12,000 Coloureds, 2,000 Asians and, officially, a mere 52,000 Africans. But these government figures distort the true picture. There are anything up to a quarter of a million blacks in the bulging township of Mdantsane — but that does not count because Mdantsane is part of the Ciskei. Yet the vast majority are dependent on East London for everything from grocery shopping to employment.

East London's insularity is also explained by the lack of industry to attract new people to the city and by the fact that it has no university (the nearest for whites is Rhodes, 110 miles away in Grahamstown; for blacks it is Fort Hare in Alice, 80 miles away). It must also be a product of a frontier heritage and the new Ciskei and Transkei borders imposed by Government, combined with decades of economic neglect. East London sold itself to the rest of South Africa for years as a holiday resort and a pensioner's paradise: there was an almost deliberate policy by the City Council after the Second World War (which gave the country a massive impetus to industrialization) not to go for industrial development.

Yet 200 miles down the coast, East London's virtual twin city of Port Elizabeth opted for factories and business: today it is a much bigger, wealthier industrial sprawl while East London has been trying belatedly, and generally unsuccessfully, for little more than a decade to attract the industries it desperately needs. When the city council did wake up to the fact that industry equalled both money and employment, it sited its new industrial complex in Berlin, 25 miles away. The reasons were complicated, tied in with the presence of Mdantsane nearby, government policy to encourage new growth points rather more than expanding existing ones, and (it is rumoured) not unrelated to the fact that some people in influential positions had been shrewd enough to buy land beforehand in Berlin which could be sold at a nice profit. But Berlin has been a disastrous failure and an expensive one.

What industry there is in East London cannot hope to employ even a percentage of the job seekers. Some factories are labour intensive: Wilson Rowntrees and Cyril Lord, for example. But most of the firms that started in East London's mini-boom in the 1960s and early 1970s employ only a few hundred people each. Leaders of commerce and industry have tried in vain to bring prosperity to the city by persuading the government to make East London a free port — a kind of Tangiers of the south. Pretoria remains unmoved. East London, which has South Africa's only river port, on the Buffalo River, handles a mere 3.5 million tons of cargo a year, compared with Port Elizabeth's 7.3 million and Durban's 35 million. Yet at one stage East London was the country's biggest exporter of wool. It imports and exports for the Border and Transkei, but both Bantustans plan new harbours of their own, and existing dock facilities are ill-equipped for containerization.

The city once hoped to attract the nationalized iron and steel corporation, Iscor, to set up a plant but, like so many others, it went elsewhere. Good Hope Textiles, British-controlled, was established in the late 1940s near King William's Town, 40 miles away; Cyril Lord came in the 1960s shortly before its British parent company went bankrupt; British Leyland's Chairman Sir Michael Edwardes received some of his early executive experience at a battery manufacturing company on the West Bank (where most of the industry is located); Parker Pen, CDA (makers of Mercedes cars) and a few canning companies and some light engineering firms are also on the West Bank; the American-owned Johnson and Johnson is a few miles from the city centre. East London contributes somewhere between 0.5 and 2 per cent to South Africa's industrial output; Port Elizabeth (its once-similar twin) with its adjacent Uitenhage 7.4 per cent.

Yet East London provides a comfortable living for most of its whites. The beaches are superb; the climate temperate although the wind blows constantly; there are reputed to be more sports clubs and golf clubs for a population its size than in any other South African city; the beachfront hotels are adequate. White unemployment is close to zero.

For blacks it is a different story: figures for black unemployment are not readily available, but it has been estimated at 20 per cent throughout South Africa and certainly is higher in a depressed area like East London. The pace of white living is measured, and virtually alone of South Africa's major centres, there is time for office and shop workers (if they are white) to go home for lunch. Signs of white prosperity can be seen in the new ranch-type houses — three bedrooms, garage and sometimes a swimming pool — in the new suburbs.

Two concerns govern the lives of blacks in the frontier territory of East London and its environs: the hunt for work and the search for political freedom. Employment is not easy to come by, pay is low (probably the lowest of any industrialized centre in South Africa) and job security minimal. There is also a large reservoir of unemployed which makes any attempt at unionizing workers hazardous and difficult: labour 'agitators' can be fired without fear of legal repercussions. Managements seldom if ever take into account the views of their black workers: even at the *Daily Dispatch,* probably the most liberal employer on the Border, there is no formal machinery for consultation, let alone negotiation, between the mass of black employees and the management.

The search for political rights is equally haphazard and hazardous. Historically, the black versus white conflict occurred first in the Eastern Cape and Border, from the clashes over land and cattle that led to a succession of frontier wars beginning in 1779 and continuing for the next century. But the various tribes were not united at all times against the whites, and successive generals and administrators, sometimes aided by white missionaries, made clever use of tribal rivalries and splits to divide and rule. Tribal and political divisions remain a force today, although there is concern particularly among more radical blacks that there should be unity. Historically, too, as blacks started and developed their own political organizations, a significant number — if not the majority — of leaders came from the Eastern Cape, Border, Ciskei and Transkei. They stretch back at least to the formation of the African National Congress in 1912. Among the more famous are men like Z.K. Matthews, Joe Matthews, Nelson Mandela, Govan Mbeki, D.D.T.

Jabavu, Robert Sobukwe and Potlako Leballo, all with their roots in this area, and, more recently, Steve Biko and his black consciousness movement.

The banning of the ANC and its off-shoot, the Pan-Africanist Congress, in 1960 drove both organizations underground and into a campaign of violence against a government that had determinedly ignored and trampled on black calls for freedom. More recently, the black consciousness movement was also banned and driven underground. But these prohibitions, which recall in some ways the century of conflict in the Frontier Wars tend to obscure the last half of the eighteenth century when, it seemed, an accommodation could be worked out between black and white.

The blacks had been forced off the land by the importation of the British settlers in 1820 and German settlers in 1857. The latter settled in the immediate hinterland of East London; Berlin, Sterkstroom, Stutterheim and Hamburg, among others, are all towns on the Border that show their German origin from that period. In 1853 some of the responsibility for government passed from the Colonial Office in London to Cape Town when the Cape colony was granted limited powers of self-government. All Her Majesty's subjects 'without distinction to class or colour' were entitled to the franchise if they could meet the property and financial qualifications. That ushered in 57 years of a relatively liberal tradition that influenced generations of black leaders for years afterwards.

Even during this allegedly liberal period, however, white politicians perceived a threat to their interests and those of the white voters: Cecil Rhodes in the 1870s raised the franchise qualifications to exclude the 'red blanket' blacks — a euphemism for unwesternized peasants, many of them concentrated on the Border — who could have attained the vote. Yet by the 1880s there were still more than 12,000 blacks on the Cape common voters' roll, and in the five Eastern Cape constituencies they made up 47 per cent of the electorate — a proportion that no politician could afford to ignore.

By the 1900s, after the Anglo-Boer War and when unification of the Cape with the other colonies of the Transvaal, Orange Free State and Natal was beginning to be discussed, 16 per cent of the Cape common roll was black — 10 per cent Coloured and 6 per cent African. Peter Walshe, a white liberal academic, writes in *Black Nationalism in South Africa:*

The Cape system offered a new method of political adjustment, an alternative to the wars of resistance. The non-racial qualified franchise, allied to the right to purchase land outside the [black] reserves, meant that the Cape offered a working system for the governance of varied peoples under the integrating forces of modernisation. Here was an important precedent, not some vague theory, but a practical example of the non-racial principle enshrined in legislation.

Walshe's view is probably too sanguine, and would be disputed by more radical historians and politicians, whatever their colour. Yet it is undoubtedly correct to say, as he does, that this Cape tradition 'exercised a profound influence on African political thinking for decades into the 20th century'. That influence was particularly strong in the Eastern Cape, where the majority of Cape Africans lived. There was no similar tradition in the other three colonies that joined the Cape in 1910 to become the Union of South Africa. The Boer republics of the Transvaal and Orange Free State enshrined the principle of 'no equality in church or state' in their constitutions, and when they surrendered to the British in 1902 after the Anglo-Boer War, the colonial administration generally ignored the blacks. Natal, like the Cape a British colony, practised apartheid under an ill-fitting disguise of tokenism: fewer than a dozen Africans were on the common voters' roll despite the fact that there were probably as many blacks as in the Cape.

The Cape liberal tradition first broke in the discussions leading to the formation of Union. The Transvaal, Free State and Natal refused to contemplate a non-racial franchise. The Cape Government, despite black pressure, compromised in accepting that electoral apartheid would remain in force in the three provinces; it also began the process of disenfranchising its own black voters by agreeing that no black would be allowed to sit in the new House of Assembly or Senate. The Cape thought that the other three provinces would eventually see the error of their ways and adopt the Cape system: the exact reverse happened and in the following 60 years Coloureds and Africans were gradually stripped of their parliamentary rights.

Yet the gradualist Cape tradition survived among black leaders. It was perhaps bolstered by the activities of missionaries, particularly in the Eastern Cape, although Marxist historians and politicans argue that one of the missionaries' main functions, together with teaching the gospel, was to be an advance for capitalism and imperialism. Mission schools gave Africans their first Western education, several of the more famous, like Lovedale and Healdtown, on the Border. In addition, the University College of Fort Hare, established from a missionary base, provided a non-racial education and encouraged the Cape liberal tradition, despite decades of increasingly strict apartheid. This lasted right until the late 1960s, as Fort Hare clung to its heritage despite being taken over by the government and turned into a 'tribal college' supposed to cater only to the Xhosa tribe, one of the largest in South Africa. Fort Hare, 80 miles from East London, also provided most of the black leaders of the twentieth century in South Africa, including, in the past few months, Mr Robert Mugabe of Zimbabwe, and even further afield as far north as Kenya; it was a black Oxbridge. But there were few black students at the 'open' English-speaking universities.

The most important keeper of the Cape liberal conscience, among blacks, was initially the African National Congress, established in 1912. Before that, local organizations had sprung up throughout South Africa as it became obvious in the wake of the Boer War that Britain was focusing on wooing the loyalties of the Afrikaners in the Transvaal and Free State rather than extending rights to blacks. The first pan-South African organization, the Native Convention, lobbied the meetings of white politicians negotiating to establish the Union in 1910. It failed to prevent segregation becoming institutionalized in the new South African Constitution, and failed also to persuade Westminster to veto these colour-bar clauses.

From 1910 on, black leaders attempted both to persuade white South Africa, in the words of the 1909 Native Convention, to give 'full and equal rights and privileges ... without distinction of class, colour or creed' and, at the same time, to protest against retrogressive legislation which diminished the few rights the blacks had. They did not have to wait long: the Native Land Act of 1913 laid down the basic provisions of territorial segregation that was to reach its apex in the Verwoerdian ideal of independent Bantustans. But the Act gave Africans only 13 per cent of the land despite the fact that they formed (then as now) nearly three-quarters of the population. A significant proportion of this 13 per cent was in the eastern half of South Africa, so it was natural that Transkei would be the first Bantustan in the 1960s and that the Ciskei would soon follow. A series of further restrictions followed in the 1920s and 1930s under Prime Minister Hertzog, culminating in 1936 with the abolition of the Cape common roll. As a lopsided *quid pro quo,* the Africans removed from the roll were put on a separate voters' list to elect three white MPs and four senators. Two decades later, as Bantustans entered official government terminology, they too were abolished.

The 1936 'deal' — about which blacks were not consulted — promised more land for Africans which later was to be the basis of Bantustan territory. But it did not increase the 13 per cent reserved in 1913 by more than 1 per cent. At the same time, a Native Representative Council was established. A talking shop with no legislative powers, it became known sardonically as a toy telephone and collapsed shortly after the Second World War — to be formally abolished when the National Party came to power in 1948.

That year was the turning point. The Nationalists came to power on a slogan of 'Kaffir op sy plek en koolie uit die land' — the black in his place and the Indians to be thrown out. If it had not become obvious before, it was now clear that the tactic of blacks going cap-in-hand to the white government to ask for amelioration of their economic plight and for political rights was over. The decades of mass organization were to begin, not least in the Eastern Cape.

There had, of course, been attempts before. The Industrial and Commercial Workers' Union had been founded in Cape Town in 1919 and spread throughout the country a few years later, developing political aims along the way. But the organization which had a paid-up membership of 50,000 to 80,000 in 1927 collapsed within a few years. 'By the late twenties,' says Walshe, 'only a residue persisted — small groups of followers clustered around local figures, the most important of which were Clements Kadalie in East London and George Champion in Durban'. The Joint Councils of South Africa — white liberals and black leaders — had also enjoyed some popularity in main centres around the country in the 1930s. Bantu-European Conferences had some vogue as well, but all these organizations and the ANC (plus the opposition of fewer than a dozen white MPs) all failed to prevent more legislated apartheid in the 1930s and the rise of the National Party to power.

The 1950s saw the beginnings of mass action on the part of what grew to be called the Congress Alliance — the ANC, the Indian Congress and the Congress of Democrats (regarded by the government as another name for the predominantly-white Communist Party which had been banned in 1950). The issues of the 1950s were many: boycotts of buses in protest against increased fares, calls for better pay, protests against the pass laws which were increasingly tightened and spread to every black over the age of 16 and protests against forced removals from shanty towns to newly-established 'locations' generally miles from the white cities and places of employment.

In 1952 the ANC launched the Defiance Campaign, warning that unless a number of racist laws were abolished, blacks would embark on a programme of passive resistance throughout the country and court arrest just as white South Africa was celebrating the tercentenary of Van Riebeek's arrival at the Cape and, by implication, 300 years of white rule. The government did not budge, and thousands of blacks from Johannesburg to East London were arrested. In East London in October of 1952 black anger turned into a riot — against Congress' wishes — and two people were killed. Similar riots occurred elsewhere, but the government refused to appoint any judicial commissions of inquiry into the causes, blaming instead ANC agitation. Within a few months 52 ANC leaders were banned, preventing them from taking part in any of their organization's activities.

This pattern of protest, counteraction by the government, sporadic violence and the arrest or banning (sometimes both) of the leaders continued throughout the 1950s, and set a pattern first for the events of 1960 and then for the mid 1970s. Sharpeville, in 1960, began as a peaceful protest against the pass laws; it ended with 69 people killed by police bullets, a State of Emergency, the banning of the ANC and the PAC and a lull in legal black politics until the black consciousness movement began to emerge in the late 1960s. In the interval, legal black political activity was channelled into the Bantustans; illegal activity into two organizations, *Umkonto we Sizwe* (Spear of the Nation, an underground wing of the ANC which had now abandoned its policy of passive resistance and non-violence) and *Poqo* (the underground wing of the PAC). In the Transkei, there had been the Pondoland uprising against chiefs thought to be stooges of the government and also against a number of administrative plans. Throughout the early 1960s there were sporadic outbreaks of violence and sabotage, and dozens of political trials, many of them in the Eastern Cape, of people charged with belonging to the now-illegal ANC and PAC and their underground wings. Hundreds of people were jailed and sent to Robben Island or dispersed to prisons elsewhere. Strangely, many of those who had served their sentences on Robben Island were on release banned to East London and, to a lesser extent, Port Elizabeth — the two cities that had long been centres of ANC and PAC activity.

White repression continued unabated throughout the 1960s, and for some time it appeared as if the ANC and PAC were crushed: their potential members frightened off by thousands of informers and by the knowledge that even discussion of the liberation movements in the privacy of one's house could lead at best to Special Branch interest and harassment, at worst lengthy spells in jail.

It was in this atmosphere that the black consciousness movement began. It was formulated first in Durban by people like Steve Biko and Barney Pityana (both of Eastern Cape stock), and the decision to start the first organization, the South African Students' Organization, was made after a conference of the multiracial, but white-dominated, National Union of South African Students in Grahamstown. From there, the movement spread and other formal organizations were established until, by 1976, it could be said to be the dominant black organization — or at least movement — in South Africa, fuelling the anger of the Soweto schoolchildren in June of that year and providing most of the emotion for the wave of riots that spread rapidly around the country. The movement's informal headquarters were in King William's Town, to where Biko had been banned. The movement was tolerated by the government initially, in the mistaken belief that it tied up with tribalism. But by 1973 Pretoria came to appreciate that it was the beginning of a new liberation movement, albeit one that wanted to work legally. Its leaders were harassed, detained, banned and jailed and on 19 October 1977 — a month after Biko had died in detention — all the movement's formal organizations were banned. Today many of its old leaders, like Pityana, now in London, are in exile, trying to form a common front with the ANC and the PAC. The wheel — limited protests, calls for dialogue with the white establishment, demands for full equality, ruthless government action against the leadership, the banning of the organizations — has come full circle again.

To some extent, the same cycle has operated in the affairs of Coloured people. South Africa's Coloured people were once called, by Sarah Gertrude Millin, 'God's stepchildren'. Of the 2.4 million people of mixed race — their forefathers the product of liaisons between Dutch settlers, slaves from the East Indies and native Africans — about 12,000 live in East London. On a countrywide basis, 78.9 per cent are said to be Afrikaans-speaking, a fact that has made some 'enlightened' Nationalists refer to them as 'brown Afrikaners' and to hope for a union of common interests against the Africans. This hope appears slim, and is receding rapidly. In East London, the percentage of Coloureds speaking Afrikaans at home is lower than the national average, partly because Afrikaans is a minority language in the city and partly because it is increasingly perceived as the language of the oppressor.

The Coloureds have borne much of the brunt of apartheid oppression. The Group Areas Act has been used to move them from their homes close to city centres: East London's North End, Port

Elizabeth's South End and Cape Town's District Six were all once thriving and vibrant Coloured communities, but now the people have been removed to spartan, soulless townships and their old homes razed or, in the case of District Six, taken over by whites and 'gentrified' into smart little desirable residences at vast profit to all but the Coloureds.

The Population Registration Act, which classified all South Africans into strict racial groups, hit the Coloureds particularly hard. With their mixed backgrounds, many passed for white for years until they were reclassified Coloured: families were split as one branch was classified white and another Coloured. Jobs and housing were lost and suicides reported in many cases as people were downgraded from white to Coloured or from Coloured to African after arbitrary tests for racial purity and official snooping among neighbours, friends and enemies.

The dividing line between 'white' and 'Coloured' is thin; it has been reckoned that any South African family stretching back more than six generations has some 'Coloured' blood — a matter of shame for those whites who put a premium on their skin colour and support the National Party government, but also a blot on Afrikanerdom for those who are more sensitive to the discrimination meted out to Coloureds by Afrikaner whites. The Coloured reaction to apartheid has varied from Uncle Tom-like supplication to the white establishment through to violent opposition. Increasingly Coloureds have realized that they are forced to make common cause with Africans — hence the growing use of the term 'black' to describe all those who are on the receiving end of apartheid. These also include the country's 750,000 Asians, the majority of them Indians imported as labourers to Natal in the last half of the nineteenth century. About 2,000 live in East London, while most remain in Natal, and in Cape Town there is a large Malay community which, for the purposes of apartheid, is lumped together with the Coloureds and Asians.

The Coloureds enjoyed the right to vote in the Cape from 1853 (together with Africans under the non-racial qualified franchise) until just over a century later when, after a lengthy and passionate battle, the National Party Government removed them from the common roll. This fight occupied parliamentary attention for years, arousing intense opposition from the white opposition United Party, ex-servicemen in the Torch Commando (which at one stage looked as if it was about to mount a *coup* on the issue) and Coloureds themselves. The fight also brought into being an organization like the Black Sash, liberal white women defending the Constitution against its cynical rape by the government.

The government's attempts to deprive the Coloureds of their common roll vote was fraught with difficulties and high passions were raised. A Bill removing them from the roll was passed by a simple parliamentary majority; this was challenged successfully in the courts on the grounds that the Constitution demanded that the Bill had to have a two-thirds' majority which the National Government could not muster. The government got around this problem by the simple means of creating more senators and packing the Senate with its supporters until it had the necessary two-thirds' majority. This, in turn, was challenged in the courts, but only one Appellate Division judge out of twelve said that the spirit, if not the letter, of the Constitution had been violated.

In part compensation for taking them off the common roll, the government gave the Coloured people of the Cape four MPs in the House of Assembly and a number of nominated senators — the senators all being white Nationalists. But when the Coloureds showed signs of supporting the anti-apartheid Progressive Party, the Government dispensed with the four MPs. Instead it set up the Coloured Representative Council (CRC), first composed of both elected and nominated members. When the bulk of the Coloured people supported the anti-apartheid Labour Party instead of the Uncle Tom-like Federal Party, the government promptly nominated many of the defeated Federal candidates to fill the nominated seats and thereby ensured that Labour was kept out of power. It was a device that could not be repeated indefinitely, however, and by the 1970s Labour had a clear majority on the CRC. Labour has always held the Eastern Cape seat that includes East London, but in recent years the party has been split as more Coloureds have withdrawn their cooperation with any apartheid institutions and as various leaders have compromised — or have been thought to have compromised — Labour principles.

The CRC, always a stormy institution, was run for several years by a government-nominated chief executive after the Labour Party refused to operate within the Nationalist Government's demanded framework. In early 1980, the government tacitly admitted that it had become a farce and closed the CRC, while attempts were continued to negotiate the 'new deal' that would establish a new constitution for the country, setting up two new parliaments — one for Coloureds and the other for Indians — and a Cabinet Council of white, Coloured and Indian members.

Closer to home than the now-disbanded CRC, and more tangible than the government's new constitutional proposals, the Coloured community's interests in East London, as in most other cities, are supposed to be looked after by a Coloured Management Committee. It is composed of both elected Coloured representatives and members of the white city council, but it has no legislative powers and the city council is not bound to heed any of its wishes. Coloured opinion in East London seems split between the acquiescent attitude of the old Federal Party (now little more than a skeleton) and the increasing awareness of a community of interest with the Africans, particularly in the black consciousness movement. A number of Coloureds and Indians, many now banned or jailed, have held senior positions in the movement.

In limbo, as they have been for so many years between black and white, Coloureds have suffered tremendous social problems: prostitution, illegitimacy, alcoholism and drug addiction are rampant. Their crime rate is high: 38,000 jailed every year. In East London, they work as skilled and semi-skilled artisans, storemen, waiters and chefs. As some of the earlier rigidity of Nationalist thinking has slowly been eroded, many Coloureds have moved upwards economically. Yet although they can enjoy, or aspire to enjoy, some of the economic fruit, they are still deprived of their rights as citizens. Their housing in East London is more spacious than that of the blacks in Mdantsane, but they share with blacks an almost total lack of those amenities that whites take for granted. The 2,000-odd Asians of East London have slowly intermingled with the Coloureds, although there are still Asians who maintain a rigid caste system — generally the better-off merchants. Their political influence is minimal in the city.

This, then, is the background to East London and its people, a microcosm of the land of apartheid.

The region is facing probably its most critical time. How the future works here will determine to a large extent how the future of South Africa will develop. The government has looked into the future and declares it works through Bantustans. The black consciousness movement, with the ANC and PAC, see it working through an undivided South Africa ruled by the majority with a major redistribution of the land and its wealth. The Bantustan leaders see it working through acquisition of more land and skills — not an ideal future, perhaps, but one that is within their grasp, particularly if they are at the helm. The white liberal, to a large extent, has consulted the crystal ball and despairs of the future. The white businessman and entrepreneur see the future working through capitalism with a slightly more human face — but with segregation continuing. Perhaps most see only a short distance ahead. They see the prospect of East London being handed back to the original native inhabitants. Those who have read the history books and learned the lesson of Port St Johns see either no future or a great future.

In the short term, East London's major problem is an economic one: its black population desperately needs more employment opportunities. Its white entrepreneurs need a bigger market that only the blacks can provide. On the horizon looms the prospect of the West withdrawing its economic stake, perhaps even imposing sanctions. Politically, there is potential for yet more conflict — and to date the region has seen relatively little conflict for the past century since the end of the Frontier Wars.

Just why there has been so little trouble in the Border is something of a mystery. Only 200 miles away lies Port Elizabeth where, in the wake of the Soweto protests in 1976, the black townships exploded and exploded again. But in East London and King William's Town, the townships were relatively quiet. There were boycotts of classes by black schoolchildren, but nothing on the scale of the Witwatersrand, Cape Town and Port Elizabeth. There were few riot deaths. The gravest outbreak was the day Steve Biko was buried when two black policemen were stoned to death in Mdantsane.

Why the calm? One reason is that the government's policy of divide-and-rule through Bantustans has worked to some extent; many blacks have been absorbed into the Ciskei civil service and their political energies diverted into the party struggle there rather than into the broader fight against white domination. Another is that the black consciousness movement, which provided the moral and intellectual force behind the Soweto protests, had its headquarters in King William's Town. Once it saw that protests were being met by bullets, it established some kind of discipline among the youth and persuaded them not to throw their lives away at that juncture. A third is that the *Daily Dispatch* was a radical newspaper; it was perceived by blacks to be interested in their welfare and problems, and that riots were not necessarily the answer at that stage.

But all this may change — may have changed already. The Ciskei and Transkei governments have resorted to bannings, banishments and detention without trial to keep power. Resentment and anger have built up that may be difficult to control — just as Pretoria was unable to handle the fury that exploded at Sharpeville and Soweto. The black consciousness movement is banned and its members radicalized; most of the leaders from King William's Town are dead, banned or in exile and those remaining may well be unable to control the youth. The *Dispatch* has grown more conservative; it is not the safety valve it was once perceived to

On the other hand are the proposed relaxations in apartheid foreseen by the Prime Minister, P.W. Botha. These will be tested in the Border as throughout South Africa. Conservative-to-liberal whites see this as a way of defusing black anger. The contrary view is that Mr Botha may well arouse expectations that cannot be fulfilled except at the price of burying apartheid completely. That, in turn, may herald new unrest.

In this context and setting, and facing an uncertain future, the people of the Border area have spelled out their attitudes, fears and hopes. The interviews that follow flesh out the dry bones of apartheid. They give an insight into South Africa and all its problems that has not been seen before. This is not a dry sociological examination of a region and its people filled with graphs, tables of figures and jargon incomprehensible to all but practising sociologists. These are real people living in a real world: a world that is a microcosm of South Africa.

The interviews were given at a critical time in South Africa's history. It is post-Soweto; the period of black quiescence, which lasted from Sharpeville until 16 June 1976, is over. The black consciousness movement is emerging as a real force. Steve Biko is not yet dead. The 1977 general election that saw the Border switch to the ruling National Party is about to take place. The Muldergate scandal that divided the country and led to the disgrace of half-a-dozen of South Africa's most powerful whites is still only a newspaper rumour. Transkei has just become the first independent Bantustan. The Ciskei seems to be on the same path. The 'security' clampdown that immobilized dozens of black leaders and 18 organizations is a little way off.

South Africa is in critical flux, and these interviews freeze South Africans caught in that flux. They are dated only according to the calendar, not in relevance or importance. They give an insight undiminished by the time lapse. They illuminate not merely the Border but the entire country and its range of opinions and problems.

Note on Terminology

South African racial terminology often is confused — and confusing. The way one group describes another sometimes indicates political leanings: for example a hardline Nationalist would call those of African descent kaffirs; more politely the government insisted on the use of the word 'Bantu' (literally 'people'). But this term, too, was regarded as an insult and has now fallen into official disuse.

The term 'black' originally was used to describe those of African descent. Now, however, particularly as the ideas of the black consciousness movement have spread, it is used to describe all those at the receiving end of apartheid — Africans, Coloureds and Indians: those people whom whites group together as 'non-whites'. The term 'non-white' itself is now seen as an insult.

The word 'Coloured' also is disliked by many of those so described — the mixed-race descendants of unions between whites and Africans, whites and Indians and whites and Malays. But although the term may be disliked, it is in common usage and there is no other, generally-acceptable word to describe them.

Perhaps even more confusing, some people — white or black — now describe themselves as African to indicate that their first loyalty is to the continent of Africa. While colour is still a factor they allow themselves to be described as 'white Africans' or 'black Africans' but hope that one day the need for the adjective will fall away.

It is almost impossible to arrive at uniformity of description, but the context in which each term is used, and the views of the people interviewed, make it clear what racial group is being referred to.

'What do you think of this country?'

At five in the afternoon on 22 September 1977, Fraser and I stood with our baggage on the docks at Durban where the taxi had dropped us. Nearby were stacks of cartons and rows of containers. Beyond these was the SA *Tugelaland,* the freighter we were to take to New York. I looked around and saw no one: 'Well, what now?'

'I guess we'll carry these aboard ourselves', Fraser said.

We had flown to Durban that morning from East London, a city some 400 miles south, where Fraser MacLean and I, both Americans, had worked for the last twelve months, he as chief photographer for the *Daily Dispatch,* I as features editor. Scheduled to leave the next day, we had checked into a Durban hotel. Within an hour, the call had come that the ship would sail a day early and that we must report to F Shed between five and six.

We hauled our gear across the concrete apron and up the gangway. Uncertain of what to do next, we waited on a lower deck. After several minutes, a deckhand appeared and we followed him through corridors to a dining room. He left us there, returning in a few minutes with a heavily built, blond man who told us he was chief steward and off duty. The *Tugelaland* was a German ship leased to a South African line and the steward spoke heavily accented English.

We went with him into the bar adjoining the dining room and waited while he checked papers, 'MacLean,' he said, 'cabin 105'. He took our passports and locked them in a drawer. 'We'll do the paperwork later', he said. We carried our bags down another corridor to our cabin. We saw no one else.

The cabin was large and nicely furnished. At one end were a couch, two armchairs and a table. On either side of the couch were cabinets and lamps. At the other end of the room was a long counter, a mirror above it, drawers beneath. Next to these, against the wall, were bunks. Fraser put the suitcases on the bed and stowed the odd bags underneath. I began unpacking. The suitcases were half emptied when the ship's radio officer, a woman, knocked at the open door. 'Customs is on the phone', she said. 'They say you have not been cleared and you must go to the terminal right away.'

'You're kidding', I groaned. 'No one told us to report to customs, the agents told us to come here.' The idea of repacking our bulging suitcases was overwhelming.

'Well,' the radio officer said, 'I can try talking to them ...' She left for the radio room, reappearing a few minutes later with the bad news. 'They're very angry. You're to pack everything up and go the customs terminal at once.'

'How are we supposed to get there?' I asked. 'I don't even know where it is — and we don't have a car.'

She explained this was her first voyage as radio officer and she was uncertain of how to handle the situation. 'I could ring for a taxi. Or perhaps they could come here. I'll call them again.'

After she left, Fraser said: 'Maybe we should have gone to them.'

He sat on the couch and turned pages in a magazine. I looked out of the porthole as we waited for our intermediary to come back. Of the many ships directly across from us, two flew US flags. I wished ours did.

The radio officer returned. 'Now they say you mustn't leave the room — they'll come here', she said. 'They're very angry.' Then, as she walked away, she shook her head saying, 'I wish the captain were on board.'

We waited silently for the customs officials. The previous day Fraser and I had both worked until 5.30 as usual, then gone home to pack and close the house. We had dinner with a friend down the street and went from there to the Belonskys' house where we would stay the night. The Belonskys' are good friends. Bernie is an architect, Ruth a city councillor. We talked until late, rose early the following morning then lingered over coffee around the kitchen table. The stable door opposite opened onto the garden and we watched a monkey swing from tree to tree. It was early spring in South Africa and the blooms of trees and flowers were bright against deep-green leaves.

My thoughts were interrupted by a sharp rap on the door. Three men entered the room and shut the door behind them. One wore a dark, naval-type uniform and introduced himself as the customs officer. He gestured at the other two and explained, 'These are my men.' One was dark haired and wore a safari suit. The other, tanned, good-looking, had sun-streaked hair and looked like Robert Redford.

I sat at the table with Navy Uniform and filled out forms as he gave them to me. The other two men rifled through what was left in the suitcases, then walked to a duffle bag that Fraser had shoved under one of the bunks. My vague anxiety became more specific. What did we have that we shouldn't? I had no idea what was in the duffle. When we had packed the night before, we had been concerned only with getting everything in. Customs hadn't entered our minds.

When we had arrived at the docks that afternoon, our taxi had stopped at the gate. A uniformed man asked our destination. 'The SA *Tugelaland*', Fraser had replied. 'We're passengers.'

'Do you have anything to declare?' the man asked.

'No.'

He waved us through. Perhaps he thought we arrived in Durban on the *Tugelaland*. I had stupidly thought him to be a customs officer.

'A lot of expensive camera equipment here', said Dark Hair. 'What did you do in South Africa?'

'Photographer', Fraser replied.

Robert Redford pulled cans of negatives out of the duffle bag. We all watched him as he passed strips of negatives in front of the light above one of the beds. He was taking a long time. There were a lot of negatives. While this went on, Navy Uniform went over each answer I'd given on the forms and Fraser talked rugby with Dark Hair. Robert Redford kept unrolling strip after strip of film. I wondered which negatives these were and which we had packed in the crate of household goods that had been loaded when the ship stopped a few days earlier in East London and which was now in the ship's hold. Robert Redford lowered his arms. 'You have pictures here of Steve Biko.'

'Oh, do I?' Fraser said. He went to look at the tangle of film on the counter between the beds. 'Where are they?'

'You tell me', ordered Robert Redford, waving his hand over the mess. Fraser began passing negatives in front of the light.

I was frightened. My breath was short and I fought an urge to race out of the room. These men were looking for specific things and I knew that in the cupboard behind me were pages of interviews with South Africans, many of whom had been openly critical of government policy. Transcripts of our taped conversations were incorporated into a manuscript which I had worked on for most of the months we'd been in South Africa. In the same folder were photographs of those interviewed, including Steve Biko, the black leader who had died in prison ten days before.

'Is this the one you mean?' Fraser asked handing a negative to Robert Redford.

'That's Biko.'

Fraser corrected him: 'It's a photograph of a portrait done by the cartoonist at the paper. If you look closely in the corner you can see the signature.' The *Daily Dispatch* had published the portrait on the front page of the edition that announced Biko's death. Following the usual procedure when colour was used, Fraser had taken a black-and-white photograph of the drawing to be used in case there was a foul-up in the colour process.

No one spoke. I remember thinking that in East London we'd feared violence at the hands of angry blacks, yet I was more afraid at that moment than at any time during the past year. Robert Redford broke the silence. 'Do you have any more film at all? If not, will you sign a paper to that effect? Think very carefully.'

Fraser rubbed his beard. 'Yes,' he said finally, 'I believe there is more.'

My pulse doubled. The only photographs I knew of were the ones in the cupboard behind me, but Fraser walked to the dresser, pulled from his camera bag a blue leather folder containing prints. Robert Redford went through them, putting a few aside. 'We'll take these and mail them to you later', he said.

Then he turned to me. 'Where are your personal belongings?'

'In those suitcases. Some things are already in the drawers.'

'Do you have any film?'

'No.'

'What about your handbag?'

I unhitched the strap of my bag from the arm of the chair. 'You're welcome to look', I said, holding it towards him. He declined and looked at Fraser. 'You took photographs for Donald Woods of Steve Biko's body in the mortuary.' Donald Woods was the editor of the *Daily Dispatch* in East London. Less than a month after we left he was banned.

'No', said Fraser, 'you're wrong. I didn't photograph the body.'

There was silence for what seemed a very long time. I became aware of a letter in my handbag to be mailed in the States for a South African friend — I didn't know what was in it — and of the tape recorder next to one of the open suitcases on the bed. The recorder was in a plastic shopping bag, the cassette in it used last at a dinner party on Saturday. Donald had been there. I'd recorded what he said about the condition of Biko's body, which he'd seen that morning at the mortuary. Someone else had taken the pictures Robert Redford was so eager to have, but Fraser had gone to the paper on Sunday morning to develop and print them.

In a drawer under the counter was a history of South Africa, given to us by friends at the airport that morning. I had opened it before putting it away. The handwritten message on the first page referred to *Azania*, the black South African term for South Africa. Was that usage considered treasonous? Was the book itself banned? Had our friends signed their names?

'Will you spread hate propaganda about South Africa when you are back in America?' Robert Redford asked. But he didn't wait for us to answer. Instead he said, quietly and more to himself than to us, 'We have so many enemies now, what difference will two more make.'

The rest of us waited, again in silence. Our passports were locked in the ship's bar. What was our position without them?

'What do you think of this country?' Robert Redford asked Fraser.

Fraser thought a moment, then said, 'I think it has problems.'

'I asked your opinion.'

'I could ask you the same question about America and you could tell me it has problems too', Fraser said. 'Opinions are only opinions.'

'What do you think of Donald Woods?' Robert Redford asked, turning to me.

I found it difficult to breathe, much less speak. 'I think he's a brave man.'

'You sound worried about him', Robert Redford said. 'Why? Do you think something will happen to him? We've put up with Donald Woods for twenty years and nothing has happened to him yet.'

I offered no comments and that, for all intents and purposes, ended our inspection. I looked at my watch as the three men filed out the door — over an hour had passed. The pictures that Robert Redford set aside still lay on the counter; either he'd forgotten them or they hadn't really been all that important. One photo showed a black fashion model, the other, Biko leaving the East London courthouse during a trial earlier in the year.

Fearful that the men might have placed a bug in our cabin — in South Africa, one frequently feels a certain degree of paranoia — we didn't talk right away about what had happened. Later we went on deck and whispered about it as we watched cargo being loaded. We concluded that Robert Redford was not a customs agent. We thought him to be a member of either the Special Branch or the police or of BOSS, the South African equivalents of the MI5 and MI6, respectively. It seemed obvious that his sole concern was obtaining photographs taken of Biko at the mortuary.

Two other passengers were sailing on the *Tugelaland* and they had boarded during the time the trio were in our cabin. They too, we learned, had unwittingly bypassed customs, but their belongings had not been inspected.

Once at sea, we relaxed a bit. Bad weather closed in and, for a while, our first priority was to avoid seasickness. It was still rough the next night when the ship neared Port Elizabeth on its way south to the Cape of Good Hope. It had been a Port Elizabeth prison where Biko had been held after his arrest. We stood at the window of the cabin, still talking in whispers.

'Do you think we'll be searched again in Cape Town?'

'I think it's possible', Fraser said. 'There were so many places he could have looked but didn't. He's likely to wake up in the middle of the night and remember what he missed. If he does, he'll call Cape Town and tell them to give us another go.'

We put coats over our pyjamas and went on deck. 'We'd better think about that manuscript', Fraser said. 'If they were to get their hands on it, we'd put a lot of people in the shit.'

'I guess I wouldn't have any problems with just getting rid of it', I said after a moment.

We discussed how to do this and then went to our cabin to look for anchor potential among our belongings. 'It's got to be something heavy enough to sink it all. We don't want pages drifting off and floating ashore', Fraser said. I looked in a cardboard box under the counter. 'What about the wine bottle?'

We'd bought a half gallon of wine on our way to the ship. It was dispensable we agreed. So while Fraser filled our coffee mugs with wine, then refilled the bottle with water, I went through papers that would have to go — about 500 typed pages, 50 photographs and copies of correspondence outlining the book's contents for an overseas publishing house. Using a stout cord he'd found in his camera bag, Fraser tied all of the papers together then secured the package to the handle of the bottle.

We went back out on deck with our mugs of wine. The lights of Port Elizabeth had disappeared when we tossed the bottle and papers overboard. We leaned over the rail, saw the bundle float on the dark sea for a moment, then disappear.

East London: Microcosm of Apartheid

Donald Woods. Steve Biko. I worked for Woods and knew Biko; before his death the black leader had been banned to King William's Town, unofficial headquarters for the emerging black consciousness movement, just 40 miles from East London.

I went to South Africa for the first time in 1972 and worked as a columnist for the *Daily Dispatch* for nearly four months. The next year I returned as features editor and stayed 14 months. In September 1976, I went back for the third time: same job, same paper, same town.

From the beginning it had been my intention to write a book about South Africa, to explain it through the people who live in it. The second time I went back to the US, I struggled to write about what I had seen and heard but finally gave up when I realized I did not yet know enough. This was the major reason for going back in 1976. This time Fraser MacLean, a California photographer hired as chief photographer for the *Daily Dispatch,* accompanied me.

Before we left, it was apparent that the situation in South Africa was changing. Overseas papers carried front-page stories of continuing racial unrest though it was three months after Soweto. On my last day at work in the US a wire editor brought over a wire service telex datelined East London. A reporter from the *Daily Dispatch* had been detained by police. A political prisoner had died in a jail near East London. Change was there when we filed off the plane at Jan Smuts International Airport in Johannesburg. A uniformed man with an automatic weapon slung over his shoulder waited at the terminal entrance.

Inside, immigration officials routinely stamped my passport with its proof of permanent residence but spent a long time studying Fraser's papers, finally marking them for three months though a work permit gave him six months and his visa a year. Through intermediaries this time was extended but by order of the government we left South Africa late in 1977.

It was by no means a shocking, stereotyped picture of racial injustice that met me when I first arrived in 1972. The lifestyle of South African whites is elegant, gracious and leisurely. They might have been well-to-do residents of Alabama before the civil rights movement or prosperous, uncrowded Californians before the rest of the nation began its mass migration there. South Africa, at first, felt like the good old days with all the modern conveniences.

I had come to observe I told myself, but gradually, as I saw the gnarly underbelly of what seemed a Utopia, I became involved. I saw what it means to live without habeas corpus, so that a man can be put in prison by order of a government official and held indefinitely without recourse to lawyers or courts. I met people who had been detained in this manner and others who had been banned — a kind of house arrest also imposed without court sanction. I saw the poverty of blacks and the thoughtless paternalism of whites — some insisting that blacks were 'not ready' for equality, others more hypocritically engaging in the same kind of oppression while professing a belief in equal rights.

Over 100 interviews were conducted with people of East London, trying to get inside this microcosm of apartheid, trying to explain a nation under moral siege — people living with apartheid, living under the crushing weight of world opinion. Politicians, servants, clergymen, school teachers; white, Coloured, black and Indian. We talked, sometimes becoming friends. They shared their feelings about their curious, beautiful country, their dreams and fears — thoughts they were willing to share with an American but not their South African neighbours.

Their words explain what South Africa is doing to their lives as men and women confront a dilemma that popular authority can no longer hide. South Africans are sitting on a powder keg. Before the lid blows off and everything changes forever, the rest of the world should meet them.

'The basic fear we all have is of an uprising'

After work on a Friday in early October, Roger and Mary Omond, Fraser and I drove north from East London to Haga Haga, travelling parallel to the coast on tarred road for about half an hour, then turning off to the right on a dirt track which wound up and down rounded hills.

Now and then we passed clusters of round mud huts with thatched roofs. Near them, chickens scratched in the dirt, and clothes, stretched into distorted shapes, dried on thorn bushes. Women walked single file along paths from dirt-sided reservoirs balancing pails of water on their heads. Some had babies, tied with blankets, on their backs. The women's skirts were ankle length and the colour of clay in the clearings. Heron-like birds stood on long legs in grass by the road. Since there were no fences, goats and cattle — lean and long-horned — wandered where the grass looked best. There were only a few trees, scrubs with gnarled trunks and tangled branches that looked, in silhouette, like twisted 'T's.

Roger stopped the car to wait as a cow considered us through red eyes before crossing. When the road ended at a gate three black youngsters ran up the hill, tattered shirt tails flapping around their knees. They pulled back strands of barbed wire then waited in silence while Mary peeled lollies from a paper strip kept in the glove compartment.

We went on through the grass and other gates, stopping just below the crest of a hill that sloped to the sea. A ship on the horizon was white in the last light and at the bottom of the hills, breakers rolled in on the sand. Near the house, whose roof was below us, a boy trailed through the grass behind a line of red cattle. Above was a small house and two or three outbuildings. A man came from one of these to unload boxes from the car.

The rambling, rustic house, built about five years before, and the 50-odd acres around it, belonged to friends who live in East London. In October the land and house were for sale for £23,000. A year later they sold for £20,000.

In the kitchen Mary — who was taking Xhosa lessons — talked to the woman while her husband helped Roger and Fraser stack wood by the fireplace. Later when the hamburgers were done, we ate them at a long wooden table by the sliding glass doors. It was very dark by that time. The only light, except for the paraffin lantern on the table, dots along the coast far to the south.

Mary and I cleared the table. The woman would come in early the next morning to clean up and make tea. Fraser and Roger put more wood on the fire and when it burned well, they turned off the lantern. Inside the wood crackled and snapped. Outside insects chattered and wind bent the grass into the hill so that it sang too.

We drank wine from glass tumblers, talked. Roger noted that the price of wine had doubled in a year — but it was still half of what we'd paid in London. The wine was very dry and when held before the fire, the colour of cranberries.

Later Roger and Fraser found flashlights and went across the courtyard to the bedrooms. Mary and I added their cushions to our own and stretched out by the fire. We had met shortly before I left in 1974. She had married Roger in London and come back with him to East London. I thought of her as a friend because we'd exchanged many letters. She knew about the book I hoped to write and had agreed to be part of it. Though it hadn't been planned, that night at Haga was the time I heard her story.

She grew up near East London, she was Mary Powrie then, living with her parents and elder sister in a rambling house wrapped in verandahs on a hillside called Blue Bend above the mouth of the Nahoon River three or four miles north-east of the city's suburbs. There were no neighbours and this isolation was the attraction to Noel and Patricia, Mary's parents — both descendants of 1820 English settlers who homesteaded the smooth, easy hills of the Eastern Cape. She remembers life at Blue Bend as being open and free. 'We used to swim and fish and chase the cows, and it was only lonely in that when I went to school, I was isolated from classmates.'

School began when she was five: 'My sister and I would walk toward the river mouth then down the cliff to the ferryman, called Aaron, and off we'd go in his row boat. Then we'd walk across the beach on the other side to a path that led through tangled roots and trees full of monkeys to the road and the 7 o'clock bus.'

After high school at a convent boarding school in the Orange Free State, Mary went to Rhodes University in Grahamstown, an English educational centre about 110 miles north west of East London. 'I was one of those blinkered students there for a good time', Mary said. 'I had little sense of social responsibility. Though I think I was fairly conscious of a privileged way of life, I didn't do much about it.'

After teaching for a year in a primary school in Johannesburg, she went to London. 'I liked the life London offered', she said. 'I think fundamentally it was that one was much more independent. I had lived a very closeted life in Johannesburg. For example, I couldn't go out in the evenings and take a bus to the cinema because the people I lived with would worry. It was the basic sort of South African fear. Young girls, whites, just don't go to the movies by themselves on public transport. In London I liked going to movies by myself if I wanted.'

When she returned to East London after her marriage to Roger, Mary went to work for the Institute of Race Relations which she described as 'your basic South African liberal organization — liberal in the sense that it aims to bring about friendlier relations between blacks and whites. My job', Mary said, 'has as its aim simply to get black and white youth together. To set up educational and social occasions where they can meet relatively unselfconsciously. For example, we hold various workshops in art, music and drama, sending invitations to all scholars in Duncan Village, the North End, Mdantsane and in the white schools of East London.'

After about two years of the programme, Mary believes it virtually impossible to measure degree of accomplishment. 'Generally, I think it's a liberal dream that these kind of meetings do knock down prejudices and barriers of intolerance and plain ignorance. I think', she said, 'that there may be tiny ripple effects now and again. I don't think it achieves the effect we'd like it to.'

But Mary's own contacts with blacks have widened through her job. Before she had known only rural people and domestics. Now there were others she met through Institute activities and, more recently, through Window Theatre.

'Window Theatre is one of a kind in East London though there are others in Cape Town and Johannesburg', Mary explained. 'Anyone can go there — it's not restricted to either white audiences or black as are other theatres and cinemas. One gets around the legalities by saying, "This is a club". People pay subscriptions, a rand a quarter [one rand equals 60 English pence], and become members. With admission being dependent on membership, this apparently meets the legal requirement for a non-racial organization.'

Window Theatre is an old building in the centre of town, opposite City Hall. Originally begun by a local white man interested in black theatre, it is now run by a board of directors. These include Mary; Leslie Xinwa, a reporter at the *Daily Dispatch* and one of the actors for whom the theatre had been opened; and Errol Theron, Coloured, also employed by the *Dispatch*, who had been in another multiracial amateur theatre group. Since both organizations are inactive, whatever productions are staged must be brought in from larger cities. As presentations are relatively few in number and the membership is small, without grants from Anglo-American (the largest and wealthiest of South African companies) Window Theatre would probably fold.

Mary said her community involvements were limited to Window Theatre and Black Sash, a national women's organization.

I asked about their friends. Donald and Wendy Woods, Errol Theron, the Jan van Gends and Ruth and Bernie Belonsky were names she mentioned. Friendships in South Africa are usually based on common political beliefs and the people Mary talked about — who later told their own stories — hold views commonly thought of as liberal.

Mary said: 'A friend of mine in England — also South African — and I used to spend hours trying to define our views and we came up with "emotional socialists". I wouldn't say I am an emotional South African now, but I do have a basic sort of liberal concern for an equal South Africa. Like the end of apartheid, like equal opportunities, majority rule. In that sense I suppose people would call it a liberal view like that of the Progressive Party, but they are for qualified franchise and I would rather have majority rule — no matter what the shit and pretty quickly. I think just an even deal for everyone.'

Just as friendships follow political lines, so do politics affect the daily life of everyone in South Africa, black or white.

'One is always conscious of the divisions', Mary said. 'There is the whole knowledge of a disenfranchised majority who are denied — through government legislation — the right to work where they want to, to have their families with them; that there are job restrictions and reservations in that blacks can only reach a certain level. There's this basic heavy sense of injustice generally and the particular enormous guilt. It's very easy to pick up your white guilt here. It's difficult to escape feeling guilty and I would like not to feel guilty.'

I asked if she and Roger had made plans to leave the country. She said, 'Increasingly I feel an involvement here with the developments after the June riots in Soweto. But although I'm excited by what I see as movement and the sideline role I can play, I also have a wish to live for some time abroad — particularly in London where I did a job that was not politically committed at all. But I think I would always have this strong umbilicus with South Africa. Many of my friends in London are South Africans, some exiled, some voluntarily living there, and among them is a terrific nostalgia for this country, for its problems as well as its obvious pleasures. The diversity and richness of contact with people of other races that I have here, I'd miss that. And the simple vigour, fundamental bluntness, honesty and lack of sophistication. I'd miss living in a country and a climate where physical enjoyment is important. I'd miss weekends along the coast, breathing smog-free air and swimming in the sea and catching a wave. Just feeling you can walk down the main street without having your elbows jostled.'

But to Mary and to many others, the problems of South Africa had become increasingly disturbing. 'I think the basic fear that all white South Africans have is of an uprising, a bloody revolution, where you — as a white — will be victim to organized or haphazard violence'. Mary said, 'It's something instilled through many years of living here,

I think. Much as one would like to ignore it and say, "Well, hit or miss, one may get knocked over by a bus or a shark attack in the sea," this is no longer possible. I don't feel any fear from thugs or robbers, though I know many people do, and I don't feel particularly vulnerable to white vigilante attacks except for the time Roger did the Mohapi story.'

This is her account of that particular time in late August, a few weeks before our arrival: 'It was a Friday night and pressures were mounting. Arrests were being made daily. Steve Biko and a reporter from the *Dispatch* had been arrested. Mohapi had been found dead and Donald felt he might be arrested because of the fuss the *Dispatch* had kicked up.

'Over the weekend we began to feel we too might be picked up. We began to discuss the one who would be arrested — I for my involvement with Race Relations and Window Theatre, Roger because of his association with the paper. I said when they are pulling out my toenails asking, "What are you guilty of?" I would say, "All I ever said to the young people was 'have another hot dog'." But, despite the knowledge I'd not been involved in anything subversive, I felt vulnerable and we knew Roger had been of interest to the security police for years.

'That night,' Mary continued, 'in that particular climate after Mohapi's death and the whole after-Soweto anxiety, we went to bed and I said, "People are picked up in the dawn." Every night someone else had been arrested. I said, "I feel a bit anxious. I don't know whether there will be a knock on the door." And Roger, who manages quite a good panic himself, got to the giggling stage and we were a bit hysterical.'

Vigilantes had, a month or so before, attacked the editor's home. The article about that attack plus the Mohapi article, following his death in detention, made Roger feel vulnerable Mary remembered, and he had described how people could come in, bash through the kitchen window and shoot up the flat.

'As we wryly tell the story,' Mary said, 'at dawn the next morning someone buzzed the bell. I wouldn't go to answer it. The evening before, Roger had said, "Well, look, the security police could come or the vigilantes could come." I think we were more scared of the vigilantes though the people who come at 4 o'clock in the morning are security police. But when Roger finally went to the door, he found a woman looking for work.'

'We publicly accuse the captors of Mapetla Mohapi'

After getting back from Haga Haga, I pulled out the Mohapi file in the *Daily Dispatch* library. An editorial had run on the front page on 8 August 1976:

> When a man commits a crime for which he is charged, convicted and sentenced, then dies in custody for any reason other than neglect, torture or murder, no blame attaches to officials of the state.
>
> But when a man is detained without trial then dies a violent death in captivity, his captors are automatically to blame for his death.
>
> Therefore, today we publicly accuse the captors of Mapetla Mohapi of being responsible for his death. Theirs is the guilt, and it is shared by every person in this country who supports the atrocity of detention without trial.
>
> The Editor

Donald Woods wrote of how he met Mohapi. It was about a year before his death in a country jail not far from East London. Mohapi had come to the *Daily Dispatch* following a request by members of the black consciousness movement, which included SASO (South African Students' Organization) and the BPC (Black Peoples' Convention) that they, like the white, Coloured, Indian and black homeland political parties, be permitted to explain their viewpoint. Donald said the *Dispatch* would publish their information if it infringed no law and if they could find someone able to write it.

'That was how I got to know Mapetla Mohapi', Donald wrote. 'Aged 28, he was well-built, striking looking with pleasant features. He had graduated from Turfloop University with a BA in social science. We had a mutual friend in Steve Biko who had been banned a couple of years previously and was now under so many restrictions that he had less freedom of movement than a bus in a riot.

'At first, Mapetla was reserved and obviously had a battle to overcome his suspicion of me as a white man, but as he grew to realize I was genuinely prepared to publish his viewpoint, his reserve melted somewhat and the better we got to know each other, the more

he relaxed into his basic good nature. I liked his sense
the philosophical way he accepted pretty harassm
authorities. Not content with his banning, they kept threa
evict him from his little house in Zwelitsha township nea
William's Town where he lived with his wife, Nohle, and their
small children.'
Following that meeting, several of Mohapi's columns were
published. Donald described them as moderate, reasoned in tone.
Then, in July, Mohapi was detained by police under Section 6 of the
Terrorism Act. While in prison, he smuggled out two letters to his
wife which indicated he was in good health and spirits. Mohapi had
known what to expect in prison. He had previously spent 180 days in
detention, a good part of that time in solitary confinement.
'That hadn't got him down either', Donald wrote. 'He was
essentially a survivalist who lived for a cause. Like most detainees, he
knew more about the insides of prisons than about the inside of court
— never having been charged, tried or convicted of any crimes.'
It was late at night when Steve Biko called Donald to tell him
Mohapi was dead. According to his captors he had hung himself by
his jeans in his cell. His death prompted Donald to look through
records to find out those South Africans known to have died in
detention. He published the names of 24 who, from 5 September
1963 to the death of Mapetla Mohapi in Kei Road on 5 August 1976,
had died 'from causes not yet disclosed'.

'Five men waiting at the door'

Mary referred to others in East London, among them Leslie Xinwa.
In spite of the fact we both worked for the *Daily Dispatch* I didn't
know him well. He did a Friday column for the editorial page but
much of his reporting was for *Indaba*, the once-a-week English- and
Xhosa-language newspaper published by the *Dispatch*. Added to
that, the laws of South Africa discouraged association between whites
and other races.
Leslie lives in Mdantsane, the government-built township 13 miles
from East London. Meetings after working hours are inconvenient

...ved. In the city, hotels and restaurants
...ough blacks can buy food at the counter
...e agreed to an interview, we picked up
...licatessen and brought them back to the
...paper.
...word that comes to mind is 'hyper'. He
...p speed. In the newsroom he was either
...trying to get through on the crackly
...owards the lab for a photographer; taking
...vay downstairs to approve an *Indaba* page;
...hips, with the *Indaba* editor, a position
Leslie is, without a doubt, qualified to fill but probably never will
because government policy prohibits blacks from holding supervisory
positions over whites.

Leslie is a round-faced, slim man, about 5 feet 4 inches, 36 years
old. His hair is close cropped, growing to a deep widow's peak. No
one at the *Dispatch* would consider himself an intimate of Leslie's
though he is friendly, his intent expression changing immediately to
a wide grin when he is stopped. A basic reserve still comes through.

He's been with the *Dispatch* since the middle of 1971, is married to
a nurse at Frere Hospital, East London, is the father of two sons.
Educated in anthropology and English at Fort Hare, a black
university in Alice some 80 miles northwest of East London, he
worked holidays on a Rhodes University anthropology project which
ended when he left Fort Hare. Unable to find another post in his field
he took a job as a welfare officer with the City of Port Elizabeth and
it was there he was arrested for involvement with a black rights
movement while at university.

He explained it this way: 'Trouble started at Sharpeville [21 March
1960] when police shot and killed 69 blacks, wounded many more.
At about the same time there was an attempt to assassinate the Prime
Minister, Dr Hendrik Verwoerd, then the banning of the African
National Congress [ANC] and the Pan Africanist Congress [PAC].

'The purpose of the ANC, which started in 1912, was, basically, to
get equal rights. One of the basic principles in its constitution was
that this would be achieved by non-violent means. This type of
thinking predominated until about the 1940s when the ANC tied up
with workers' unions.'

This, Leslie explained, was part of a plan to get everyone into the
fold of one organization. Groups such as the South African
Communist Party and Congress of Democrats joined the alliance. In
1955, the South African Indian Congress, Congress of Democrats,

the Coloured Peoples' Organization and the ANC adopted what came to be known as the Freedom Charter, now a banned document. Basically, it was an enunciation of policy and beliefs: that South Africa belonged to all the people and all should enjoy full rights to home ownership and land.

'Soon afterwards PAC broke away, claiming the ANC was dominated by racial groups who did not feel the pinch of oppression to the extent blacks did, and two, that the Freedom Charter was a Communist manifesto. On its own', Leslie said, 'PAC initiated a campaign against the pass laws. This involved blacks marching to police stations, showing officers they didn't have reference books which, unless otherwise stamped, restrict blacks to areas where they are registered. Protestors asked to be arrested. Demonstrations ended with Sharpeville but other acts of defiance, such as the burning of reference books, followed. The government retaliated by declaring both ANC and PAC unlawful organizations. From then on, both organizations operated underground.

'There is a point that needs to be cleared here', Leslie said. 'The government claimed that black leaders had told them there was a need to give blacks a share in the running of the country, that if they did not get this, they would resort to violence. Blacks claimed that after Sharpeville, extreme measures [on their part] were understandable — the government had suppressed them for years and when they took the initiative in a peaceful way to make the world realize their plight, they'd been shot. They said they could pursue a course of violence because the government had shot first. On the other side, the government said, "We've had to ban you because you've resorted to violence."'

Acts of sabotage followed and in 1962 the General Laws Amendment Act was passed. People could be held for twelve days without trial. Further Acts increased the detention period, allowing imprisonment without due process in cases where subversion was suspected. More arrests were made in late 1962 after the murders of whites on the Bashee River in the Transkei and murders in the Western Cape.

The government concentrated on cutting down PAC first, then went after the larger, well-organized ANC with its multiracial membership. Most of the ANC arrests came in 1963 though more followed in 1964, 1965 and 1966. Every disturbance was attributed to one or the other of the banned organizations, even tribal conflicts in rural areas. In many cases, according to Leslie, crimes had no subversive origins, but it was easy to find witnesses who would testify

that the person charged had attended an ANC or PAC meeting:
'People got to the stage where they realized, "To save my skin I can do
anything the government asks me to do." '

Leslie was picked up in Port Elizabeth in late 1964, charged with
attending illegal ANC meetings in 1961 while at the University of
Fort Hare. What happened to him then happened to hundreds of
others during the same period. He tells the story as if it was yesterday.

'I had just arrived home from work. Card was the man who picked
me up, Councillor Donald Card. It was about quarter-past-five. I
was living with my cousin and she had gone to make me some coffee.
I was sitting on the couch. There was a knock on the door. I looked
up, saw a white man and a black man. I said, "Come in." I thought
they were meter readers. They said, "Who are you?" I gave my name.
They said, "Yes, we're looking for you. We'd like to ask you some
questions." I said, "In connection with what?" Card said, "Don't ask
me that. You'd better wear some warm clothes. They might keep
you."

'I walked from where I was to a room a few feet away. Got in there,
opened the wardrobe. Took off the tie and white shirt and got a
warm jersey. As I put it on, I turned around and saw five men
waiting at the door. I didn't realize what it was all about. As I went
towards the gate, I saw a car with a CFD registration which is Alice.
Then I saw [Gerhardus] Hattingh, the same man involved in Donald
Woods' and Alan Paton's case. He was in the security police in Alice
at that time. Then it dawned on me, with Hattingh around, what it
was all about.

'They drove me straight from Port Elizabeth to East London —
non-stop. We got to Cambridge Police Station at twenty-past-nine.
They took my watch, all the money I had, my belt, and locked me in
a cell. I was there for 15 days.

'Now I *was* involved. I *did* go to a meeting in 1961. But I wasn't
questioned at all until the final day. I just slept there for 15 days and
then they said, "Look, we've got this information about that
meeting." And I said, "This is true." Then I was released, to my
surprise. This was in September. I went back to work early October.
About 3 or 4 December I came home at half-past-five and a
policemen informed me I was required to go to East London and give
evidence.

'I said, "Evidence on what?"

'He said, "I don't know. I've just been asked to serve this subpoena
on you." I read it and saw some of my ex-colleagues were appearing
in court and I was to give evidence against them. I wasn't prepared to
do this.

'When I came to East London, I saw there were about 40 people. Some of them I didn't know, most of them I did know. On Tuesday I was called. I refused to give evidence and they locked me up immediately. I thought, "Look, I was involved with these people, and I knew very well that at some stage or another I'd be caught for carrying on with an organization that was banned, and I wasn't prepared to save my skin at the expense of my ex-colleagues." If there was anything to suffer for this, I felt we all should suffer.

'It was 8 December. I was taken to Cambridge, locked up. Kept Tuesday, Wednesday, Thursday. Friday they took me to court and charged me with membership of an illegal organization. I was kept in East London through December, January, February and March and taken to court in Grahamstown on 22 April. I pleaded guilty, was found guilty, and sentenced to 12 months in prison. I spent the first 10 days in Grahamstown, was taken to Port Elizabeth prison, spent 10 days there and then was taken to Fort Glamorgan in East London where I stayed until 16 March of the following year.

'The day before I got out, the security police came to the prison and said, "Please come to see us tomorrow at our offices. We want a few details." I got out at five-past-nine the following day. They were there waiting for me. They took me to their offices, had some unpleasant things to say, then took me to the labour bureau and ultimately to my home. The labour bureau said I couldn't stay in Port Elizabeth and wanted to send me to Port St John's where I was born.

'What actually helped me to stay in East London was that when I was in prison, I had interpreted on Sundays for a Dutch Reformed minister. When I came out, he wanted me to help him on a study. He pulled strings for me — Dutch Reformed people can always pull strings. During this time, the security police in East London would take me into their offices and make all sort of offers. "If you get us information, we'll get you a job." In the end I didn't do much for the Dominee [Dutch Reformed minister]. I just couldn't. After all that time in prison, I was scared of people.

'I didn't really settle down until I got a job with an engineering company. I got the job by chance. An old friend of mine who was also at Fort Hare, but who had left there long before the arrests, had then got involved with the ANC in East London. He got arrested, sentenced to two years. I arrived in East London in May, he was released from prison in June. We spent most of our time together. His name is Cyril Mjo and he now has a classical music choir in Mdantsane. He was well known here. He had been born here and grew up here. He played rugby. People were organizing jobs for him.

It so happened he got two jobs on the same day so he gave one to me. It was a poor job. It paid R13 [£7.80] a week, but I had no responsibilities. I intended staying for about three months on that job, but I was there for almost five years.

'I started work on 1 August. In October I went to Port Elizabeth, returning to East London on 10 October. On 12 October, the security police phoned my boss. They asked him how I was at work. He said he was happy.

'They said, "What type of people visit him at work?"

'He said, "He's never bothered."

'They said, "Well, he's a political prisoner and under surveillance." They also told him about my academic qualifications.

'I'd decided earlier that these should never be known for two reasons: one, if they thought I was well educated, they would think I was going to be cheeky; and two, they would feel they were underpaying me and couldn't keep a man who should be better paid. My boss said: "I'm very happy with your work. All I can say is, look after yourself. I know these men can be very cruel."

'On 11 November, I was given banning orders restricting me to East London for two years. It was the general sort of banning order. It means basically that you're restricted. I had to move from home to work, work to home. I couldn't go anyplace like factories, schools, churches, the harbour, halls, cinemas, any place where people might gather. It also meant I couldn't go to any African, Indian or Coloured area outside of Duncan Village where I lived. I could not have more than one person talking to me at a time. Every movement of mine was under surveillance.

'At the end of two years, 30 November 1968, the banning order expired. But they continued to call me from time to time. The last, I think, was in 1974. But I know, even now, people are asked about me. As Card put it: "Once in the ANC and refusing to give evidence, you'll always get called back." '

It was through Card, the man who had arrested him, that Leslie got a job at the *Dispatch*. Leslie had called Card to ask his help in getting a house in Mdantsane. Leslie was planning to marry and his house in Duncan Village was rundown and too small. After talking about housing, Card asked if he liked his work. Leslie replied he could always do with a better job. Card then called Donald Woods. After an interview Woods hired Xinwa.

At the moment, Leslie is out of politics and into other things. He has done some acting, served on the Window Theatre committee since its inception and on the board of a prisoner rehabilitation group; he is involved in the Methodist Youth Guild. 'I'm not a very ambitious person', Leslie said. 'I suppose I know my limitations. I'm happy in journalism. I'd like to develop my skills and also to provide for my children.'

Since his youth, he said, he's had a concern for general justice. 'I've always felt that the problem with South Africa is that justice has become divisible. Social factors have become more important than the basic tenets of justice, and I think unless we can settle this — until law, equity and equal chances for all are achieved — we cannot solve the problems of South Africa. Hundreds of people are murdered in the townships every year. If they were white, the whole murder squad would be sent to investigate, but perhaps half the cases of murder in the townships get to the courts. That bothers. If a man dies, wherever he is, it is a man who has died.'

He regards the Nationalist policy of separate development as 'the worst thing man has ever thought of. If people were to be separated and given equal opportunities in every respect, then I don't think anybody would be so hard on separate development. But why would you separate them if you're going to given them equal opportunities? The expense of separation is so much as to negate the idea of equal opportunities.'

He said that he, himself, had no white friends outside his office associates. 'We who are brought up in this situation, if you are among whites — especially whites you don't know — you don't feel free. The other thing is, that in the South African context, almost every white is a stranger.'

'Baas, pause to consider ...'

David and Mary Saunders have a house at Gulu which is on the coast and about 15 miles south of East London. It's a few miles less from Gulu to David's offices in an industrial area near the airport. I'd known them since 1972, considered them friends though it was, from the beginning and continued to be, a different relationship than that with the Omonds or the Woods or the Belonskys.

Thinking about it now, perhaps being with them was, in a way, a kind of vacation from the problems of South Africa. With the others, conversation always related to — or came back to — politics. This did not seem of special interest to David and Mary Saunders nor to people I met through them. At least politics was not what they talked about. One asked Mary Saunders if her golf game was going well, if she was playing in the next tournament, or about their horses; one asked David when his next trip overseas was scheduled. The same kind of questions could be put to their friends who, like them, are part of East London's business and industrial community.

It was safe to assume that David and Mary Saunders had not been to the Window Theatre. Nor would they know Leslie Xinwa. They would have nodded at Roger and Mary Omond if they met because East London, in spite of a population of about 130,000 is, in many ways, a small town. People knew about one another, even if they had no reason to be with each other. To me, as an outsider, East London's white society of 54,000 seemed surprisingly well acquainted, made up of interlocking circles based on a common language, political persuasion, income and status in the community.

I met the Saunders at a cocktail party, one of those large functions which blurs the edges of social circles. The following weekend I went to their home. It was the first of many spent with them.

The Saunders' rambling house with its low, beamed ceiling, polished wood floors, the bar with dark panelling and hunting horns on the plate rails and bougainvillaea-shaded verandahs, had a colonial, Somerset Maugham air about it. The Saunders, English-born and raised, had come to Southern Africa on their honeymoon 20 years before, David having been posted to the Zambian outback by British employers. He'd gone on to other jobs, eventually had come to East London.

At Gulu we swam in the lagoon and in the cooler waters of the Indian Ocean, walking there with the dogs from the house on the hill. Mary put out plates of English biscuits with afternoon tea, and in the evenings, David built fires of driftwood in the fieldstone fireplace. There were horses to ride, a fully-equipped pottery studio. Sometimes there would be parties, sometimes it would be just the three of us. We'd drink Pimm's on the lawn and watch the sea through palm fronds and the twisted limbs of a giant kaffirboom tree. In the afternoon, I'd go to the cottage behind the main house, to read or sleep in the room with blue rose wallpaper and white wicker furniture.

Since David knew about industry, it had been my intention to talk with him, and there was an opportunity to do this later in October.

Fraser and I had been assigned to cover independence events in Transkei. To get there we'd had to rent a car. We picked it up a couple of days early to go to Gulu.

On Saturday morning there was time to talk. David is 50, a big, robust, cheerful man, the managing director of a firm which manufactures and markets lead acid batteries. Once exclusively producing for the automotive market, it was moving into industrial batteries for power systems. For that kind of development, David said, his company, like others, relied heavily on overseas technology since the size of the South African market did not justify its own research and development. David's company now operated on a licencee basis with a major US battery manufacturer. The association had begun some years before.

'Initially,' David said, 'when they quoted their terms and conditions for a licensee arrangement, I said, "You could buy the company for that." So I thought, that's that deal finished here and now. Then they said, "Have you got your balance sheet with you?" Which, of course, I did. They looked at that and popped up. "Hell," they said, "we'd like a bit of that action. How about us coming in as a shareholder?" That gave us a free exchange of technology and, in return, all we had to do was see they got a reasonable return on their investment which, so far, cross fingers, they've had.'

Annual turnover of David's firm is now about R7 million [£4,200,000]. In the ten years he's been managing director there's been a growth rate of 380 per cent.

David divides his time between two plants, one in East London and another in Benoni, near Johannesburg. About 400 people are employed, most of them blacks.

The June 1976 riots in Soweto had little effect on his operations: 'Most of the unrest occurred on the western side of Johannesburg and Benoni is, plus or minus, 40 miles on the eastern side. The Benoni African township is rated as a model and perhaps this had something to do with it', David said. 'Facilities are better so their lot is less complicated than in Soweto. Soweto is a thing that's grown like Topsy because of the sheer volume of people [an estimated 1.5 million] who want to work in Johannesburg. Soweto was one of those dreams that just got out of hand.'

I asked if the employment of almost exclusively black labour presented unique problems.

'The basic problem is, as in other parts of the world, one of education', David said. 'From an industrial point of view, if we could solve the educational problem, it would make our life a lot easier and in turn give the labour force tremendous scope for their own development. Recently, we have been getting more literate people because of government education programmes, but we're not keeping up with population growth. The Department of Health is opening family planning clinics and so on and so forth, but you've got a problem with virility complexes with Africans. It's, "My gosh, if I don't produce children, my manhood hasn't been proved."'

I asked David about the current state of the country's economy. Since coming back, I'd heard a lot on that subject. At the paper, we had been told that business was down, that we should watch every cent spent in our department. I'd heard the same thing periodically on any newspaper where I'd worked, but it always blew over and things continued as before. The *Dispatch* seemed a different situation. In 1974 there had been women's pages every day. Now, because of less advertising, there were fewer pages in the paper which meant women's pages came along once or perhaps twice a week.

David replied that what was happening at the *Daily Dispatch* was, in one form or another, happening elsewhere as well. After 20 years of phenomenal industrial and commercial expansion, the country had, in mid 1974, entered a period of no-growth. He attributed it to a number of things. The South African economy, he explained, relied principally on exports — not solely to Europe and the US. 'If you take the southern part of Africa up to Angola, the Congo, across to the top end of Rhodesia and Mozambique, this in itself was quite a little trade continent. It remained relatively stable after the fall of the Congo many years ago, but then when Angola went out, this brought pressure to bear on Rhodesia and the whole thing started to fall apart.' Added to this, was the general slowdown in the world economy and South Africa's own political problems.

I asked if, in view of the current unrest, he had thought about going back to England.

'I never think about leaving', he replied. 'Heavens no, only when I'm going on trips — that's the extent of my thought about leaving the country. I have no fears for my personal safety. It hasn't got to that stage yet. To answer that for the long term is difficult anywhere, I should think. Revolution, violent change, is not a worry because it hasn't happened yet. There's no breakdown in law and order. It hasn't got to the stage where terrorism is rampant. Obviously, if this does happen, one would have to be reassured of the sustaining of law and order or have another think on that question'. He smiled then added, 'Having said that, I'll say, as a close friend of mine did the other day, "On the other hand, if it goes wrong, I'm not going to be the last bloke here to switch off the light."'

While David is not involved politically — 'I haven't got the patience for it, very few business people do' — he would like to see changes. 'We're all together here, we might as well make it comfortable for each other. The pressures on apartheid, from both outside and in, are beginning to be felt. And while I've never gone along with the apartheid kick myself, I will say there's a devil of a lot of comment on the neighbour's dirty washing in the world today.

'Maybe we're no more subjected to it than anyone else is but it complicates things somewhat. You resist change if you think you're being forced into it by outside influences. The pressure within the country is the one one should take most notice of, I think. South Africa is comparatively strong economically, militarily, technically, so it could probably afford to cock a snook at its neighbours, but it can't afford to ignore internal pressure. That's a whole new scene altogether. Internal pressure can be repressed, but only to a degree.' The pressure, he said, is coming from two strong opposing forces, 'The man with a strong feeling — and with a certain amount of justice — of repression; a system which is against giving too much too soon'.

Later in the day, David spoke of his feelings about South Africa, why he and Mary had become citizens, made it their home: 'I think what we like is the opportunity we've been given here. You come out of a society like Britain, it's a rat race. You're one of millions. There's far more opportunity here, more scope.

'Naturally, climate is a big factor. But you can't live on climate alone. One might say, as a white man I've had it easy. We've got servants and all the rest of it. Still, we didn't know what it would be like before we came and, in fact, South Africa was going through the whip then. It was on the verge of withdrawing from the British Commonwealth and the Sharpeville blow-up came just two years after we got here.

'Quite simply,' David said, 'I like this place. It's a great country. It's vibrant, it's got unlimited potential — and this is what really appeals to anyone who thinks. It's the great attraction of this country.'

That night Corder and Suria Tilney, who lived on the next farm, were coming to dinner. While we waited, I asked Mary if she were ever afraid staying at Gulu. David was away a lot. There were no close neighbours. She said she was used to being alone but took 'reasonable precautions'. In the past year, Mary had learned to shoot, kept a gun by her bed. She personally locked all windows before dark. Those left ajar had burglar protection. Then, of course, there were the dogs — four of them including an alsatian and a mastiff. Mary appeared to be quite capable of handling any situation at Gulu.

The Saunders had lived there for 10 years, the Tilneys about 15. The Tilneys' 6,000 acre farm, Shelford Pineries, had originally been owned by Suria's father, a grape grower with large holdings in the wine country of the Western Cape. Following university and marriage, Corder worked as a civil engineer in East London. One of his reasons for coming there had been to observe operations at the farm, which had been showing steady losses.

'As it turned out,' David explained, 'the manager had his hands in the scrum. Corder eventually took it over and he's been enormously successful. He bought out his father-in-law, added to the original acreage and bought half interest in a cannery that processes their pines [pineapples] for export. He's now the biggest exporter of pineapples in the country.'

I'd met the Tilneys through David and Mary, had spent several weekends with them. They were a strikingly attractive couple. Suria's family was Afrikaans, of French descent. Corder came from an English-speaking family. Both languages were used in their home along with Xhosa in which Corder and their four children were fluent.

At dinner there was talk of what Transkeian independence might mean in terms of black unrest. Transkei, a Denmark-sized piece of land whose southern boundary was some 50 miles north of East London, would be the first homeland to become independent. As the date for that drew near, whites speculated whether it would cause new rioting. As it turned out, independence was calm and uneventful in the Eastern Cape thought violence erupted in black townships near Cape Town and newspapers reported several hundred wounded.

Homelands are the heart of the Nationalist Government's plan for separate development. Most urban blacks scorn the idea of arbitrary citizenship in a land where they may never have lived. Nine ethnic territories, all slated for eventual independence, have been established on 14 per cent of South Africa's lands. The Transkei, as well as the Ciskei which borders East London on the west, are homelands for blacks of Xhosa descent.

Corder told of a conversation with one of the Xhosa labourers on his farm: 'I said to him, "Well, one of these days you chaps are going to be independent and maybe the Ciskei will take this land." And this chap said to me, "Please Baas, you mustn't leave us." I said, "Why not? You'll have your independence, you'll be OK." And he's a fairly

bright chap, he said, "Baas, pause to consider. The white man, he makes sputniks, goes to the moon, builds motorcars, builds airplanes. Baas, the black man can't even build a bicycle."
'Now, I hadn't thought of it that way', Corder said. 'What he was trying to say to me was they needed the white man. And I believe they do need the white man. While I don't think they should be oppressed in any way, I don't see that they can carry on alone.'
He said that if his farm were handed over to blacks tomorrow, for a few years they'd have crops, then nothing. 'It happened in Swaziland and it happened in Kenya. I simply do not believe that it would continue without white supervision, at this stage ... I'm not saying that in 10 or 20 years they wouldn't be able to do it, but I think we, as South Africans, would be shirking our responsibilities if we handed it to them on a plate and said, "Get on with it." You might as well give it to a child'.
David referred to our earlier conversation, said that Corder's experience with black labour was far more extensive than his own. Approximately 1,100 people live on the Tilneys' farm. Men from these families are the basis of his labour force with older children employed as casual labour. Approximately 150 additional blacks from nearby tribal areas are brought in on a weekly basis: 'We arrange with the various headmen and our trucks go in on Monday morning', Corder said. 'They stay at a farm compound during the week and are trucked back home Saturday morning'. On the farm, workers were separated according to tribes. 'They don't mix with each other, these people, so if you keep them apart, you have more peace', Corder said.
Permanent families lived in five other areas, kept their own cattle, goats, fowl, had land for gardens.
'My philosophy, as far as all employees is concerned', Corder said, 'and I don't care if they're black or white — is that if you expect respect, you must also give it. I've based my whole attitude towards my labour force, whether they are top managers or ordinary labourers, on the basis of respect. I don't believe in shouting at these people or swearing at them because you're not going to achieve anything. You must be straight and honest and open as far as terms of employment as well. Bear in mind that most of these people can't read or write. You must spell out for them exactly what their wage will be, privileges will be, what the side benefits are and what you expect from them.'
He believes, as a white South African, that he has a responsibility towards their development. A school has been established on his

farm: 'When I arranged that, I had a lot of opposition from my neighbours who said, "Once you educate these people, you're going to lose out." But they were wrong', Corder said. 'The school has worked out well and I can now rely on a more educated labour force. Today pineapple farming is a highly scientific business. If you're going to rely on absolute barbarians to do the work, you're going to come unstuck.'

Seeing the Tilneys made me think of a time at their house. I had been in the guest cottage and awoke during the night when dogs began barking. Rain poured down outside, blurring the light that came on in the main house and the talk that came from there though I recognized Corder's voice. After half-an-hour or so, there was the sound of a vehicle. A red light revolved on the road above the house. Still later, the whole routine was repeated — dogs barking, light, talk, another red light. Next morning Corder explained that the first ambulance had taken a woman in labour to the East London hospital. The second call had been in response to a stabbing in one of the compounds. A search crew had been organized to look for the assailant who, Corder said, according to witnesses, was a young man back from the mines on furlough — 'drunk and stirring up trouble'. He was found hiding in one of the warehouses. Corder had had him locked in a shed until police could pick him up on Monday. Later he got word that the victim had died.

I reminded Corder of that night. He shrugged it off, calling it a routine thing. Blacks, he said, tend to look on an employer as a father figure — a 'Big Daddy' who controls everything and solves all problems.

He had more to say the next morning as he showed us the farm, steering a yellow Datsun pick-up with two-way radio along dirt tracks between fields. Modern farming methods enabled him to harvest through the year and some areas had young plants while others had been harvested, the spikey, palm-like stalks brown and drooping. Other fields lay fallow.

'I think we need still more scientific help on the research side,' Corder said, 'but where in the world don't you need that? We've got to become more mechanized, but you can't until you have the hands to run your mechanization, but more important than that, to maintain your mechanization. Labour is plentiful but inefficient. Your Xhosa is basically not a hard worker.'

Pineapple planting remains a hand operation no matter where in the world it is done. An American expert had worked out planting rates in various pineapple-producing countries. In Hawaii, Filipino labourers average about 8,000 plants per man during an eight-hour shift. Corder's workers average 6,000 plants each in a ten-hour shift. But, on the other had, he said philosophically, it could be worse. A worker in Guinea averages 1,200 plants in a ten-hour day.

'The one big problem I encounter here is that unless they are under white supervision, Xhosas won't work. You can appoint boss boys and the boss boy will work very well when there's a white man there, but as soon as he turns his back, everything grinds to a halt.'

He stopped the truck at the top of a hill and pointed to a hill nearby where a cluster of buildings were under construction. 'I'm busy with a housing scheme at the moment', he said. 'The sort of thing you have at Mdantsane. Full houses with water laid on and everything. I'm going to go for different areas, each a cluster-housing development. A maximum of ten houses in one area, spaced to give each house about four acres of land around it. They'll have their own gardens and they'll have beautiful views.' The houses were being built in part with government loans at a 1 per cent interest rate.

I asked about profits and Corder said the average return on his investment was about 15 per cent annually, 20 per cent in a good year. 'As a foreign exchange earner, we're in the vicinity of about five million rand [£3 million] annually.'

Workdays begin at dawn, end at sunset and, he added, 'my hours are the same as anyone who works for me'. He explained wages in this way: 'If you take into account food that's given, housing and everything else that's included, I would say our wages range from R2 [£1.10] a day up to R5 [£2.80] or R6 [£3.40]. I realize that is probably low by western standards, but for the work that is actually done, well, it's a going wage here'

I asked if he were concerned over the future of South Africa.

'I'm not a worrier', Corder said. 'I go home at night and I switch off. I watch television awhile, read a book. One is concerned about the economy and one hopes the worldwide recession will recover. Since we're in the export business, I probably worry more about external influences — and I mean by that, economic influences — than I do about South Africa itself. Sure, we've had problems in this country. I think sometimes we are moving a little bit too slowly in ridding ourselves of some of the petty apartheid — which I don't agree with — but at the same time, I don't think we should move too quickly.

'I think I know the odd Xhosa fairly well. I know how much responsibility they can take. They can't even sort out their home problems — mind you, a lot of white people can't either — but their whole approach to their home indicates to me that they are not ready to run a country. We must be realistic about what is possible, what is practical.'

He found support for his viewpoint in the United Party, then the opposition party, and contributed to it financially. 'I like to see a stable government with a good opposition', Corder said. 'If only for that reason, I would vote the opposition.'

He suggested that a talk with William Deacon, the United Party Member of Parliament from his district, would be helpful.

That same day, at the large midday cocktail party at the Saunders, a direct contact was made with another member of the UP. One of the guests, John Malcomess, member of the Provincial Council, agreed to an interview.

'In this country the law is very often against you'

Perhaps this book would never have been written except that in the beginning of our year in East London, pieces of the jigsaw puzzle came together very quickly and without a lot of effort on my part. There were new questions to ask of old friends and things happening — Transkei independence, the death of Mohapi in prison. During those first weeks I felt the quickening turbulence under the surface. In 1972 there had been the sense of something about to happen, but in 1976 I felt violent change could come at any moment. The Soweto riots had provided the catalyst, pushing up unpleasant realities into individual and national consciousness. It was like seeing a terminally ill person after being away: the failing that those who were constantly with him did not see.

The day after Fraser and I got back from a visit to Umtata in the Transkei, a case involving Donald Woods came before the courts. In Grahamstown, seat of the higher courts in the Eastern Cape, the Supreme Court would hear Donald's appeal of an earlier, lower court verdict sentencing him to a year in jail.

It was a confusing case which had begun early in 1975, or at least it was then that Donald became involved. He went to Pretoria to make an unofficial complaint to General H. van den Bergh, head of the Bureau of State Security, and to the Minister of Justice, Jimmy Kruger, concerning alleged actions by Warrant Officer Gerhardus Hattingh of the Special Branch — the same man who had, with Donald Card, arrested Leslie Xinwa in 1964.

Woods told the two government officials that an eye-witness reported to him that it was Hattingh who was responsible for a recent ransacking and burglary of the BCP (Black Community Programme) offices in King William's Town. Since that witness wasn't prepared to disclose his identity for fear of reprisal, there wasn't much chance of successful prosecution, but Woods suggested to Kruger and Van Den Bergh that Hattingh should be told of his complaint and cautioned accordingly.

A few days later, back in East London, a Security Branch officer came to Woods' office, asked for a formal statement and an oath on the matter Woods had discussed with the two men in Pretoria. Donald repeated the story and added another, also concerning Hattingh: that on the evening of 21 September 1964, Hattingh had followed South African author Alan Paton's car to the Hogsback Inn, a mountain resort about 100 miles inland from East London.

Woods told the officer that, according to his information, Hattingh had waited outside the hotel until all was quiet, then smashed the windshield and rear window of Paton's car with rocks. Though there had been no witnesses, Hattingh later boasted of what he had done and these were the words relayed to Woods. (Presumably Paton was of interest to the Special Branch because of the anti-apartheid views expressed in his novels, *Cry the Beloved Country* and *Too Late the Phalarope,* in university speeches and through a now defunct political opposition party.)

A few days after his talk with security police, Woods was subpoenaed under a law that compelled him either to reveal his informants in both incidents or spend up to a year in jail. The man to whom Hattingh had boasted of vandalizing Paton's car was Donald Card, a long time friend of Woods. At the time of the window smashing, Card was, like Hattingh, a warrant officer in the Special Branch. Since then Card had resigned and headed a security firm owned by the *Daily Dispatch*. He had also been elected to the East London City Council.

Because of the subpoena served on Woods, Card became so irate he threatened to take matters into his own hands. If Woods did not tell the authorities that he, Card, was the informant, he would do it himself. As a result, Woods duly relayed this information to the authorities but said he still could not name the witness to the BCP break-in for 'fear of his victimization'.

A few weeks went by and then the government notified Woods that it had decided to act only on the BCP case. Woods was again ordered to disclose the identity of the witness to the incident in King William's Town. Again Woods refused, claiming that journalistic ethics required him to protect his informant, and that special circumstances made the informant 'particularly vulnerable to the possible consequences' of disclosure. My own guess was that it was either Mohapi or Biko who had seen Hattingh go through the BCP offices and both, having already been imprisoned, had good reason for not wanting further attention from the police.

In December 1975, Woods' case came to court and an East London magistrate sentenced him to six months in jail. There was an immediate appeal and Woods was released on bail. It was almost a year later, 29 October 1976, when the Supreme Court scheduled the appeal hearing. Late the following day the word came from Grahamstown: judgement postponed.

Woods' lawyer's case had been that the first verdict had been issued irregularly in that Woods should have appeared before the same magistrate issuing the subpoena and that Woods was not in a position to give 'material evidence' about any offence. The government had never admitted there had been a break-in at the BCP offices. Therefore there could not be an inquiry into a break-in and therefore no need of witnesses and no need for Woods to reveal the name of his informant. A few weeks later, on 9 December, Woods won his appeal at the Supreme Court in Grahamstown set aside the magistrate's ruling.

The day after the hearing Fraser and I sat across a desk from Alan Paton in the book-lined study in the Woods' house. Paton and his wife were staying there before going on to their home near Durban. Donald had asked that Paton be interviewed for a *Dispatch* editorial page piece. I'd been nervous before meeting him — I consider Paton an exceptional writer — but he proved easy to talk to.

At 74, he was a remarkable man, articulate, aware and the possessor of a keen mind. Physically, he looked like an ageing eagle. The features were craggy, the eyes hooded and piercing and he sat with shoulders hunched, head thrust forward. Though he gives the impression of having no time for fools, he was unassuming and gracious during the interview.

I'd read *Cry the Beloved Country* when it was published in the US in 1948 and reread it on the ship coming over in 1972. Initially I enjoyed the book as fiction and because it was written so well. After being in South Africa, I regarded it with even more respect, seeing in it a remarkable reflection of the tensions and tragedy of the country.

It was when he was principal of Diepkloof Reformatory, an institution for black youths just outside Johannesburg, that Paton came to realize 'how much of this delinquency was due to social conditions. Broken homes — very often a boy didn't know who his father was, sometimes didn't even know who his mother was. Leaving school at a very early age, living in the townships where he could do quite well on stealing, this undoubtedly affected many boys.

'Seeing the great hopelessness and the struggle by many parents to bring up their children decently in a township where there are great world temptations and the world is present. The way they continued to struggle and to save, to dress their children nicely and to send them to school. All these things made a tremendous impression upon me.'

Towards the end of the years of Diepkloof Paton went to Norway. 'I got there late in the afternoon', he said. 'The girl at the desk couldn't speak English. A chap came along and said, "Can I help you?" He was an engineer, a Mr Jensen. He said to me, "Well, you've got some time, would you like to come and see our cathedral?" So we went to the cathedral and it was dark there. We sat in the front row and I looked up at the rose window. It was a most beautiful window and I was very homesick. Then he said, "I'll take you back to the hotel and in an hour's time I will call for you." And in that hour, I wrote the first chapter of *Cry the Beloved Country*.' After that came another novel of apartheid, *Too Late the Phalarope*, and several non-fiction works.

Paton believes that much of what he said in *Cry the Beloved Country* is being said again, mentioning in particular one passage where Msimangu said to Kumalo: "I have one great fear in my heart. That one day when they turn to loving they will find we are turned to hating." These words Paton said, were realized during the Soweto riots. 'When you're really thinking of making changes, when you've given that promise at the United Nations, then two years later you get these terrible happenings at Soweto, it makes many people remember those words written in 1946.'

At one time involved in politics in South Africa, Paton still is deeply interested in politics — 'not only the life of a country but my life and my children's too' — but said he would never be a member of a political party again.

'I've had my party days', he said. 'I was a member [and one of the founders] of the Liberal Party from 1953 until 1968 when it was

outlawed. It was then made an offence for any member of a white
racial group to join in a common political cause with any member of
another racial group. We could have changed ourselves into a white
party and a black party, but we decided no, that would be doing
exactly what the government wanted us to do. We would be
practising apartheid ourselves. This was discussed very fully and our
black members agreed.' (The multiracial Progressive Party chose at
that time to continue with whites only.)

'But many of the things that we were doing and saying in 1953 —
not all of them by any means — are what the government is coming
to today. It's taken them all these years to come to see the truth about
South Africa as we saw it then', Paton said.

During that period, he served as an honorary vice-president of
NUSAS (National Union of South African Students). Roger Omond
had been a NUSAS member while at Rhodes University and asked
that Paton be questioned concerning his falling out with that group.

Paton admitted to differences with them: 'But I would like to say
that I never criticized them on the grounds of their being too radical.
I criticized them', Paton said, 'on the grounds that people like myself
whom they put into positions of honour never knew what was going
on.

'For instance, there was one thing I remember objecting to. A
leading member of NUSAS gave the black power salute at a public
meeting. That's the kind of thing I disapprove of very strongly. In the
first place, because I can't identify myself with the black power salute
and I would think the vast majority of the membership of NUSAS
couldn't either. I'm not a black power man. I believe in black
identity and I believe in this upsurge of black consciousness, but
when it comes down to hard politics, black power means, I should
think, the eventual end of white tenure just as much as Communism
would, and I have no doubt that both black power and Communism
would use each other in any opportunity.'

Paton had made several trips to the US, in particular to the south,
and sees many parallels in their racial problems but many differences
as well. 'For one thing', he said, 'the population ratio in the southern
states never approached what it is in this country [approximately 1
white to 7 blacks]. Even in the south there wasn't a single state that
had a black majority. Mississippi was the nearest with about 49 per
cent black.

'I think with the Supreme Court decisions — in the first place
dealing with places of entertainment, sports, then with jobs,
everything — it was much easier to obey the law of your country since

there wasn't the same fear that there would be in South Africa. For one thing, America has the great fortune of having a constitution. Oh, we have a constitution, but it doesn't mean anything. But the American Bill of Rights is very powerful in the hands of those who are trying to change society because you actually have the law on your side.

'In this country', Paton continued, 'the law is not on your side. As a matter of fact, the law is very often against you and will put you into prison or detain you or make you suffer for what you believe in.'

Paton said that the changes he would like to see in South Africa and the changes which he thinks are possible to make are two different things: 'I would like to see a common society, one South African society. But I don't think you could get that without armed revolution and resistance to revolution — without the desolation of the whole country. If you're black and radical, I suppose you say, "The hell with it. Let's desolate the whole country. What does it matter? Everything that's standing is rotten. Let's knock it all down and start again." And I couldn't possibly bring myself to agree with that.

'Whether or not we go into this period of desolation would depend on the outside powers leaving us alone. I'm coming to think more and more that the outside powers — African nations with Russia and Cuba in the background — are determined to bring this particular regime to an end, and the Afrikaner, particularly the Afrikaner Nationalist, would, I believe, fight to the death to stop majority rule.'

The United States, he predicted, would stand on the sidelines, reluctant to go in after Vietnam. However, he believes there has been covert involvement by the US, that it was on the advice of the CIA that the South African government sent troops into Angola in 1974: 'Our Prime Minister has indicated that we did not go in without encouragement from the US. It obviously did not come from Congress or the President so it must have been the CIA.' Paton sees South African intervention in Angola as a tremendous error and one that weakened South Africa's moral position in the eyes of the world.

He went back to what he called the period of desolation: 'If it is an armed revolution between the people in this country who are determined either to have no change or little change and those who are determined to make great changes, then I think that our cities would all fall to pieces. I think the harbours would fall to pieces, the medical services and, most serious of all, agriculture would fall to pieces. The great bulk of the food in this country is produced by white farmers and if white farmers are all off fighting for their country, it would bring agriculture to an end. I think it would be too terrible to contemplate. But, on the other hand, I'm white. If I were black I might say, "I don't care. After all, we've struggled all these years, what is it going to hurt to struggle a few more?"'

Paton pondered the question of how South Africa would meet its racial problems. 'One possibility would be for white people just to hold on to everything that they have. And that would be their death warrant, no question about it. White tenure in South Africa would be destroyed completely. There would then be no room for a white person in this country except some poor chap who doesn't own anything — a white man working for a white man — who would have no spirit to go anywhere else and who, quite easily if there weren't any Immorality Act or Mixed Marriages Act, would fuse with the other people in the country.' Paton believes that revolution is the second possibility: 'Whether this would last a long time or a short time would depend entirely on the strength of outside intervention.

'The ideal,' Paton continued, 'and there doesn't seem to be much hope for it at the moment, would be if we really made determined efforts to get away from race discrimination. If, for example, I could go and live where I liked, among whom I liked. It seems to me quite feasible to say, "Now look, from now on there are certain areas in East London that are open and anyone can go and live there and there are certain areas which will remain white neighbourhoods and black neighbourhoods."

'The opening up of certain schools would be another thing that could be done. I wouldn't suggest immediate fusion of all schools because I think the educational consequences for both black and white children would be very severe. Tremendous improvements have to be made in black education before that kind of thing can be done, but at the university level, open them all.

'Certainly what they call job reservation should be done away with altogether. And great changes would have to be made in what they call influx control which means migratory labour — hundreds of thousands of men living their lives away from their families. The damage that has done to African family life is incomputable.'

The most difficult change for whites to accept would be 'a different standard of living and a different way of living'. The average white income is, Paton estimated, at least ten times as great as the average black income, 'And there's no doubt at all that our high standard of white living is very largely based on a very low standard of black living. Our gold mining industry which has brought such wealth to our country couldn't have been done in any other country. If you want to be very cruel, you could say that the wealth of the gold mining industry never came from gold at all, it came from black peoples' wages.'

Which, if any, of these changes would occur, Paton said he could not predict, mainly because he did not understand Afrikaner Nationalist thinking. 'It's a completely closed book to me', he said. 'And I'm beginning to think that even many Afrikaners don't know what's going on. How many people really know what Mr Vorster thinks he could do to improve things? He never speaks about it. All he is going to do is maintain law and order. A preposterous cliché really.

'I had hoped that when he appointed Pik Botha as Minister of Foreign Affairs he was more or less saying, "Well, I can't do it. Psychologically I'm unable to do it. Pik, you have a go at it." But as I read Mr Botha's speeches, I wonder if he can do it either. If you have been living — as Afrikaners have — as a superior race for generations and particularly when during the last quarter century you've been passing one law after the other to maintain your differences and your superiority, how then can you start changing?'

Going back to the office, I thought about Paton. I had liked him enormously. What he said was logical and reasonable and in 1972 Donald Woods and Roger Omond — the two people I thought most in touch with South Africa's racial problems — had said many of the same things he did. Now there seemed a certain irrelevance in Paton's solutions. Blacks now were willing to die to change South Africa. Soweto had shown this. I couldn't believe that they would now settle for anything less than rights fully equal to whites.

'Detention without trial is a disease'

Black Sash is a national women's organization which formed in the 1950s to protest the proposed disenfranchising of Coloureds. Though the measure was passed, the group continues to oppose — with about equal success — discriminatory acts and legislation. Until the early

1970s when the government outlawed mass outdoor gatherings, women would stand silently in a public place, holding placards and wearing black arm bands.

National membership, largely white, is about 1,100. In East London about 50 women belong. Ten or fifteen met at the Donald Woods' home one night to hear Kingsley Kingon, a local attorney who represented Woods in many of his court cases. His topic was South Africa's repressive legislation.

Married and the father of three children, Kingon was, at 42, a senior partner in a nine-member law firm, the largest in East London. Though he now specialized in commercial law, Kingon continued to represent Woods who was a personal friend.

That night he told the Black Sash: 'Detention without trial is a disease — one might say a cancer — which has invaded the body of South African law. It certainly is not the only disease with which our law is affected. There is a lot of other repressive legislation in force in South Africa in terms of which people are banned or silenced. There are laws which prevent freedom of speech, which prevent us from reading what we want to read and seeing what films and plays we want to see, but these are not the disease which I am going to talk about tonight. The way to understand a disease is first of all to understand what the healthy body looks like ...'

Kingon began to trace the history of the English legal system and I looked at the women around me. Their wealth was there to see. I knew most of them. With few exceptions they were housewives, married to professional men and voted Progressive. Trudi Thomas, a doctor, was one of the few exceptions.

'... but there are other constitutions and other bodies which recognize fundamental human rights', Kingon was saying. 'In 1948, the United Nations passed a resolution titled the Universal Declaration of Human Rights which set out the fundamental freedoms which the authors believed were inherently the right of every human being:

'That all persons shall be equal before the courts and tribunals; everyone shall be entitled to a fair and public hearing by a competent, independent and impartial tribunal; that any judgement rendered in a criminal case or in a suit of law shall be made public; that everyone charged with a criminal offence shall be deemed to be innocent until proved guilty according to law.

'In the determination of any criminal charge there are the following minimum guarantees to the person charged — to be informed of the

nature and cause of the charge; to have time and facilities for the pre-
paration of defence; to be tried without undue delay; to have legal
assistance assigned to him; to examine or have examined the witnesses
against him and to obtain the attendance and examination of witnesses
on his own behalf; to have the free assistance of an interpreter if he
cannot understand; not to be compelled to testify against himself.

'Everyone convicted of a crime shall have the right to his
conviction and sentence being reviewed by a higher tribunal; no one
shall be tried or punished again for an offence for which he has
already been finally convicted or acquitted ...'

(A black man had worked in the *Dispatch* photo lab the first time I
had come to South Africa. You had to be careful when you went
back to talk to him — since he was banned, he could talk to only one
person at a time. He had had to get special permission to work and
when he was through working he stayed in his house. Originally he
had been charged with membership in the banned ANC. Acquitted
of charges brought under the Suppression of Communism Act, as he
left the courtroom, he was rearrested under the Terrorism Act. He
spent a total of 16 months in prison, half of that time in solitary
confinement. When he came to trial the second time, he was again
acquitted but then banned for five years.)

'We in South Africa have no such built-in constitutional
safeguards', Kingon continued.

Women around me were intent on his words. Black Sash members
had been accused, as one told me, of joining to 'assuage their guilt'.
How could you avoid feeling guilty, but what really could these
women do to make things any different? They probably paid their
servants the minimum wage recommended by the Institute of Race
Relations: R60 [£36] a month. They did some kind of volunteer
work. They voted Progressive. But beyond this, well, they had no
answers.

'The first example of repressive legislation in South Africa which
provided for detention without trial is the War Measures
Amendment Act passed during the Second World War by the Jan
Smuts government', Kingsley was saying.

'The act provided that the Governor-General [later to become the
State President when South Africa became a republic. It was then
part of the British Commonwealth] would be permitted to make, by
proclamation, such regulations as appeared necessary for the defence
of the Union of South Africa. In 1953 the Public Safety Act was
passed. This act provided that the Governor-General could at any
time declare a State of Emergency allowing summary arrest and

detention. The State of Emergency was proclaimed on 30 March 1960, immediately following the shootings at Sharpeville and far-reaching emergency regulations were framed.

'In the General Law Amendment Act of 1962, a new crime was created which was called sabotage and a new type of detention without trial and this was called house detention. In 1963, the 90-days detention authorized the arrest, without warrant, of anyone whom a police officer suspects, on reasonable grounds, of having committed or having intended to commit, any offence under the Suppression of Communism Act or any person who, in his opinion, possesses information relating to such an offence. He may then cause that person to be detained at any place that he thinks fit for interrogation until the person has, in the opinion of the Commissioner of Police, replied satisfactorily to all questions.

'It also provided that no one other than a person authorized by the Minister of Justice or a commissioned police officer may have access to a detained person and that no court had jurisdiction to order the release of any 90-day detainee. In 1964 the 90-day measure was extended for a year and then replaced by a similar clause for 180 days.

'Then in 1966, section 22 of the General Law Amendment Act provided that a commissioned officer may cause a person to be arrested without warrant and detained for interrogation without trial for a period not exceeding 14 days if he has reason to believe that that person is a terrorist. A terrorist is defined to include any person who favours terroristic activities. This is, of course,' Kingon said, 'an exception to the rule that the thought of man is not triable. "For the devil himself knoweth not the thought of man" according to a judgement given in an ancient English case.

'In 1967, the Terrorism Act, section 6, states that a commissioned police officer may, if he has reason to believe a person is a terrorist, cause that person to be arrested without warrant and detained until the Commissioner of Police orders the detainee's release on being satisfied he has replied to all questions.

'In 1971, the Drugs Act was passed with the frightening subsection 4 that stated: "No court of law shall pronounce upon the validity of any action taken under this section nor order the release of any person detained."

'Subsection 5 is even more frightening: "No person other than an officer in the service of the state shall have access to the person detained or shall be entitled to any official information relating to or obtained from such detainee."

'Finally we come to the cherry on the top and that is the Internal Security Amendment Act of 1976. This act amends the Suppression of Communism Act, the Public Safety Act, the Criminal Procedures Act, Riotous Assemblies Act and the Terrorism Act. Section 12B repeats the 180-day clause for security crimes whenever, in the opinion of the Attorney General, there is any danger of tampering with or intimidation of any person likely to give material evidence for the state.

'In April 1968 the Department of Foreign Affairs of the Republic of South Africa published a 68-page booklet called *South Africa and the Rule of Law*. The introduction states: "Allegations are frequently made that persons are detained and persecuted for their opposition to the South African Government and that South Africa is a police state where the rule of law is continually being violated. Nothing is further from the truth ..." '

In response to this, Kingon quoted an article by a South African lawyer from a national law journal: '"The Rule of Law requires that no person should be detained or punished without trial in open court and without the opportunity of denying the charge and defending himself." After considering the Suppression of Communism Act, the 180-day detention clause and the Terrorism Act, the author,' Kingon said, 'concludes that the Rule of Law is being infringed in South Africa since a person can be deprived of his liberties legally and subjected to a variety of pains and penalties without a formal charge and a trial in open court.

'The author of the official booklet said that while the South African government subscribes to the Rule of Law, it is not prepared to "expose the peoples committed to its care to terrorism or aggression because of a dogmatic insistence on the immutability of certain selective legal rules and procedures. It is and remains the responsibility of every state to ensure the security of its people."'

Kingon concluded: 'I have no quarrel with anyone who believes that in times of emergency and crisis, emergency legislation is called for. But I do join with people who sneer at what they call the "dogmatic insistence on the immutability of certain selective rules and procedures". As Mr Justice Frankfurter of the United States Supreme Court pointedly observed, "The history of liberty has largely been the history of observance of procedural safeguards."'

Later in the evening, I talked with Kingsley, asked if he understood the Nationalist Government's increasing reliance on repressive legislation when these tactics were so obviously abhorrent to the

Western powers, though it was with them — not the Communist countries — that South Africa wished to be aligned.

'The South African government has this thing', Kingon replied. 'They feel threatened all the time and they believe the only way to overcome the threats is to use force and power — all the sort of right-wing stuff they go in for. If I must try to psychoanalyse the South African government, I would say they are great believers in law and order. But law and order to them means, "Do as I tell you to do." They are not permissive which is the modern trend. This is just the way they are.'

He told about travelling from Pretoria to Johannesburg recently with four Nationalists — among them Senator Geoff O'Connell, an English-speaking Nationalist who heads a successful civil engineering firm in East London.

'I was the only Prog among them', Kingsley said. 'Eventually, of course, we got to talking politics. The thing I found so depressing was that these guys genuinely believed that they had the only right and correct solutions to this country's problems. And why it was so depressing was because it is clear to me they are heading straight into disaster if they carry on the way they're going. One of the things we talked about was this banning legislation. The senator's attitude to me was: "Look, my boy, if these people had done no wrong, they wouldn't have been put inside. You can't tell me that all these people who have been put there are innocent. Where there's smoke there's fire." I tried to talk to him about the fact it's only fair that both sides of the case should be heard in open court, that every man has got a right to a fair trial. He said, "No ways. If you're a Communist, you're not entitled to a fair trial. If you're a terrorist, you're not entitled to a fair trial."'

Kingsley referred to the question and answer session after his talk, specifically of the question put to him by one of the women: 'What has the legal profession done to oppose and object to these laws?'

The question troubled him. 'As I told her,' he said, 'we have objected. Papers have been submitted to the Minister of Justice from time to time, but she, and I suppose many of the others, feel this is not militant enough. And they might be right, I don't know. Speaking for myself, I'm not a political animal', he said. 'I do my job. There are people who are dedicated — like these Black Sash women, like Donald Woods and Wendy — but there are other people like me, the millions, the masses. We don't stand up and make speeches. Maybe we should. Maybe we should make ourselves heard ... But the English press makes itself heard. What is difficult, is that people are not listening. You look at this little town of East London. We've had a liberal newspaper for over a hundred years and for the last 15 years or so it's had probably one of the most outspoken editors in the country. You would think that if the newspaper did have an influence, the city would be filled with raving liberals. But if you talk to the common or garden variety person in this town — the ordinary nice person who lives in Vincent, he's English-speaking but he's a Nat deep down.

'I've heard it so often', Kingsley continued. '"The kaffir should be kept in his place." Or, "Once a kaffir, always a kaffir." But, these are very nice people. They don't kick dogs, beat up their children. They work regular hours, they don't get drunk. They look after their wives, cut the grass in front of the pavement and they're good citizens. This attitude has just been bred into them. I know my wife and I — we have to make a conscious effort to be non-racial. It isn't that I think I was brought up to be racist, it was just accepted that blacks were not as good a race as we were. A fact of life.'

'We meet again next Thursday'

His eyes down, the heavily built black man slumped in the straight backed wooden chair, waiting as Prince Ngxolwana, the interpreter, relayed his story to the two Black Sash volunteers across the table.

'I have', Prince continued, using the man's words, 'a five-year-old daughter. The child is deaf and dumb. I have been given letters by doctors at Frere Hospital ...'

'Yes, yes', said Mrs Johnson, fingering papers in front of her.

'In these letters', said Prince, 'the doctors are pleading with the authorities to give me a house because I keep on changing my address since I live here one day, the next day pushed out, live with someone else, then different the next day and the next year and so forth. Now I've been running from office to office at Mdantsane trying to find this accommodation.'

'Where is his name on the list?' asked Mrs Johnson, a dour-faced woman in her fifties.

Prince repeated the other man's reply: 'I put my name on the list last year.'

Mrs Johnson looked angry: 'Does he know that some people have had their name on the list for years and years? If he gets his name before anyone else, what is going to happen?' She glanced at Mrs Davis, a pretty woman in her mid-thirties sitting next to her. Mrs Davis nodded. Both are volunteers staffing the regular once-a-week session of the Black Sash Advice Office which is held in the Window Theatre. They sit opposite rows of empty chairs. Sunlight coming through long narrow windows is filtered through dusty panes onto the rough, uneven wood floor and on the bilious green peeling walls.

The women had already dealt with several people and more waited in the small landing outside. One woman, with a listless child tied to her back, had been referred to Care, a local self-help charity programme; another woman saddled with four young grandchildren had been sent to the Dutch Reformed Orphanage in Mdantsane. If the children could be cared for, perhaps she could find work.

Mrs Johnson explained to Mrs Davis, a recent volunteer: 'This man wants a permanent address in Mdantsane. So does everyone else. I'm wondering if he doesn't have a friend who can get his letters?'

The man spoke softly to Prince who repeated his words to the women: 'I know I am not close on the list. My case would be a special one.'

'Mr Prince, the others are special too', said Mrs Johnson impatiently. 'That is the problem. The school just wants an address or someone who can take messages. Isn't there someone in Mdantsane who can do that?'

Prince gave his opinion: 'There's no point in beating about the bush. The problem is housing. He must be thankful the child will be in school.'

A black man came into the room. Prince told him he must wait outside. The man argued with him in Xhosa. Prince raised his voice. The man left.

Mrs Johnson, half angrily, half amused, said to her companion: 'What happens if they bring out the pangas [machete-like knife], for goodness sake?'

Mrs Davis turned to Prince. 'So that is the situation. Housing is impossible. There's nothing we can do. It's hopeless.' She shook her head. 'The whole thing is a nightmare really.'

'I don't even like to think about it', Mrs Johnson replied. 'It's lucky his child will be cared for. If a friend would just let him use his name, there'd be no problem. But it's the same thing, they don't want their name used in case they get into trouble. You see, he's not even supposed to be here.' She turned to the interpreter: 'I'm sorry Mr Prince, we can do nothing.'

The man thanked them and went away. A woman took his place at the table. She was there to find out if the Advice Office could give her money since her rent in Duncan Village, an older black area in the city, had recently been raised from R5 [£3] to R8.55 [£5.18]. She earned R80 [£48] a month and was the sole support of her family of four children. She was told that the office offers no financial aid and acts only in an advisory capacity.

In 1976, according to records, 282 persons, the majority of them black, sought help at the Advice Office. The greatest number of cases concerned unemployment and wage disputes. Other inquiries were about pensions, housing, marital problems and insurance claims.

Mrs Johnson looked at her watch as the woman left: 'We're running late.'

'I'm all right. I don't have children to pick up', said Mrs Davis.

'Fourteen already today. No, it's all right if we can just keep up, but if Mr Prince decided to get flu or something, we'd have to pack up ...'

Another woman came in.

'It's about that fridge', Prince whispered to the women.

'Oh yes', said Mrs Davis. 'I've heard about this one.'

'My head aches', said Mrs Johnson.

In Xhosa, the woman explained to Prince who then told the story in her words: 'I have come back because Barlow's [a local furniture store] has not removed this frightening, ghastly thing from my house — that fridge. I am staying in the country now because I cannot bear looking at it.'

'Yes, just let me read here.' Mrs Davis sorted through cards in a pasteboard box, removed one: 'Didn't work. Replaced by Barlow's. Blew up after four days ...'

Mrs Johnson peered at the cards: 'And it's still sitting there? It exploded in 1974. She still owes on it?'

After talking with the woman, Prince continued: 'They send accounts but nobody bothers. They took away the tank and promised to come later for the fridge. I don't care what happens if they will only remove that fridge.'

'It's a paraffin fridge', explained Mrs Davis. 'Her daughter was there. It blew up in her face.' She shuddered: 'Those things scare me to death.'

Prince again spoke for the woman: 'Barlow's is responsible for moving that fridge. It is their fridge.'

'It sounds very tricky to me', said Mrs Johnson, rubbing her forehead. 'I'll phone the lawyer.' She went out to call one of the two or three East London lawyers who offer free consultation to the group.

'It only lasted four days', Prince said. Mrs Davis began packing up boxes. When Mrs Johnson returned she told the group at the table: 'The firm cannot be held responsible. She'll have to pay someone to get the thing out of her way. There's no legal comeback at all. Barlow's are very obviously not prepared to do it and you can't force them to. That's the point. She's lucky there's no money to pay.'

Prince explained this to the woman who thanked them and left.

While the women collected boxes and ledger books, Prince told the half dozen people still waiting that it was all over for that morning. Prince stayed behind to turn off the lights and lock up. One of the women called to him as they went down the stairs: 'Don't forget. We meet again next Thursday. Nine-thirty.'

'You can't block yourself off'

Dew Drive branches off the road from East London to Gonubie — a coastal suburb about ten miles north of East London — and runs for about half a mile along the Gonubie River. Number 32 is the only house on it. Sail and power boats are scattered around the edges of the lawn between the house and river. The house itself is on two floors. Inside it is open plan with a lot of wood and glass. A staircase, like a ladder, divides dining and living areas. That night a half dozen children sprawled on the floor watching television. Sliding doors along the river side were open to the night which was hot and humid with lightning on the horizon.

Dr Trudi Thomas, her husband Dr Ian Harris and their four children live at 32 Dew Drive and relatives were there for the Christmas holidays. Trudi and I climbed steps to a balcony outside her bedroom.

Trudi is a small woman, forty years old, who has been working in black paediatrics at Frere Hospital since she left St Matthew's, an Anglican mission hospital in the Ciskei. That was where I met her in 1974. She'd been packing to leave then after 13 years. Perhaps because of the heavy workload, Harris had developed bleeding ulcers. It was this that made them decide to go. Obviously, it had been a difficult decision. I'd thought about Trudi often since then, wondering if she would find such an intense involvement anywhere else. But, talking with her that night on the balcony, I could see that she had. In East London she was doing the same things she'd done at St Matthew's. Her particular interest is malnourished children.

'They come to the hospital for coughs or colds or runny tummies, but when they are examined', she said, 'more than 40 per cent are found to be undersized. If you see 80 or 100 patients a day, your hand will touch 50 malnourished children.'

Kwashiorkor and marasmus are the sickness forms of malnutrition. Kwashiorkor occurs after weaning, usually becoming apparent at the toddling stage.

'If they have been walking, they stop. They become antisocial, very dull. You find them sitting with little pot bellies, thin shoulders, supporting themselves over their tummies. Their hair becomes grey and sparse. I call it the mangy dog syndrome', Trudi said, 'because in addition to food deprivation, very often there has been emotional deprivation. People treat this kind of child roughly.'

The background of the problem according to Trudi is poverty, based on unemployment and on the poverty wage structure. 'I think it's very clear. You can correlate the weight of children with wage charts.' The average wage for an African family is R80 [£48] a month, far below the poverty datum level, which is between R110 [£66] and R120 [£78]. In the East London area, many people earn only R10 [£6] per month.

'Something gives in a situation like this and usually the protein goes because that is so expensive', Trudi said. 'The immediate thing is people are eating very poor food. Mainly it's a maize diet. You ask them, "What did you have to eat?" And they say porridge. "How often do you have meat?" And they say once a month and at Christmas. Vegetables two or three times a month. "And do you get milk?" "Well, two or three times a week."'

A survey made by Trudi at St Matthew's showed that less than 2 per cent of the kwashiorkor and marasmus children (she treated 3,000, about a third of those in the district) came from families who could afford pauper's rations. The other 98 per cent had even less.

'Some people', Trudi said, 'say malnutrition is much worse in the rural areas, but I haven't found it to be so. In the country it is very markedly due to migrant labour. In town there is the effect of the migrants being here and having girlfriends.'

Illegitimacy is a major factor in malnutrition, according to Trudi.

'If a child is cared for by its own mother, it's very likely to be well-nourished. Over half of the kwashiorkor and marasmus babies are illegitimate, less than half are looked after by their mothers. About 80 per cent are not supported by their fathers. There's a lot of unemployment, a lot of desertion. Father in jail is also quite a high reason why there is no breadwinner,' Trudi said, 'which fits with our pass laws, our set-up'.

Most white South Africans, she believes, are unaware of the breakdown in black families and assume the traditional structure of three generations in a house is still in effect. But these days, people go to the towns and send the children back to the villages, leaving granny with an extended family of illegitimate and legitimate children and erratic support. It is this sort of unit which produces malnourished children.

Trudi set up a nutrition clinic at Frere Hospital which works in the same fashion as the one she established at the mission. Each child brought to the hospital is weighed and measured. If the child shows signs of malnourishment, the mother is routinely referred to the nutrition clinic. There, on alternate weeks, her baby is weighed and she is given milk to last until the next clinic. 'Under the white government, we're very lucky,' Trudi said, 'we can supply full cream milk for babies under six months.' If a child is very ill, it is sent into the hospital, providing a bed is available, but space, she said, is a very big problem.

The whole idea of the nutrition clinics began when a check of malnourished children treated at the mission hospital revealed that 10 per cent of those released healthy had died within the first three months. Another 10 per cent were thriving and the rest just hanging on. 'We realized then', Trudi said, 'that we must follow them up'.

Trudi and a black woman, serving as interpreter, initiated small groups in schools or homes in the villages. 'It became a sort of community event', she said. 'The truck would come, the hooter would blare and the people would arrive. Those whose babies were doing well would get patted on the back. If baby didn't do well, everyone said, "Tut, tut. How disgraceful." The whole thing, the comparing, the praising and the shaming, had an educational effect.'

At the mission, Trudi's next step was to set up a cottage industry. Mothers of malnourished babies — and their grandmothers — came to Trudi's front porch where they learned to knit sweaters, to make stuffed toys and to sew simple articles of clothing. Trudi found retail outlets for the items and the profits came back to buy food. When she moved from the mission, the programme continued under the woman who had worked with her and Trudi began a similar one in East London called Care.

Trudi is South African born and has never been out of the country. Her mother is an Afrikaner, her father English with an Afrikaner father.

'When I was about five or six I knew I was going to be a doctor', she said. 'Nobody knows why. My own father just got Standard 6 [aged 13] and my mother, who comes from a family of 10 children, stopped in Standard 9 [aged 16].'

Trudi studied medicine in Johannesburg at the University of Witwatersrand, met her husband there. They married the day after graduation. 'At that stage we were extremely religious', Trudi said. 'We decided we wanted to go to a mission. We were interested in black medicine because it is pure pathology. White medicine can sometimes drive you up the wall — coughs and headaches — lots of neuroses. We dealt with real problems.'

I made some comment about the selflessness of her efforts. She replied, 'I do hate people who say, look what I am doing for everybody, because I get very well paid. There's nothing wrong with my salary and it's nice work — exciting — though sometimes very depressing. I'm not particularly materialistic. I suppose if I had gone into more lucrative medicine, I'd be rushing around all the time making lots of money but having little time to use it.'

I asked what she earned.

'I don't have exact figures because I just give my money to my husband,' Trudi said, 'but as a white doctor, I think I earn about R800 [£480] or R900 [£540] a month.'

I asked if she were involved in politics.

'I'm not very politically oriented,' she said, 'but it's difficult to keep out of politics. I find that I don't want to rush around with posters, but here you have to get involved to some extent. I'm in Black Sash which is politically inspired — sort of a protest group against what you think is not right. I've never voted in my life, but I suppose I would call myself a Progressive.

'As far as other interests, my husband is terribly keen on sailing and unfortunately, I'm not interested enough. He would like to sell the house, everything, and sail off.'

'What do you think will happen in South Africa?'

'The future looks unhappy to me', she replied. 'I think there's going to be polarization, white against black.'

She doesn't believe the situation to be entirely the fault of the

Afrikaners, that it is simply the whole white atmosphere. 'What whites have got, they certainly feel they deserve, and they are not going to give it up. There's a very great lack of awareness of the needs of the black people. Even quite *verlig* [enlightened] people whom I know haven't seen the light and nobody gives up what they've got easily. I wonder if historically they ever did? Without giving it up, black nationalism will increasingly make its mark. Just a natural reaction. Black consciousness is very healthy. "I am a man. Regard me as a man."

'But there is hope, I think. There is the women's peace movement [similar to the one in Ireland] and some people seem to be realizing we can't go on like this. I hope so. I do want to stay here. I don't want to leave. I want to keep on planting my garden. And I think, "This is my country. Why should I have to get out of it?" I'd like to stay, to see a multiracial country.'

I asked if she were ever afraid.

'I grew up in a town where we always locked our doors and big black men were frightening', Trudi said. 'When I went to the mission, I was frightened at first. I remember when Ian went out, I used to build up things against the doors and put a pail on top so if anyone opened it, the pail would fall and make a big noise. But in a few years we left everything, absolutely everything, open.

'Now, personally, I have very little fear. I think if you walk down the streets of the townships trustfully, your trust shows. At least this has been my experience, though other people disagree with me. I'm not frightened. But, of course, what about people who don't know who I am — or who my children are?'

After a moment she said, 'I think what I do worry about is our lack of realization of what a terrible thing it is not to have habeas corpus. After I wrote that little book on malnourished children, I was worried about people coming round to my door at 4 o'clock in the morning. And it is purely psychological, but you are a little bit frightened. You worry about if you've got a banned book on the shelves. Now that's silly. Why can't you have this book? But nevertheless, you are frightened.'

She talked a little about what it was like to be a white South African: 'Most of us live in circumstances like these. My possessions surround me as I sit here now. We've got a huge joint in the oven, a telly in the lounge, and we think this is it. But once you've had an insight, you can't block yourself off from the insight and you've got this niggling thing and sometimes I wish I'd never gone anywhere and I could have enjoyed my things. It's purely something that's been shown to you and not everyone has seen it.'

I asked what her personal goals were.

'What are my dreams? To be serene, to be thin, to have my children happy. And I'm a complete malnutrition nut. I've written something but haven't been published in the medical journals yet because I'm too long-winded. I'd like to get these figures over to the medical profession.

'Sometimes I think it would be nice to go into a black business. To start up a sort of — I must be careful here — business along social lines that I read about in England where all the workers have their own share. I sometimes think about that.'

She waited a moment, then said, 'You know, people see malnutrition now as a sort of charity thing, not as a socioeconomic turnaround for all of us. We must equalize wages, but not in the present way we're doing where we put up the black wage by 17 per cent and white wage by 10 per cent. If you work it out arithmetically, the wage gap just gets greater.

'If we can put people over this poverty datum line, we can have a viable middle class where people can look after themselves. You see, we mustn't put people in the position where they need charity or, if we forget them, they starve.'

Khayalethemba, Home of Hope

Writing for the *Daily Dispatch* gave me an opportunity to go to many places and talk to people which would otherwise have been difficult to arrange as a private individual. Because of the conversation at the Advice Office, I wanted to visit the Dutch Reformed orphanage. 'Could you use a feature on the orphanage in Mdantsane?' I asked the *Indaba* editor.

'Fine', he replied. 'Talk to Leslie. He can make the arrangements.'

A day or two later Leslie told me when and how to get there. 'The man to see is Gozongo', he said.

Fraser, who would take pictures, and I stopped at the main gate into Mdantsane. A black man came to the car, asked what he could do for the 'baas', then pointed out the office that issued permits. With the duty schedule, Fraser was in the township about every other weekend. Usually I went with him.

Though it was illegal for whites to be in a black area without a permit, after talking to the other photographers, we came and went freely without official recognition. The only time we picked up permits was when arrangements were made for us, as in this case by people at the orphanage. Forms asked who we were and why we had come. The white man behind the desk looked them over before stamping them.

'You must be out by 4.30', he said, putting the forms in a basket on his desk. 'No whites allowed inside after that time.'

'Why is that?' I asked.

'It's not safe', he replied. 'Even the policemen are gone by then.'

Leslie's map took us to a one-storey cement building on a grassless hilltop, its windows protected by thick grids. In the distance, as far as you could see, stretched long straight rows of square houses, concrete in colour. Winds stirred up the dirt on a playing field nearby and whipped leaves in the rows of a vegetable garden.

A short, scholarly-looking man with shaved head and spectacles came out. 'I'm Mr Gozongo.' A stutterer, he spoke with difficulty.

Inside smelled of cheap food, rancid grease and over-used lavatories. We went through the foyer and out to the courtyard, following walkways next to concrete drainage ditches where water stood. Two boys crossing the enclosed courtyard looked at us out of the corners of their eyes. Gozongo stopped at an open doorway. In the room were four to six cots, neatly made.

'We have 192 children now, though our number is supposed to be 140', he said. Further along we passed a larger room with a dozen cribs.

The orphanage, called Khayalethemba, a Xhosa word meaning home of hope, takes boys from birth up to 12 years, girls to 18 years.

Gozongo was director of the orphanage. Before coming to it he had worked as a clerk in the magistrate's court in Grahamstown. Students at Rhodes University helped him complete high school and when he graduated, they provided money for him to register with the University of South Africa, a correspondence school open to all South Africans regardless of colour. Rhodes students tutored him for three and a half hours a night, also made arrangements with the library for him to not only study there but to check out books — though libraries are for white use only. After getting his degree in history and systematic theology, Gozongo was hired by the Dutch Reformed Church and sent to Khayalethemba.

Though Gozongo was director, one got the impression that most of the decisions were made by the secretary-treasurer, an Afrikaner named C.A. Gouws. In his mid sixties, Gouws had a placid, unlined face and a pious though cheerful manner.

Children at Khayalethemba are Xhosa, admitted only by court order through welfare agencies. Though the Dutch Reformed Church makes the decisions on policy and staff (it is referred to as the Dutch Reformed orphanage), the Church's actual support is minimal. According to Gouws, its single contribution in the past year was R500 [£30] from a women's aid society.

Funds come from the government: 'We get 75 cents a day per child', Gouws said. 'Out of that we've got to feed him, clothe him, pay for his education, books, school uniform, everything.'

An enormously fat black woman came into Gouws office with a tea tray which she placed on his desk. Gouws introduced her: 'This is our housemother and cook. I can't imagine how we could carry on without her.' In addition to the three in the office, there were a housefather and seven 'nannies' for the infants.

Holding my saucer with one hand, I swatted flies with the other. The little office was hot and airless, permeated by the same strong odours as in the other rooms. I asked Gouws how he had come to the orphanage.

'I used to be an engine driver on the railways', he said. 'Then I had a coronary and started getting quiet. I had always said that when I go on pension, I want to sell off everything and go into the missionary service, but it did so happen I went off three years before my time and, funny enough, this job was waiting for me.'

'Do you like being here?'

'I'm very happy', he replied. 'You know, being a child lover, it makes no difference what colour or creed. If you can do good, you do it. That's how I feel.'

Fraser wanted photographs so we went into the adjoining section which was for girls. Children rushed towards us in a pack, pushing and shoving and fighting for our hands. Some crawled and it seemed they would be trampled. Around us was a sea of shaved heads and bright eager eyes. Sores scarred many arms and legs and crusted noses dripped mucous. Gouws and Gozongo each scooped up a child or two and carried them as they walked, calling to an older girl to take the smaller ones still fighting for attention.

'For the children to get resettled here, to get accustomed, it's not so easy', Gouws said. 'Mr Gozongo and I were talking this morning. It's up to us to build them from scratch bottom, you could say. They come from a broken home or no home at all and yet they cry, "I want to go home ... " It's heartbreaking, you know. Honestly, sometimes I feel like crying with them. But you have to live with it.'

'It's not so easy', echoed Gozongo. 'However much the institution tries to act as a home, it is no home and there is always a craving for home. Some people feel that even the best children's home is not as good as the worst home.'

Fraser peeled off the children's hands and took his pictures. Gozongo went with us to our car. Older children were beginning to return from school. I asked where the boys went when the orphanage released them.

Finding suitable foster homes was a problem, he said, since most blacks already had large families. What usually happened was that they simply stayed on at the orphanage. This had not always been the case.

'It had been the custom', Gozongo explained, 'to put them into a reformatory outside of King William's Town, but we found they had great difficulty in adjusting to the more rigid rules. They were like those imprisoned for crimes, confined to the institution. Even their clothing was the same.'

Once this had tragic results. 'Two of our boys who had been admitted to the reformatory tried to escape one night. They were making their way down the road when a policeman saw them. When he shouted at them to stop, they became afraid and began to run. Seeing their clothing and thinking them to be escapees, the policeman shot at them.'

One was killed, the other wounded critically. Both were 12 years old.

'Some of us decided we wanted to do something'

Anne Coppinger, her three-month old son under one arm, carry-cot in the other, supervised the loading of boxes in her car.

'Most of that was food parcels', she said as she drove along the quiet suburban streets. 'Things like skimmed milk, dried vegetables, samp [crushed maize] and beans. When we can, we add peanut butter or tea, but that's not very often. Our finances are usually in a dreadful state and we just lurch from week to week.'

She left the baby at a friend's, came back with a bag of yarn and needles. 'We're stuck a bit for storage space at the Window', she said.

Blue-jean clad Anne, about 30, is one of four or five young women — among them Trudi Thomas — working with mothers of malnourished children. Several months before the *Daily Dispatch* ran a series on malnutrition among blacks. 'Some of us decided we wanted to do something', Anne said. She and the others give money each month and try to round up other contributions.

'The basic idea', Anne explained, 'is that if there is a malnourished child, there's usually a problem family behind it. The father may be dead or, what is more likely, he's deserted them. So you have a case of a woman with a small child or children who can't get work. When she seeks help at the hospital, that is how we find her. The idea, of course is not only to care for the malnourished child, but to tackle the problems of the family as well.'

Sometimes it's a case of a lost reference book or a pension eligibility and the woman will be directed to the proper agency. Usually it's a question of work, which is more difficult. 'If we could find a job for everyone, I think our problems would be solved', Anne said.

Rather than take on continuing support of families, the women hold knitting classes hoping that the mothers can eventually become self-supporting and still be at home with their children.

We got out of the car at Frere Hospital. Prince Ngxolwana waited. Between two buildings a long line of blacks waited to see doctors at the outpatient clinic. It had rained and dirt had become mud. People sat on the ground next to a steel mesh fence. Infants bound to their mother's backs coughed or whimpered quietly. The line straggled on for the length of a football field.

In a far building, Dr Thomas and a black woman in a white uniform saw patients. Trudi smiled when she saw Anne, reached in her pocket for a R10 [£6] note. 'It came to us from a woman in church when I spoke there about Care', she said.

'This is how our money comes in', Anne explained.

A thin woman in native dress came to the door and Prince talked with her. Her name was Mrs Blanket and she had come for a food parcel. Anne tried to lift one of the boxes and couldn't. 'Can she carry all this?' she asked Prince.

'Yes. She said she can.'

Anne brought out a packet from the box. 'Does she know how to use this soup?' Mrs Blanket shook her head. 'Tell her to put a spoonful in boiling water and stir.' Mealie meal and samp and a can of sardines were also in the carton and would provide Mrs Blanket and her four children with 'reasonable nutrition' for a week. Health authorities would contribute powdered milk.

Together Prince and Anne lifted the box onto Mrs Blanket's head. Mrs Blanket smiled. 'She said thank you', Prince told Anne.

'Good luck', Anne said.

'Did you notice her bare feet? That is a very good indication of poverty', said Trudi. 'If they have any money at all, the first thing they do is buy shoes.'

Another woman came in. 'She's got one son and he's in the hospital with TB so she's destitute. She's got a grandchild to care for and chest disease too.'

Mrs Majompela produced a carefully folded letter from under her blanket. 'We filled in the disability form for her', Trudi explained. She and Anne read the paper. It said Mrs Majompela was to report to the Bantu authority yesterday. Prince asked her if she had. She said no.

'This is what we run into', Anne said. 'They don't tell them. Prince, she must go the Bantu affairs place tomorrow at eight and take all her forms with her.'

Mrs Majompela smiled. 'No problems', Prince reported.
among the creases of a scarf which she then tied around her waist.

'Prince, ask her if there are any other problems.'

Mrs Majampela smiled. 'No problems', Prince reported.

Anne gathered up the remaining parcels. We went back to the car, again passing the line of people which seemed as long as it had earlier.

'If we take 20 or 30 families — or however many we can afford to help — and support them until the mother can earn a bit of money by selling what she makes, I think it is better than giving out one grand food parcel to many and then that's all', Anne said. 'As you can see, it's very unstructured, but I don't think it would work any other way. It's rather depressing, because you see an endless string of people and you can't possibly solve their problems. It's not only the pass laws and influx control and migrant workers, it's the unbelievably high birth rate and the men who don't take responsibility for their families.'

Downtown, boxes were unloaded in front of the theatre. 'Birth control', Anne said grimly. 'If we could only get this across.'

We went up a wide wood staircase with three landings. At the top landing, tables and chairs had been set out. Eight women and four or five small children waited. 'We also have coffee and high protein biscuits and it becomes a social occasion as well', Anne said.

Another volunteer arrived with skeins of yarn and more needles. 'One of us bought needles, two of us got the wool', she said.

Anne pointed out a woman who waited. It was the first time she'd come to Care. 'I've organized a food parcel for her, and I don't like the others to see it. It's very difficult to determine the need. You have to go on trust and give with love.'

The woman teaching sat down between two black women: 'Now, you see, you hold the needles like this... '

Later I talked with one of the women. She spoke only Afrikaans and Xhosa so Prince translated her replies.

'My name is Emily Cisha', she said, 'and I live in the location. My parents came down from the Transkei and when they died, I came to East London on my own. I have four children. The eldest was born in 1961 and there is this baby. All of them are well now. I have no husband. I feed them with the help of Care.'

I asked how she had come to Care.

'The doctor introduced me to these people. These children were unwell and I was attending the clinic and the doctor asked me about these children's history. I explained it to her and the doctor came to know my destitute position.'

I asked if she worked.

'Before the last one was born I used to go around jobbing then when I got the last baby, nobody would take me.' She shifted the infant in her arms. 'I can do domestic work. Before I had this baby, I made R11.50 [£6.90] a month. I have no income now. The only income I get is what Care gives to me. First they taught me how to make a jersey, now they are teaching me to make a mat. When I am perfect, I will sell these things. I am so destitute I must take what I am offered.'

The women who had been working began filing out. The volunteers stayed on to pack up the yarns and needles and to wash the coffee cups. One had brought her daughter, about three, and she played hide and seek in the hallway with a black boy about the same age.

I asked Emily what plans and hopes she had for the future.

'I have my wishes of being somebody, but it is a pity that I have nowhere to start', she told Prince. 'I have no, what they call it — diving board. As far as marriage is concerned, I have my doubts because men have a tendency of not wanting another man's children.'

Anne came down the stairs with the keys in her hand. Emily

adjusted the baby on her back and tied the blanket around him. At the bottom of the steps we said goodbye and went our various black and white ways.

'I believe in peace, in coexisting'

Across the table, Errol Theron finished lunch. Short, solidly built, his features have an Asian cast and his skin is the colour of honey. Like Mary and Leslie, Errol was on the Window Theatre board. He'd acted in local theatre, but this had been before I came.

We'd been friends since 1972. He'd come into my office then — he worked in the advertising section of the *Dispatch* — and we'd begun talking. I remember mentioning I hoped to come back. He asked why the hell would I want to do that. The answer he got was so glib and thoughtless that after he left, I wrote down some reasons and sent them on to him. We talked a lot after that and I'd spent an occasional weekend and many evenings at his home in Buffalo Flats.

At 30, Errol is jaunty, self-confident — even arrogant. I liked him. Many people found him abrasive. There was no façade to Errol. You always knew where he stood. That day, for instance. Fraser and I had moved into a grand, old Dutch-style house in the centre of town. Errol walked in as if he owned it.

Ida, the maid who'd come with the house, gathered up plates. She looked at Errol with interest. Knowing the elderly pair who owned the place — the first thing they'd said to us was how much they despised Donald Woods — it was a safe bet that no one but whites had ever sat at their table. I wondered if she would tell 'the madam' about Errol.

He's Coloured which is, in the South African context, any person of mixed blood. Coloureds come in seven different classifications: 'I'm Cape Coloured I think — or maybe it's just Coloured', Errol said. 'I can't remember which kind actually. But I consider myself black. I decided a long time ago who I wanted to identify with.'

His father is the illegitimate son of an Afrikaner and a Coloured woman. Some of his half-brothers, same name, are leading businessmen, one the mayor, of the small inland town where Errol's father was born. Errol's mother's people came from Mauritius. He believes her family to be of French extraction.

Errol had this to say about them: 'My father was a mechanic and a driver, general handyman. We were never very rich. He drank a lot 25 years back but then just kicked it completely. My father was head of the house, but I think my mother exerted a strong influence too. At the moment they are very religious, very devout, members of the Pentecostal church.

'The overriding thing in my parents' life was education. To illustrate a point, I've got a brother who's brilliant. He came first right through then one year he came second. He got a hell of a hiding for it. That's not true to form in our family. If you come first, there's no reason you're not first straight through.

'My brother, the one I spoke of, he's about fourth down the line [Errol is one of ten children], got a scholarship to study medicine at the University of Cape Town. But he was 15 when he matriculated and completely and emotionally unprepared for a big city and he failed. But he's a teacher now and a very good one. My eldest brother is a teacher as well and here again the same thing: he went to varsity and it was too much for him. He was free, let's put it that way.'

All of his sisters became teachers as well. 'My sisters had a big influence on my life because I am the youngest and they were quite old when I got on the scene. As I grew up, my parents, who had been very strict, were mellowing and my sisters had already been teaching and all of this helped to shape me. Then when I went to school I had good teachers. I grew up very aware of a lot of things.'

When he says 'aware', Errol means politically aware. In South Africa this is no advantage. Especially if you are not white. When Errol's brothers and sisters finished high school they could go on to a South African university which would accept blacks with special dispensation from government ministers. But by the time Errol graduated, the University of the Western Cape had been established for Coloureds. He did not apply there however, but to the traditional institutions. Accepted by all of them, he was refused the necessary permits from authorities.

'They gave no reasons', Errol said. 'Possibly it was my political attitude. So, in the interim, I got a job at the *Daily Dispatch*. The prospects seemed reasonable and I didn't want to go to this new Coloured university. I wouldn't have lasted in any case — a so-called Coloured university with all the lecturers coming from Stellensbosch, indoctrinating you with Nat philosophy.' (Stellenbosch University has produced every Nationalist prime minister of South Africa and is where the intellectual justification for apartheid was formulated.) He said his concept of a university is of a place where students are taught how to think, not what to think.

The facts about the University of the Western Cape are, for him, borne out by seeing the products of it: 'These people cannot think for themselves. They're programmed along a certain way. A lot of them are teachers and I suppose if things had developed normally I would have been also because that is the tradition in my family. In the black communities when we were growing up, the leaders in the community were teachers. A teacher was someone to be respected. But with the advent of Coloured education and Bantu education, all that was swept away. The teacher now is someone to be despised because he has to be so careful of what he says and of who he says it to. People who have become principals are people who toe the line, follow the syllabuses as laid down — even if the syllabuses are all lies.'

At the time we talked, Errol was taking correspondence courses through the University of South Africa but finding that less than satisfactory. 'I thrive in a competitive situation', he said, 'and this is what I lack at present. And in my job situation I'm completely frustrated as well. Such authority as I have is a tacit authority with no weight to it. I'm just rolling along, kicking doors open, clawing my way into certain situations by sheer cussedness.'

His attitude offends many whites and Errol is aware of this.

'I think what a lot of people hold against me', Errol said, 'is that I don't have a complex because I'm black.

'South Africa is geared so that anything that is beautiful, is good, is affluent — anything that's nice — the white man has got. Therefore, what you aspire to be or what awes you as a black person, because of the brainwashing, is a white. I don't have this. I went to this place the other day and we mixed freely. And it was treated by everyone as a wonderful thing. All of us sitting together, drinking tea. That's beautiful. As far as I'm concerned, that's rubbish. What the hell. I'm giving you a status higher than me because I am thrilled that I can sit down and have a cup of tea with you? I marvelled at that, but a lot of black people have that attitude. That's what black consciousness is trying to eradicate.'

Errol was at that first meeting in Durban when Steve Biko articulated black consciousness and he believes in it. 'We're not interested in concession here and concession there — not that maybe I won't take advantage of them if it suits me and furthers my ends. Our goal is direct to where the power is. The law-making machine, that is what must be got ahold of first. It must happen. It's inevitable.'

I asked how he thought this would come about.

'The Afrikaners', he said, 'will not give away power. But, make no mistake, I do not advocate a bloody revolution. I mean, look at my set-up. I've got a family, three children. I believe in peace, in coexisting. I believe in being fair, in being just. I believe that if I take a right away from somebody else, I will be taking a right away from myself. So I don't believe the white man must be chased into the sea, but I also don't believe that he must continue with his criminal acts against me and my family which is what is happening, day in, day out — morning to night.

'My children's whole future is being shaped by them. I really have no say in it. They've got to grow up in a certain environment, they've got to go to a certain school. Their horizons are limited as mine have been.'

Errol said he believes he is an average person but that even his average potential has been stunted, his development stalled by the denial of a university education. 'And I've got no bargaining powers really, with the *Dispatch* or with anybody.' After 14 years with the paper he is earning R510 [£306] a month. Fraser and I each earned R624 [£364]. I asked how much he would earn in his job if he were white.

'I don't know,' he said impatiently, 'but I wouldn't be in that job if I were white'.

I asked what he thought about Afrikaners and he said that, at least, unlike white English-speaking liberals, you always knew where you stood with them. 'If an Afrikaner hates you, he hates you. If he likes you, he likes you.' Errol, who grew up near Afrikaners, says their outlook, religion, language, are common to Coloureds. 'If you would put a Coloured in an Afrikaner household, it would not be a traumatic experience.'

As far as his own future goes, Errol would like to study law — 'not to become a lawyer, but maybe one day to help shape the South Africa that I want — to get everything sorted out after the mess and there's going to be a mess.

'I feel my first task is to myself — to equip myself. I feel inadequate. I wouldn't like to be a politician as such, but I would like to help shape things. I think this is my first priority at the moment, to get myself sorted out. But I get involved all the time. If it's toward that goal, I get involved.'

It's dangerous to get involved in South Africa and Errol is very aware of that. 'I also believe that one must not over extend one's resources', he said, 'because then you get chopped. Martyrs are useful, but I think we must first get the necessary muscle power. Not compromise, that's the other thing. I don't believe in it. You might be flexible in attaining the ultimate aim, but I don't believe you can compromise with that aim.'

His ultimate aim? 'To be free in the land of my birth.'

He doesn't believe that working within the system is the answer. 'I don't believe you can use something like the CRC [Coloured Representative Council] as a vehicle for meaningful change and I feel the guys who are doing it are ruining their reputations because, ultimately, they will also be called to book. They are neutralized to such an extent they make fools of themselves. Take for instance the CRC. Five hundred or something rand per month plus all the other perks. They're growing fat on it. How can you pay me to fight you? When you pay me you're going to influence me in some way or another.'

One of Errol's brothers has moved to Australia and I asked if he had considered getting out.

'I've thought of it fleetingly, but I won't', he said. 'I think I can be happy in this country. I know it. It's a good country. I feel it is the place for me and I'd like to stay.'

He believes there will be change but doesn't know exactly how it will come about.

'Can you imagine a huge mass of jelly struggling and moving? It just goes in any direction where there's a crack or where there's a way out or to move forward. I believe that's the nature of things for the foreseeable future.'

He talked finally of how it would be worked out under black majority rule: 'I feel the capitalistic system won't do — particularly as it's practised in South Africa, an elitist thing in the hands of the oppressors. But I don't believe in a communistic or socialistic state', he said. 'In fact, I don't really know very much about these. What I think is completely from my own experience and what I feel. There must be adequate reward for labour, for initiative, but not to the extent it's practised in the capitalistic society, where it's completely disproportionate. I feel there must be some sort of meriting, but it must be on real ability, not on the ability to manipulate.

'I also feel it is up to the state if, for instance, a person with the capability of being a labourer earns only a labourer's salary, his children must not be held back because of the father's limitations. I feel there's going to have to be some sort of mix between a capitalistic society and socialistic state. Where initiative is not completely stamped out, because people like to achieve and people like to see their efforts recognized, but it must not be as disproportionate as it is now. There must be a fine balance struck and perhaps some revaluation of what gives us a sense of satisfaction.

'But the system we have now — where a few people have a fantastic standard of living and the rest are starving — can't continue. All the safeguards and policies have to be worked out, but basically what it should be is that initiative as such must not be stifled, though it must not reach ridiculous extents either. That's the reason I would like to study law and constitutional matters, to try and work out these things.

'So, I guess the way I see it is that it will have to be a marriage of the two, a compromise, until our sense of values has changed. You find even ardent revolutionaries being impressed by a beautiful, smart car — a nice house. This is contrary to everything they espouse. And while I feel materialistic standards are wrong standards really, I'm also realistic enough to accept that one can't change them overnight.

'Whether the kind of thing I've talked about can ever work, I don't know', Errol said. 'But I think it's worth a try.'

'South Africa is a paradise as long as you don't think'

The Hogsback is in an inland range of mountains and gets its name from the highest of the ridges which is bare, rocky and striated. Below it, however, the slopes are forested with pines and firs. Streams run fast and clear among the trees and waterfalls plunge from great heights to the valley floor.

Hogsback weather is wetter and colder than in East London, some 100 miles away. Damp grey fogs roll in frequently, hiding tree tops and muffling sounds. But it's a place loved by the few hundred year-round residents — most of them retired and English-speaking — and by summer visitors who flock there to escape the heat of the flatlands.

Mary Omond's parents, Noel and Patricia Powrie, had lived on the Hogsback for about five years. Many years before that, they'd bought acreage with a cottage and Noel had gradually converted it to a full-size house. Noel loved the Hogsback. Living there continued to tax his considerable talents for invention. He'd rigged his own electrical system which began with a waterwheel at the stream. After lightning demolished his TV antenna and blew up the set, he built another antenna which he can lower, single-handedly, from the ground when storms threaten. Noel, by choice, seldom left the mountain.

On the other hand, Patricia, his tiny, sociable 70-year-old wife, left whenever she had an excuse. With an income of her own, she spent a month or so every year with their married daughter in England, drove to East London, about two hours away, whenever there was a concert or play she wanted to see.

Their political views were as different as their interests and while Patricia, overcoming conservative beginnings, grew ever more amenable to racial equality, Noel became more against it. At the Hogsback one could always count on hot political arguments.

We had drinks on the Powrie's verandah and watched darkness come to the valley on Christmas day. Dinner, turkey with all the trimmings, was followed by the exchange of presents. The next day, Boxing Day, was a holiday for the servants and after breakfast other people began to arrive. Initially, families who lived on the Powrie's land and worked for them. Then came blacks from nearby, among them many children who, on request, would sing and jig. Casual visitors got coins or hard candy. There was a lot of drinking as well and as the day wore on, many slept by the side of the road.

In the evening I talked to Roger Omond.

Roger was born in East London. His parents lived just outside of Alice then — his father principal of a black school. When he was promoted to inspector, the family moved to Kokstad, a small town between Durban and the northern border of Transkei. Roger describes it as 'insular, very English-speaking, very United Party. The polo playing centre of South Africa'.

From Kokstad they went to Port Elizabeth. Roger was 12. 'In those days, in the circles in which my parents moved, again very much English-speaking, United Party, in an apoliticized society. Deliberately so. In spite of the fact my father was in black education, there was never any social intermingling among him and his school principals, his subinspectors. There was also in them then, and I think still, a fairly strong element of English versus Afrikaans.'

His initial involvement in politics came with membership in NUSAS when he was a student at Rhodes University. During the years Roger was involved with NUSAS it was an activist organization and many of its members had been arrested and subsequently charged with aiding the African Resistance Movement.

After graduation he went to work on the subs desk of the *Daily Dispatch*. At the beginning of 1968 Roger was assigned to Cape Town for the parliamentary session. It was an interesting one: 'The BOSS Bill setting up the Bureau for State Security got passed then', Roger said. 'Only concerned with political crimes, quote, unquote. BOSS was a sort of CIA but with the most incredible terms of reference in the Bill — prohibiting anyone, anywhere from discussing or writing anything about it. You could literally not say after the Bill was pushed through Parliament, that there was a Bureau for State Security. It was unbelievably widely defined. Something like, "No one may refer to any matter which may, or is calculated to be, related to state security." And the definition of state security is left up to the Minister of Justice. It was greeted as the end of all Bills. Subsequently there was an outcry, but it was passed with some opposition dissent, as was normal.'

Roger, covering another session the following year, found himself totally disillusioned, not only with Nationalists but with the opposition United Party whose English-speaking members professed liberal views.

'Came the end,' Roger said, 'and you realized that this whole gang were talking to themselves, not listening to each other, and what they were saying had very little relevance, apart from Helen Suzman [until 1974, Parliament's sole member of the Progressive Party], to what was taking place in the country. Just a lot of whiteys saying, "Shall we do this?" "Should we do that?"

'I got pissed off in the end. It's a very incestuous atmosphere. You got out of the place and slapped your head and said, "OK, so what?" No one gives the slightest damn about who said what to whom. It's all irrelevant.'

After that last session, Roger, tired of South Africa, bored with East London, left to work on a newspaper in Cardiff, Wales. A year later Donald Woods phoned him and asked him to come back to the *Dispatch* as night editor which he did at the beginning of 1972. When questioned as to what this job involved, Roger replied, 'My duties are mainly to keep Donald out of jail. This was his specific brief.' The broad definition of South African laws make this necessary, he explained.

'It requires a sort of sixth sense of saying, "We can get away with this. No one will prosecute. That one's dicey, therefore I must refer it to the editor." By that time the government had managed to narrow the area of debate down so much that even to talk or warn of violence was forbidden which in retrospect of Soweto, 16 June 1976 on, looks like some kind of sick joke.

'This was the sort of thing in those days that Donald was very worried about. My particular job then, apart from bringing out the paper every night, was to pick up the nuances. A very tricky thing, but I presume I did it successfully since he didn't go to jail. Then I landed him in the crap four years later.'

The newspaper had been running a series of debates by Mapetla Mohapi on whether blacks should enter Bantustan institutions because these support apartheid. This had led to letters to the editors.

'I got one', Roger said. 'It was very long. I didn't think it particularly impressive, but I kept it aside for a rainy day when I didn't have anything else to use. Unfortunately, the rainy day arrived about a week after the guy who wrote it had been banned.'

He found out his mistake when he got a frantic call from Leslie Xinwa early in the morning on the day the letter was printed. 'All I foresaw was court cases, hassles, problems', he said. 'I don't need problems like that. Donald doesn't need problems like that. The newspaper doesn't need problems like that. I'd cocked it up. I'd been hired specifically to avoid this sort of thing and I'd screwed it up.'

After hearing from Leslie, Roger called Donald: 'I said, "I've landed you in the shit." He said, "My god. Well, maybe they won't notice." But they did. The Special Branch came round to Donald's office about a week later.'

Towards the end of 1975, the *Dispatch*, represented by Kingsley Kingon, was fined by the court. Donald Woods, as director and editor, was cautioned and discharged. The *Dispatch* appealed against the decision. Sometime later, an appeal court reversed the judgement of the lower court. The vital fact in Kingon's defence had been that the banning order had not yet been published in the *Government Gazette* when the *Dispatch* had printed the letter — even though a short article reporting the banning had been carried by the *Dispatch* some few days before the letter had been printed.

This case was followed in six months by the other in which Donald refused to name the sources of his information about Hattingh. 'Both cases we won', Roger said. 'That's Donald's main advantage. He's the luckiest bastard alive. Like Napoleon said, "Give me lucky generals, never mind if they can fight." '

I asked Roger what he thought the future held for South Africa.

'I think there's going to be a lot of shit', he replied. 'We're going to be in a state of constant crisis and the economy will nosedive intermittently as this goes on. Apart from the Sowetos and the economy going straight down, I don't know. There are some four and a half million whites — trying to protect for themselves, exclusively, a society which cannot work without the help of 24 million blacks. I can't see any peaceful answer. The whites have got all the money. The whites have got all the weapons. They're determined to fight for their privileges, or as they see them, their rights. But the 24 million others have now got the bit between their teeth and they're not going to let the whites get away with it. Urban violence will occur, re-occur, become intensified.

'The thing about Soweto is that it has been confined to black townships', Roger continued. 'Whites have not been seriously inconvenienced. In fact, if it hadn't been for the newspapers, they wouldn't really have known that anything was going on because the milk still arrived on time, the newspaper still arrived on time, bread still was baked. But it's obvious that if there is a genuine feeling about revolution, then the fight will be taken to the white suburbs and the white centres. You're going to have petrol bombs thrown in the middle of the shopping centres. You're going to have petrol bombs thrown into the offices of the *Daily Dispatch*. What happens after that phase, I don't know.

'I get particularly angry', he said, 'that the country in which, by an accident of birth, I happen to have grown up to like and to which I owe some sort of loyalty, is being fucked up by a few people in Pretoria who are leading us into the classic revolutionary situation and expecting whites like myself to fight for them. And in any revolution it's going to be white versus black and the guy at the other end of a sten gun is not going to say, "Did you vote National or United Party? Or did you vote Prog or are you more to the left of the Progs?" He's going to pull the bloody trigger. I don't want to be on the other end of the gun nor do I want to be holding the gun. I'm not prepared to fight for these bastards.'

I asked if he had considered getting out.

'I have thought about leaving,' he said, 'but for other reasons mainly. I have a vested interest in seeing things sorted out and I hope I can help which is very irrational, I admit. I would think I would only leave for two reasons: if a job came up in London — because London is a city I love; and two, if Mary decided she'd had enough. As far as emigrating to Australia or Canada just for the sake of getting out, no.'

I wondered what he liked about living in South Africa.

'Apart from the wind, I like the climate. I like the amenities for a white South African at this particular stage. They're beautiful. It's an old quote and a true one: "South Africa is a paradise as long as you don't think." There's always this accusation about white liberals — that they're just salving their consciences by making muttering noises against the government. Like I write leaders. I don't know how many people read the leaders. I don't know how many people are swayed or changed by them, but every now and again, I catch myself thinking, "What happens if things do change? My life will certainly change."

'In some ways it's a very comfortable position to be a white liberal in South Africa. It's the best of both worlds. But again, if someone offered me a similar salary in Australia, I wouldn't leave. I've been through that scene in Wales. I got bored stiff with minor issues. In South Africa we deal with major issues.

'You choose a role for yourself. If you're a liberal, you're either out throwing bombs — I'm talking about whites — or distributing pamphlets for the ANC for which you will get sent away for five years — pamphlets which very few people read. OK, I choose newspapers and I write leaders which satisfy my own political inclinations. We can highlight various things as we did over Mohapi's death. Because we have a high black readership, we can try to tell blacks that not all whites are racist. We can try to tell whites that not all blacks are kaffirs; that a non-racial socialist society is the only way to ensure some sort of peaceful solution.' So far, Roger admitted ruefully, he's experienced a singular lack of success.

I asked if the probability of violence frightened him.

'Sure,' he replied, 'you get worried about the revolution starting. If there's trouble and you're a convenient white figure, you're likely to get killed. I was thinking about that last Sunday morning when we were sitting around the Belonsky's pool, drinking gin, eating watermelon. I think the major thing that worries all South Africans is the fact that one day, and increasingly soon, the majority of the black population is going to say, "We've had enough."

'If you're white, you obviously recognize that this is the one major factor in your life. That one day the balloon is going to go up. But to a large extent you push it to the back of your mind and say, "Not today. Not this week. Not this month. Not this year."

'I guess my overriding feeling is that I'm very, very pissed off about this bunch in Pretoria who, for the sake of their own insecurity and pathological hang-ups, are screwing the country up and I'm expected to go along with it — this crazy system. And if I don't go along with this crazy system then I'm a traitor, a Communist or whatever they want to call it.

'I just get angry at people who have arrogated to themselves the right to say what is going to happen to this country without consulting me, without consulting 24 million other people. What I feel are just overwhelming feelings of anger and distress.'

'The word "apartheid" is just "apartness" '

At the Dominee's house, a black woman in a bright orange uniform dusted a wrought iron fence which ran across the front of the lot and alongside a dirt footpath. On either side of the street silver oaks were flowering with clusters of tomato red, spidery blossoms, in front of straight rows of white stucco houses with red tile roofs. A white church of substantial size was on the corner. This was Cambridge, an Afrikaner suburb of East London.

Leslie Xinwa had referred to a Dutch Reformed minister he'd worked for while in prison and I'd hoped to talk with him. He'd left the area but in trying to find him I'd spoken with Dominee J.H. Loubser who'd subsequently agreed to a visit 'if we don't talk about politics'.

About a million and a half white South Africans are members of the Dutch Reformed Church. So are a half a million Coloureds and almost a million blacks. This fundamentalist Church, based on Calvinism, exerts tremendous influence on the country. Dutch Reformed could be called the national religion. Because of the Church, cinemas close on Sunday, no organized sport is allowed. Books and films are heavily censored.

Inevitably, towards the end of our conversation Dominee Loubser did speak of South Africa's political problems.

'Now and again we have had a few riots, but I think', he said, 'our main concern is the advance of Communism. The net is drawn closer now.'

I asked who he thought was trying to impose Communism. 'I wouldn't say it is always directed by someone. We can't blame the

Russians for everything that's going wrong', Dominee Loubser said with a smile. 'The Biblical prophecies tell us that in the final days we'll get this. But I think fortunately there is a lot of backbone in South Africa. I hope we'll be able to resist all of this, even if we are a minority. In the past — and this is a great consolation — the minority got on with their task and what they stood for. Look at the disciples of Christ. They were only a handful of uneducated people. So I don't think we should be scared too much of numbers if we stand firm.'

Personally he says he has no fear of revolution. 'Peaceful coexistence I think is not so difficult', he said. 'In fact, I get along with all groups very well. As far as being afraid for one's life, I don't think there's any cause for that.'

He sidestepped the question of whether or not he personally believed in apartheid. 'This word "apartheid", it's unfortunate it's ever been fabricated, because it isn't our idea to reject certain people. In every country, you have the difference in ethnic groups and they have their own ways and there will be a natural separation. I mean, I can't expect a German to attend my church. Every group has its own tradition and its own culture, its way of doing things. The Bible speaks of this.

'The word "apartheid" is just "apartness". I think there's something great in it. People aren't made the same. I'm against the forcing of these matters. If it comes in a natural way, it's much better. It's like a ripe peach — if you press it, you only damage it. But there's no matter of "apart-hate". I see no reason why we can't live together peacefully. People just aren't made the same and these are God-given differences.'

Dominee Loubser was born in a small town in the Orange Free State. His parents were teachers, members of the Dutch Reformed Church. 'I always had it in mind to be a minister,' he said, 'though as a small boy I had the idea also of being an engine driver.'

There's a similarity between the goals of this Dutch Reformed minister and those of the administrator of the orphanage, Mr Gouws, an engineer on the railways and later in missionary-type service for the Church. These are the directions that Afrikaners tend to go. Railroads, harbours, airlines, along with the postal service and telephone system which it administers, have staff which consist almost totally of Afrikaners. Traditionally, they have held government jobs or farmed just as, traditionally, English-speaking South Africans have chosen to be part of the business world or lawyers, doctors, educators or journalists. Divided already by culture and the part of the country where they live — the majority of Afrikaners are in the Orange Free State and the Transvaal, English-speakers in Natal and the Cape provinces — this channelling into certain types of work only increases the isolation of the two white populations.

Generally speaking, English-speaking South Africans tend to think of themselves as superior to the Afrikaner while he, in turn, resents the former. An English-speaking South African told me that you could always spot an Afrikaner because he drove a big car and his wife wore purple or orange clothes. A familiar and universal racist refrain.

Before leaving, I asked the Dominee if he could suggest other Afrikaners who would be willing to be interviewed. He would, he said, check his files and call me. Then, at the door, he wrote the name of Dr Veen on a slip of paper. 'He's not a member of my congregation,' Dominee Loubser said, 'but he's written to me about some of his ideas and you might find them interesting.'

'They sold our city for thirty pieces of silver'

East London is run by a 16-member city council, two from each of the city's eight wards. Though councillors are elected on a non-partisan basis, there's no secret about who supports which party. When I was there, five were pro-government, five liberal — either Progressive or left-wing United Party — and the remainder somewhere in between.

Ruth Belonsky is a councillor from Ward Six. She's 33, liberal, Jewish, married to an architect, mother of two. I wrote about her in 1972 after she won her first election. We became friends then. She and her husband, Bernie, are close friends of Donald and Wendy Woods and it was Donald who encouraged her to run for office and promoted her candidacy personally and through the newspaper. The *Dispatch* had absolutely no conscience regarding advocacy journalism. Liberal candidates and office-holders got more than their share of lineage, not just on the editorial page but in news stories.

Most of the racial issues considered by the council had been raised by Ruth. 'When I started', she said, 'I had no intention of getting involved in this area, but it gradually just happened.'

One of the most hotly debated issues — by both the council and the city — concerned Ruth's campaign to open the central library to all races. In 1975 the council, by a small majority, approved the measure. The vote, for tactical reasons, came when the mayor, an Afrikaner Nationalist, was overseas.

'When he came back, he was furious', Ruth remembered. 'He got on to Senator [Geoff] O'Connell and I think he had a lot to do with getting the decision changed. O'Connell then got on to the [Provincial] administrator who wrote to us saying if we did not toe the line and change back, the provincial subsidy would be stopped.'

Black Sash women organized petitions supporting use of the library by all races and within three days came up with over a thousand names. 'The people were up in arms about it and it didn't seem to matter what political persuasion they were, they just seemed to feel that something like the library should be open to everyone.' But in spite of the petitions, the council backed down in the face of provincial disapproval and voted 15 to Ruth's single vote to return the library to its all-white status.

At that meeting, Ruth vowed not to set foot in the library until it was open to all. 'I also told them', she said, 'that I thought they'd sold our city for thirty pieces of silver which they literally had done.'

Early in January, Fraser, my son Clay and I moved into the Belonskys' house for six weeks while they were on holiday. A place we'd been promised had fallen through so this suited our situation. The Belonskys' house is in the suburb of Vincent, west of the city; a quiet, residential area with large lots and tree-lined streets. Though only five to ten minutes from town, they had chickens in the back part of their property and monkeys lived in the woods which went down to a deep ravine.

Vegetables grew in a plot by the side of the house and in the backyard was a large swimming pool. Frangipani trees dropped blossoms into the water. Though the Belonskys were away, two dogs, hamsters, ducks and cats stayed on. A man came to garden twice a week, a 'weed lady' on other days. Amelia, the servant, remained to cook and clean.

During the weeks we were there, we saw a lot of Cyril Mjo, leader of a black choir for which Ruth played her violin, and of Peter

Mopp, member of the Coloured Management Committee which reported to the white city council. Cyril sold clothes in the city and when he was through for the day, he came by. Peter brought his family to swim on several Sundays.

'As far as dreams for myself, I don't think any African can say'

Many of the black people I came to know in East London had been in prison. This wasn't something they told you immediately, but something that eventually, because of some conversation, you learned. For instance, Cyril Mjo. We met him at one of the Belonsky parties. The choir he directs — and which Ruth accompanies — was there after rehearsal. There must have been about 30 that night — 20 choir members, the Woods, the Omonds and Mary's mother, Patricia and the Van Gends. Cyril was the star. Usually it's Donald but even he is no match for Cyril who, quite simply, is a magnetic person.

Members of the East London Harmony Set sang during the evening. Donald, hair rumpled, drink in his hand, added his off-key voice to a couple of African folk tunes.

When I had the chance, I suggested to Cyril that the next time a concert was scheduled, he let me know in advance and we'd run a story. So, a few weeks later, he appeared at the doorway of the features office. When I remember Cyril, that is where I see him — smiling, standing easily, filling the space.

One of the questions in a routine interview was how the choir came to be. Cyril had begun it in prison. Some of the men in it then were still with him. He asked that this not be included in the story but agreed to talk about that later.

I'd see Cyril at Window Theatre, at Ruth's, and we gradually got acquainted. When we were staying at the Belonsky house, he came by fairly regularly. One Saturday morning Fraser and Clay were gone and Cyril had the time so we talked at length then. It was hot and we sat by the pool.

Cyril's mother was a domestic and he was born in the house where she worked, not far from where we talked. The family lived in Duncan Village, in a big, ten-room dwelling, which housed nine other families.

Scholarships took him through high school. When he graduated, loan bursaries enabled him to go to university. 'I played rugby at Fort Hare', Cyril said. 'I was on the black national side, playing scrum half and utility back. I was doing a B.Sc.' His parents hoped he would be a doctor but there wasn't sufficient money for that.

His mother supported the family — Cyril has a brother and two sisters. His father was a semi-invalid. 'The kind of job he did was wool sorting and he was an asthmatic and asthma and wool don't mix', Cyril said. 'But he was in demand. His fellows would come and sometimes he would be tempted into it and go. I remember on those days I had to go to the bus and fetch him because he would not make the distance between the bus stop and our house.'

Cyril left Fort Hare in 1961, married and went to work in a pharmaceutical factory in East London. He said, 'In these parts, well, in South Africa generally, if you are black you get very little money despite your education. I went to the pharmaceutical because I thought they would help me to do pharmacy too. But they wanted me to serve three years as an apprentice and the money was too low, too low for me to live on. It was like being at Fort Hare. At that time I needed money and no education. Money.

'Then the government came after me in 1963. They caught me at work. They'd been looking for me.' He was charged with membership in the banned ANC. His brother, Zola, was similarly charged but with an added count of sabotage. Cyril was held for eleven months then sentenced to two years in prison. His brother was sent to Robben Island for 21 years.

'I started the music as an "awaiting trial" ', Cyril said. 'There wasn't much one could do so I started writing out music and making other fellows sing too and forget what was going on. Being separated from life is one thing, but the terrible treatment there is another thing.'

Initially those singing were men arrested with him. Later other prisoners joined them. 'We found them wanting this sort of thing', Cyril said. 'And the choir grew and we were joined by another group and then, Christ, big. We were transferred to another prison and stayed there for another year. Fellows from Robben Island joined us then and we made a big choir, 50 voices. Male voices. Good. Most of them didn't smoke and their voices were beautiful.' Cyril wrote out songs from memory: 'I found out afterwards that each and every part was just as it was in the original. I remember a fellow commenting on this when we came out of jail — on this "Fisherman's Good Night". We sang that one and I wrote the music but there was a small part I could not remember. I said, "Gentlemen, I could not remember so I put my part, my harmony, in it." It was felt that the part I put was better than the original harmony. When we came out we looked at the music, it's full of transitions, and this one chap said, "No, man. It's just note for note except this one part that you could not remember. But we prefer yours."'

While Cyril was in prison, his wife supported herself and their two children by teaching.

'It was nice to get out,' Cyril remembered, 'but you find, ja, you've lost a lot and a lot of time. And you've got to do a lot of work. That was why I left rugby. I thought, "Oh Christ, I must be more serious and work harder than before."' He got a job in one of East London's large textile mills, starting as a laboratory assistant at R70 [£42] a month, gradually working up to twice that amount.

'Then', he said, 'I got myself into a bit of a mess. While I was there I was arrested. What a funny thing. Someone suggested that I spoke to her in a manner that suggested I love her. This was a white girl. She felt insulted so I was charged for — what is it? — *crimen injuria.* It is to injure the feelings of somebody. So I left the factory immediately.

'What actually happened is we were in a factory clinic. There are separate doors, a compartment for whites and another one for non-whites. The nurse is black. I was in this clinic and this girl came and she spoke to the nurse and looked at me. The nurse was present. An hour later I was called into the personnel manager's office and asked to explain why that particular girl was upset. They told me she was crying and saying that she met me and I had told her that I loved her. I said, "Why don't you call the girl? Let her come and explain this to me. I don't understand. And why don't you call the nurse?" But it happened, in the end, the police persuaded the nurse to say she was not there. The whole thing got twisted, but that was understandable because the father of this girl is a policeman.'

Cyril was found guilty and fined R50 [£30]. His lawyer advised him that an appeal would be expensive, that it would be better simply to pay the fine and let the matter go.

He got into the clothing business, buying from manufacturers, then selling at factories, hospitals, schools, to individuals: 'Leslie is one of my customers', Cyril said. 'He always looks nice. The director of the Imita Players was another. I was one of them. I was leading actor. But now I'm mostly concerned with the choir and the clothing.'

I asked what plans he had for the future.

'As far as dreams for myself,' Cyril replied, 'I don't think I can say. I don't think any African can say. At my age [42], with the few resources that I have, Christ. No hope at all. Just to live and try and make a future for the children. I'll try to educate them all if they agree. For myself nothing. Not at this stage. I'm late and financially there's no hope.'

Cyril is equally pessimistic about the future of South Africa. 'If it does not change now', he said, 'it will be Vietnam here. It's going to be bad. A lot of us are troubled. Very stubborn, the government. When they change, they surprise you. They come with an insignificant change — something you didn't expect. They make you feel they don't really know what is wanted. You ask for this and you are given that. Strange. What should have been given 30 years ago is being given now.'

Blacks don't want South Africa, he said, they simply want equality, 'black participation in government. But unfortunately, if the government doesn't listen, it will be something else. I know the young people and they are furious. If the government listens ... at the moment, well, it's difficult to say. We don't want the change to come about in a bad way for South Africa. The blacks are reluctant to spill blood, but the government is preparing for war. What a pity. It's strange, they even want to call up women and they have such great manpower in blacks. But they refuse to do this. We are a part of this country. We do not deny that whites have nowhere else to go.

'There is a great joke', Cyril continued. 'They have money, why must they stay here with us? You know, I take my daughters into town and I watch their faces. Going past the museum there is this small park. They jump up then and say, "Christ, town is nice. Town is bright." That's the kind of environment a person living in the twentieth century should have.'

Cyril is also concerned about the poverty he sees among his people and the apparent hopelessness of their position: 'You fill the whole room with your sweat and you get nothing. And the next moment you are out. They can say, "If you feel the money is too little, there are your brothers, waiting outside the gate for this job." For any man to say this to a man with grave responsibilities is terrible, most frustrating. And you can't leave your area. If you're unfortunate like me, born in a poor area like East London, then you'll die poor.'

Cyril sometimes thinks of leaving South Africa; many of his friends, ex-prisoners, have done so. But he has a strong feeling of family. To go away would be to abandon them. He is particularly concerned about his brother on Robben Island. Each year, one of Cyril's family has made the trip to see him. They have 30 minutes to talk and see him through a window that is about a foot square. Guards are nearby.

I asked if Zola seemed different since his imprisonment. Cyril replied: 'It is difficult to talk in terms of changes. He must change because he is growing. He was a boy when he went in. Now he is almost 28. We don't know him so there is the problem. We don't know how he will be. From the letters he writes to us, he is good, a man of substance.'

When Cyril thinks of Zola's release from prison, he remembers his own problems: 'There was a job at the sweets factory and I qualified for this because we all went there, Leslie too, and I won the job. But they looked at my reference book and inquired about my whereabouts during the three-year period. I explained to them and they said, "No man. We can't have you here."'

'Again there was another job', Cyril said. 'A teller at Barclays. They liked me. They were excited. I went through all the tests. They said they were pleased to be having me. Then they looked at the reference book. They said, "What happened?" I told them. They said, "We'll have to refer this to the head office in Cape Town. We don't know what they will say, but we'll be terribly sorry if this is held against you." They did this and it was against me. Another gone. I wouldn't be selling clothing now if I had struck that job. It was good. One of the few good jobs for Africans.

'Money is making me old', Cyril continued. 'It's going to take me a long time to get enough money. A white fellow my age would say he was pretty young because he could acquire a lot between now and ten years from now, but not me. I'm black. I've no one to take from. You live on minus quantities you see. When you leave school you literally live on minus quantities. You start out with a bad job, on a low scale, and you have debts to pay off for your schooling. It's already late. The years are going fast and South Africa is bad. So there is really no hope.'

Cyril stopped by the house late one afternoon. 'Will you come to have dinner with us?' he asked.

We said OK.

'Will you get a permit?'

'I don't think we'll bother with that', Fraser replied.

Cyril smiled, 'Good', he said.

Whites going into Mdantsane are required to have permits. The catch is that unless it is for official business or commercial purposes, these are seldom granted.

I did not know of any whites who had gone into Mdantsane other than the paper's photographers. The first time I went with Fraser, I was apprehensive. Roads were crowded with blacks. I was very conscious of being white. Would they feel we were trespassing? Did they hate all whites? But we got only interested stares and occasional waves. After the first couple of times, it was a routine trip.

But we had never been in the township after dark. The night we went to Cyril's it was black. Only a few street lights. Most houses were dark. Pedestrians loomed suddenly in the headlights' beam. I worried about hitting someone. If we got lost, could we find our way back out? Whose door would we knock at for directions?

But Cyril had drawn a good map and we found his house. He came out. 'My daughters saw you coming down the road', he said. 'They did not think you would come.' The house he led us into is exactly like the thousands of others that stretch like ribbons across the tree-less hills of Mdantsane. Each has four rooms, the largest 12 by 14 feet. The toilet and shower are in a shed behind the house. Most houses shelter several families and Cyril is well off in having this house to himself and his family.

Since the Mjos moved in in 1964, they've plastered inside, added ceilings, hot water and electricity — the latter at an initial cost of about £225.

In the kitchen, a black maid helped Cyril's wife. His three daughters were there as well and they stared at us shyly. Cyril smiled broadly. 'You are the first white people to come to our house for a meal', he said. 'I think they have a fear of coming to Mdantsane. But there is no reason to be afraid.'

It seemed there was fear on both sides. A few weeks before Fraser had hunted for Cyril. He knew roughly where he lived and asked blacks along the street where the house was. 'Mjo?' each had answered. 'We don't know that name.' The next day, Cyril, having got a half dozen messages that a white man in a blue Vauxhall had been looking for him, came to the paper. It wasn't that Cyril wasn't known, just that none of his friends would have directed a white man to his house.

The night at Cyril's house wasn't very different to other nights spent at the homes of whites. Even the living room furnishings were similar though I saw that the reason we'd come in through the kitchen was because the conventionally sized furniture completely filled the small room, blocking the front entrance. We talked, listened to some of Cyril's jazz recordings — Dizzy Gillespie, Ray Charles, Oscar Peterson.

The maid served coffee in demitasse cups, later Scotch, wine and cheese. I remember what we had for dinner: cabbage, peas, carrots, mashed potatoes, rice, gravy and lamb ribs and, for dessert, tinned pineapple and peaches and orange jelly with cream.

'For the white man, the sun is setting'

In spite of Coloureds ranking higher on the South African racial register than blacks — they're not subject to pass laws, can work in some jobs barred to blacks, can be served liquor in the home of a white — their lot seems worse in another way. No ethnic or cultural heritage supports Coloureds. Blacks, no matter how many generations removed from tribal villages, identify themselves as Xhosas, Zulus, North Sothos, or another of the nine major black cultures. Whites are Afrikaners or of English descent. But Coloureds are part of them all with claim on none, though many Coloureds have Afrikaans surnames and a lot of their social conversation concerns white descendants and relatives with emphasis on their relative status and wealth.

In appearance, there is great variation. For instance, Errol Theron's skin is golden and his features have an Asian cast while Peter Mopp looks like an American black. His skin is slightly lighter than an African's. He wears his tightly curled hair afro-style. Peter's wife, Sonja, has straight, jet-black hair and fair skin. Their three sons are just as fair, freckle-faced with light, slightly reddish hair. In shops, Sonja is treated as white until she gives her address, Buffalo Flats, a Coloured area. Peter said that on the street, they are subject to ugly stares. Like many other Coloureds, Sonja and her sons could pass as white and one assumes they occasionally do. In certain white groups, late evening conversation sometimes concerns signs of black ancestry in whites. A woman told me, 'There's something about their hands — the shape of the little finger and the way it curves when they hold a teacup. I can always tell the touch of the tar brush. Always.'

Until Soweto, whites felt no threat from the country's two and a third million Coloureds. Whites believed that if it ever came to war between them and blacks, Coloureds would fight on their side. In Transkei, I remember talking to one of the reporters from Cape Town which has the largest Coloured population of any South African city. He said Soweto came as no surprise. That the real shock came a few days afterwards when rioting erupted in the Coloured areas of Cape Town.

Whites treat Coloureds in a strange way. There's a master/slave tinge to black/white relationships; a paternalism, and a degree of affection, in the way whites deal with Coloureds.

Soweto seemed to have polarized South Africans. In 1976, Coloureds I knew were relating to the black cause. Before, I remember no conversations on the subject. Peter Mopp explained his feelings: 'Look,' he said, 'they've classified me as a Coloured and they tell me from childhood, I'm a little better than a black. So fine, there are people who believe this: "Thank God, I'm not as bad as a black — though I'm not as good as a white." But when I leave this office, I stand in the same queue as a black man, board the same bus as the black man, sit next to him on the train, sit next to him in the cinema.'

Mopp is a leader in East London's Coloured community of about 13,200. He's been involved in Coloured politics at the national and local level and was, at that time, a member of the Coloured Management Committee. He has one degree in law and is working for another through correspondence.

He began with the background to the Coloured situation. In 1951, Nationalists passed the Separate Representation of Voters Act which took Coloureds off the Common Voters Roll and created a separate one for them. (Blacks had been disenfranchised in 1936.) Four Coloured men immediately took the matter to the Supreme Court which ruled it was unable to adjudicate because of a previous decision that the courts could not query any parliamentary action. The four then took their case to the Appellate Division which said that since the Voters Act was not passed in the manner determined by the South African Constitution Act of 1909, the Voters Act was null and void.

Then, Peter said, the government increased the number of senators, called a joint sitting of both houses and thereby obtained the two-thirds majority required to pass the act taking Coloureds from the Common Roll. A further appeal was made, but this time the court ruled the removal legal.

In terms of the new act, Cape Province Coloureds were supposedly represented by four whites in parliament. When Coloureds began to switch their votes from the United Party to the more liberal Progressive Party, Nationalists created a separate elected body to represent Coloureds. Thus ended 'direct' participation by Coloureds in the South African government. So, following an election in 1969, Coloureds found themselves represented by a 'parliament' of 20 nominated members and 40 elected members directed by a chairman approved by the State President of South Africa.

'This is not my idea of political representation', Peter said. 'How can you consider yourself as a political force if you have got to abide by the laws laid out by the white South African government? In the present set-up, we are tolerated, can make as much noise as we want, as long as we don't organize the people to do things the proper way. All the CRC [Coloured Representative Council] can do is discuss education, rural affairs, pensions and crap like that instead of the genuine thing.'

Peter was elected to the CRC, a national body, in 1972 but was forced to resign in 1975 because of his 'radical views'.

'They felt I'm not suitable', he said, 'because I told them straight, they're not a political party, they're a tea party. I'd gone into it with the hope of achieving something. Then the government upped the salaries to 500 odd rand [£300] a month so now our boys thought they had a good wicket. Why destroy the goose that lays the golden egg? Let's play along. So the aspirations and ideas we set out with have now been influenced by monetary gain. They bandy words and ideas but they don't get down to the fact. As a Coloured group, you can achieve nothing.'

Peter is a member of the Coloured Management Committee, a local advisory body which makes recommendations to the East London City Council on such matters as Coloured housing and amenities in the Coloured areas. Peter feels uncomfortable about working within the 'system' but believes by doing so he can make some contribution to the Coloured community.

Peter gives the impression of living in a perpetual state of rage. That particular morning he was angry about a statement made by the national chairman of the Coloured Labour Party and published in that morning's paper. The chairman, who had been detained at the start of the latest student riot in Soweto, had just got out of prison.

'He was released', Peter said, 'because he asked students to go back to their studies, to stop their nonsense, to toe the line. And when he was released, he thanked the Minister of Justice and the Prime Minister for releasing him. Now, if you're a political leader, why in the hell must you thank your oppressor? If you go to jail for your ideas, you go to jail and jail does not change your ideas. I've told these older ones, "Look, you're even afraid of being afraid." But with the younger generation that fear is totally eliminated and it's going to get worse.'

'Today', he continued, 'they're burning the townships, tomorrow they're going to burn the towns. Boys of nine can tell you how to make a petrol bomb. That's how far their influence has stretched. What is happening is that, in the black underground, you now find people saying, "This is the way. The way of the matchbox." '

He said he was arranging a meeting so that Coloureds in East London would be able to hear leaders of the black consciousness movement from King William's Town. As far as I knew, locally it would be the first public evidence of common goals for black and Coloured. Peter explained his own feelings: 'Look, I believe that being a part of the oppressed group, it is my duty to actively support any movement which is geared to change this present set-up. I can't be a slave forever. It's that simple. Things have changed. My father used to shiver when a white man came in the room. But I say the hell with him. I'm a human being.'

I asked Peter how he felt about whites. He dismissed them with a wave of his hand. 'Whites these days are irrelevant', he said, 'What they think is no longer important. But I can tell you what I see. I see tension on their white faces and I see their homes have burglar bars, big dogs, firearms, the works.' He laughed. 'To guard against people like me, I suppose.'

Many whites see Communism as the guiding force in black activism. Peter disagrees: 'Communism is a foreign ideology to us — a white man's ideology — and we don't want what the white man's got.'

I asked who he considered to be the leader of the country's blacks.

'He's yet to emerge in this country', Peter replied. 'The point is now that any man who gets up and says, "This is the way", it's the last he'll say. Then he'll be gone for good.'

Though Peter is openly outspoken against the government, he's never served time in prison. 'But', he added, 'I've been interviewed so many times by the Bureau for State Security and the Special Branch that I've lost track of how many. It doesn't worry me.'

He has no doubts about how the struggle will end. 'To be frank with you, the white man is going down', he said. 'He is afraid now and his fear has driven him to the point where he is trying to retain control through arms. Now that's his biggest mistake ... He thinks we are going to come down the street in a mob so we can be shot down. They're out there to show they're in control. Typical Afrikaner mentality. And what makes it worse, they believe it is their God-given right. God put them in South Africa to rule and to rule by force if necessary. At the moment, he's in control of the situation, but for the white man, the sun is setting. There's no two ways about it. I believe in a hundred years, people of my skin colour will be ruling this country.'

Coming away from the interview with Peter I had the same feelings I had after listening to Errol, to Leslie, to Cyril — to many other black South Africans. That if they had lived in another country they would have been leaders. All that great potential that would never, in South Africa, be fulfilled.

'There's such a lot of them around'

The street where the Fouries' house is is near that of Dominee Loubser which is convenient for Dollie Fourie, the secretary of Dominee Loubser's church. When the Fouries moved to East London from 'up country', Dollie worked fulltime at the local dairy but, after the third child was born, her husband, Louie, who has a good job on the railways, told her, 'You've worked enough now.' Eventually she got the job with the church; most of her work is done at home, and this satisfies them both.

Dominee Loubser had called to give me Dollie's name. She sat at the dining-room table in the modest, neat, three-bedroom house in Cambridge. School holidays were on and her three teenage children came and went. Across the hall, a uniformed servant worked in the kitchen.

Dollie is a round-faced woman, slightly plump, in her late thirties. She wears glasses, with her dark hair pulled back and tied with bright yarn.

I asked what it is like to be a housewife in South Africa.

'I think here the woman plays the main role in the family', Dollie said. 'My husband and I work out the bills together each month, but it comes down on me to do all the paying and that. Like the groceries though, we always try and shop together for the big things once a month.'

East London has three or four large supermarkets, Dollie does her buying at the one in Vincent Park Centre — the same complex where the Omonds' apartment is. 'Some say Checkers is cheaper,' Dollie said, 'but what puts me off there, there's such a lot of them around, you know. The atmosphere at Pick 'n Pay is much nicer. I'd rather pay a cent more.'

Dollie's daughter sat on a stool in the kitchen by the sink where the maid peeled vegetables. I asked Dollie if she had fulltime or daily help.

'My maid sleeps in', she replied. 'She's working nine years for me now. She came to me when she came out of school. It's quite comical, you know. I never used to have a maid. I did everything myself. Then when Erina — she's the youngest — was five months old, I broke my arm. About three days after, this girl came by the back door. She was so black. I said to her, "Listen, can you put a nappie on?" She says she doesn't know. I said, "You'll have to learn if you don't." She couldn't speak a word of Afrikaans. She couldn't speak English. And now, if I go out in the afternoon, I can ask her to help the kids with their homework. She studies all the time with them. She couldn't do a bit of cooking when she came to me and now, if I've got visitors, I've just got to tell her, "Look, we'll do this and this and this." It's finished. I don't need to worry about food again.'

The name of the woman in the kitchen is Vera. She earns about £18 a month plus extras. 'I've got another one that comes in Tuesday for ironing', Dollie continued. 'Last week she didn't come in and then I just feel that if Vera does the ironing, I give her that rand extra and whenever we have visitors for a weekend, she has another one or two rands they usually give her, so she gets about double her salary when it comes to the end of the month.'

Vera has two children and they live in Berlin — a tiny town about half way to King William's Town — with their 'granny'.

'Whenever she goes home I give her some stuff to take with her for the kids', Dollie said. 'Oh, she knows which side her bread is buttered. That's what my friends say. In fact, that's what everyone says. But I mean, you so seldom get ones like that, you've got to look after them, you know.'

Dollie grew up on a farm about 100 miles northwest of East London. She learned Xhosa from blacks who worked for the family and speaks it fluently. She understands them she says. 'At the farm we used to play with them, you know. One thing is, you've always got to be honest with them. As long as you're fair with them, they'll be fair with you. You must never try to cheat them. You've got to say, "It's like this today." If you don't, they get you down. If you treat them well, they'll treat you well.'

The Fouries, Afrikaners, had little association with English-speaking people until they moved to East London.

'I tell you, when we moved to East London, it was terrible', she said. 'I battled. I never heard any Afrikaans.' Their friends now are mostly members of the church. She believes the Afrikaner is different from the English, 'We that come from the farms, for instance, we go cook a whole full meal if we get visitors. They don't bother with pudding and all that, they take it more the easy way. They don't put themselves out like we do.'

Dollie's hopes lie with her children — that they will finish their education and be able to get good jobs. She'd like to talk her husband into adding another room at the back of the house. 'We get a lot of visitors, it seems. All the family's still up-country.'

Dollie signalled to Vera who brought in a tray with coffee and rusks. The coffee was black and thick and flavoured heavily with chicory.

'I'll tell you, I worry about my kids a lot', Dollie said, stirring her coffee. 'If things are going OK with them at school and all that. My husband's health worries me a lot — troubled with his heart and that. Well,' she put the spoon down, 'I must admit, I haven't got a lot of worries because things are running smooth in the family.'

I asked if she had concerns about the future of South Africa.

She said, 'It's hard to say what's going to happen. It's definitely changing. If you take how our country used to be ten years ago and you take it now — especially with our native side — we've just got to give in. The story of apartheid is something of the past in South Africa.'

Dollie finds the relaxing of apartheid difficult to adjust to. 'If you grew up with it, you know, and if you know their ways of living and your living, their morality can never, ever, come up to the Europeans [whites]', she said. 'Their standard of living is much lower. They can't think what's going to happen tomorrow. That's the difference. They're not worried what's going to happen tomorrow. Like we're worried about our kids, what's going to happen. Have they got food?

Are they doing OK in school? They never worry about that — that I've seen.

'The change is just something you've got to accept', Dollie continued. 'It's just the way life is going. But I must be honest about it, I can never see my kids marrying them and all that. That I can't see.'

Vera walked across the hall, stacked up the cups and took the tray back to the kitchen.

'I suppose I'm old-fashioned,' Dollie said, 'but I see some of my English neighbours — their maids with them at the table having a cup of tea. That's one thing I'll never allow. Mine knows where her place is, and I know where mine is. I talk to her because the way church is. And she gets whatever we get in the house. She is free to take. Some people, they give it to them. Mine is free to take. And, I must say, she's very honest. I've sometimes got a hang of a lot of money in the house. I'm not worried about it. If a cent falls, she'll pick it up and give it back to me.

'But there's one thing. I can never communicate with them like the others does. She must know where her place is. I'm still the boss. She's not going to mess me around, that's for sure. She knows too with the television. If we're watching, she's welcome. But she comes in and sits at the door. I won't allow her to sit on my things. As far as I'm concerned, we're still not on the same level. I suppose that's just the way I grew up.'

'We can't say it out: "Why do you do this?"'

During the weeks we lived at the Belonsky house, we came to know Amelia. She had worked there four years, cooking, cleaning the house, washing, minding children and feeding the pets. Her day begins before breakfast, winds up after dinner with the time between lunch and dinner preparations free as well as Thursday and Saturday afternoons. She lives in a one-room cottage behind the garage and likes her job.

'The pay is good and I like a nice house', Amelia said. The wages are about £33 a month. Before she came to the Belonskys, she was a maid at a beachfront hotel where she earned £12 a month and worked six days a week from 6 a.m. to 6 p.m.

All of us — Clay, Fraser and I — came to like Amelia and she seemed relaxed with us. Almost without exception, this proved true of blacks we came to know. I came to believe it was because we were not South Africans. Even though we were white, we were not part of the system.

Amelia's Xhosa name is Liziwe Kwababana. She's 56, a tall, heavy woman of great dignity with a soft voice and a broad, pleasant smile which reveals mostly gums.

'I got my English name when I was baptized', Amelia said. 'Mdantsane is my home and before that, Peddie in the country. I went to school as far as Standard 4, then I came here to East London to get further on. I passed my Standard 6 and then I did my Standard 7 by corresponding.'

At the Belonskys, she speaks English; with her family, Xhosa. She has three children. 'The first one was born in 1948', Amelia said. 'Her name is Mavis. My second one is Linda, Lorraine my third one. Linda was born in 51 and Lorraine 55.'

Amelia has two grandchildren, three and ten years old, born to Mavis and Lorraine. Like Amelia, the two have no husbands. 'The middle one doesn't have any baby because she was at school and staying at the hostel and she didn't get time to be out', Amelia explained.

The women share a house in Mdantsane with another family. 'The others have two rooms and we've got two', she said. 'We've got no kitchen. We cook in one of our rooms. I've been trying to get a bigger house, but it looks like not now because they said [at the housing office] my number is 300. When I went there in 1974, Madam rang to the man there and he said my number was 41. Now last month she rang again. She asked them what number I am because she wanted to do something to help me. They said number 300 now. I don't know how they draw it back. I can't do anything now unless I put the deposit on the house. If I can get money for deposit, then I can buy the house.'

Down payment on the standard Mdantsane house is about £173 with the balance paid off like rent. Amelia said for only four rooms, that seemed a lot of money.

She talked about her daughters' education. If they can only finish high school, their lives, Amelia believes, can be better than hers. The oldest daughter went as far as Standard 6, the middle one got as far as the final year, the youngest one dropped out of school last year at the end of Standard 7. She has promised Amelia she'll take correspondence courses. Why she quit, Amelia is not sure. 'We don't know why she didn't want to go back, but she said to me she is not going back again.' A good possibility is that she is afraid to go to school. Students spearheaded the Soweto riots and continue to be the activists in the townships. Attending the white-administered schools is seen as a sellout and those who do are harassed and threatened. This is a new scene parents don't understand. To them, an education was the great dream, the only way out of poverty, and they sacrificed to send their children to school.

In January I was buying clothes Clay would need to go to school. He, like all students, black and white, was expected to wear a uniform — blazer, slacks, shirt, tie and regulation shoes. These cost almost £50. In addition, there would be tuition of about £5 a term. Blacks paid even more, plus the cost of books — provided free to white students.

'Education costs lots of money', Amelia said. 'The middle one stayed in the hostel. I used to pay R80 [£48] at the beginning of the year, but it was not only that money, they always ask for more.' For the youngest, who attended school in the township and lived at home, the cost was about £17 a term.

I asked Amelia what she would do when she got too old to work. 'I'll try and get the pension and then stay home', she replied. 'If my children are working, I won't be pulling very hard. I'll just stay home and wait for the money from them unless they get married and then I'll just be alone. But I don't worry about that.'

When she is not working at the Belonskys, Amelia enjoys going home to Mdantsane: 'I do my garden and when I finish my garden, I'll be going to my church [Wesleyan], come back and stay home, see what's happening to the children, the little ones.'

Having enough money is her principal concern. 'My problems is to be short, always worrying about money things', she said. 'I'm the only one. When I've got my pay I have to do this and this and the money is finished and that's the worry. And sometimes when I have to go to doctor, I have to borrow from my lady. That's the worries to me.

'Things that make me happy', Amelia continued, 'are when I haven't got worries of money and my children please me by doing good things — not to worry me. If I can stay like that, not having worries, it can be right to me, but sometimes the children make me worried. This little one, she's got a baby. No one to feed the baby. I feed him myself. That makes me worry, but with money, I stay all right. I don't see anything that can worry me.'

She sees that life for black people is difficult: 'It is not nice how we live here, though we can't say straight out to the people, but as far as we see it, it is not how you can say it is nice. Some of these girls here, the maids, work for very little money. And when they leave the job [when employers take vacations] and they come back again, there's no money extra. Always troubles.'

Amelia believes that only God is powerful enough to end apartheid. 'They talk about it a little in church' she said, 'they don't put it as a matter, just talk it a little time because they don't want to talk a lot about politics. They're frightened to talk a lot and anyway, they don't know how this world can be all right.'

Whites generally don't like blacks, Amelia said. 'They think blacks are funny people. As far as I've been working in the other places, sometimes your dish stay outside so when you want to put your food, you have to bring it in. This is funny because we touch everything in the house. We're working, we touch the food. It's funny they keep away so far. But we don't say anything because we just come for work. We can't say it out, "Why do you do this?" I'm not allowed to ask that one who's doing it.'

But things are different at the Belonskys. Amelia smiled: 'But the first time to see this lady — this lady doesn't mind for everything. Black people can come here. I can serve others eating here at the table. This was funny to me because I never see it before. It's not making by everybody. Others do not like it.'

I asked if she knew why whites feel as they do about blacks.

'I think white people act this way because we're poor', Amelia replied. 'Perhaps if we were rich, they wouldn't put us off so far. I don't know. I think so. It is because here we have been working for very little money. Others are still working for R20 [£12] a month; R30 [£18], that's the big money. And the food is dear and we send children to school and we feed them and we buy clothes and go to doctor. That is why we are always poor. The food is up, clothes, up, everything up. It takes more money and that's why I'm worrying about the children. They must get jobs.' But, she admitted, jobs are difficult to find.

When I asked what she wanted out of life for herself, Amelia replied: 'The best thing I can think of is to get money and do everything that pleases you. I think the life can be better when you got money and work for money. This country, they never work for themselves because working for them, maids. They have the maids from long ago. Now they can't stay without the maids because they didn't prepare to work for themselves. There are some who can live without a girl, but most of them can't do it.' Amelia noted that even Ruth — who will tell you she enjoys keeping house when Amelia is away — isn't very handy. 'Sometimes when Madam does it, she thinks that she finishes it', Amelia said. 'But she never finishes and when you come back, you have to do this thing again.'

I asked if she thought whites were basically any different than blacks. 'I don't think so', Amelia replied. 'I don't think there's difference. But they make themselves different because they always put us far away from them.'

'We won't let it get out of hand'

People never talked about South Africa being at war, yet if you added up the evidence, you could come to no other conclusion: deaths of South African soldiers serving at the border reported regularly in the *Dispatch;* eighteen-year-old males routinely inducted into the military; radio programmes dedicated to 'the boys on the Border' — 'to Rodney: we pray for your safe return' — 'to Colin from Mom and Dad: we're proud of all you boys up there' — 'Good luck, son, if God is with us, who can be against us?'

Fraser got routine assignments to photograph trainloads of departing servicemen. You'd see men in uniform on the streets, men in camouflage gear, carrying weapons, driving dusty four-wheeled drive vehicles. Reservists were periodically called up. At the greengrocer's on the corner by Ruth's house, the owner's wife would explain she was temporarily in charge — that her husband was on Border duty for three weeks.

South Africa is bordered by Angola, Botswana, Rhodesia, Mozambique and South West Africa. Angola and Mozambique, once Portuguese colonies, have become independent, leftist, black-ruled nations, committed to aiding the struggle against white rule in South Africa. Rhodesia is gone — as whites put it — and South West Africa is going. Neighbouring black countries are training grounds for guerrilla fighters.

Clem Green, 22, fought in Angola in 1975. That was a strange battle. South Africans didn't know they had troops there until months later. Alan Paton said South Africa's decision to fight in Angola resulted from CIA recommendations.

Clay met Clem at a beach disco during the holidays and Clem would come to visit when we were at Belonskys. Clem entered the army in 1974. After basic training, he was sent to the Border. The Border is a strip between South West Africa and Angola. The Caprivi Strip fits in at the top of that strip, Rhodesia and Zambia on the point.

'They just come in and tell you, "Get your kit ready. We're moving out tonight." They don't tell you where you're going', Clem said. 'You think maybe you're just going out on a road block or something. Then 2 o'clock the next morning they come in and wake you up. You move on a troop train. It's hooked to a civilian train as far as Windhoek then it becomes military.'

Clem's company moved up to relieve a base. 'We heard different reports of what they'd done', Clem said. 'Putting two and two together you can work out the actual story — what's happening. There are some places where it's slack and nothing's going on and there are some places where it's hot and you've got to watch your sights all the time. The first time we had a party. Then we went up the second time. In July 75, we moved through to Angola. You people didn't hear it then, you heard it early in November.

'We didn't know we were going over until they called the officers forward and gave them their briefing.

'We were classed as mercenaries — though we didn't get paid extra. At that stage it wasn't open warfare. No one had declared war on anyone else. All identification was taken away — dog tags, military uniforms. We just wore straightforward brown. It looks military but doesn't have any insignia, no stamps or marks or anything.'

Clem stayed six months in Angola. 'We were in a few blazes', he said. 'We moved into this one place and found trenches dug. These were filled with bodies, then sand thrown over.' The bodies he believes, were those of civilians, FNLA and UNITA troops. The latter two were opposed by SWAPO and the MPLA.

'We were at the back fighting with FNLA and UNITA. We were backing them, but the thing is, they had no sort of initiative. It's like taking your dog into the back yard and another dog attacks it. You're going to stop the dogs fighting and you chase the other dog away. Then your dog goes out and looks for trouble again. The same dog beats him up all over again.

'We had one base,' Clem recalled, 'the same place where we found all those bodies, took it over from the MPLA, gave it to FNLA and moved on. Come back a week later, MPLA's got the base again. You've got to wipe them out and put FNLA back in again. They weren't trained. That's the thing. Even the MPLA.'

At one point, Clem's company walked into an MPLA ambush. 'They started fighting,' he said, 'and when they saw we didn't run, just hit the deck and started firing back, they broke up and ran — left all the weapons, everything.'

Early in January, Clem was injured. He was a driver and taking troops through a marsh. 'There was one set of tracks there and it was naturally hard. The rest of the place you'd walk across and sink to your knees in the mud. All the troops got off the back of my truck. I put it into first and pulled off. I had a run of about a quarter of a mile and I floored it. I think I was doing about 85 or 90 ks. Then there was a sort of noise and I was lying in the mud. That's all I remember. The front wheel was blown off and shards of shrapnel had pierced the floorboard.'

His kneecap had been shattered and bits of bone blown off. 'Then they pumped me full of morphine and I waited for a chopper to come and get me.' He was flown to a base, from there to a hospital in Pretoria. 'There were plenty of guys with me. No press was allowed in. I don't know what the story was — it would seem they were still trying to keep it down.'

Clem spent six months in the hospital then came home in late July with a steel pin, a plastic kneecap and severance pay. At the time we knew him, he worked as a shipping agent. He didn't think he would stay with that much longer. 'Nothing seems to catch my interest', he said. 'I want to go into diesel engineering. That's my sort of hope, but I just can't seem to get started. You've broken out of a routine and now you can't seem to get back into it.'

I asked him if he had considered living in any other country.

'I never think of leaving here', he answered. 'It's brilliant.'

I asked what he liked about it. 'I'll put it this way', he said. 'There are places where you can go and get away from it all — just over the rise.' Clem waved his hand towards the tall trees at the back of the lot. 'You can go down there — towards the Nahoon Valley — and there are places nobody has ever been to.' Where he pointed, Mary Omond had lived when she was growing up. That was a peaceful time. No one had yet rioted in Soweto. I asked Clem his reaction to the rioting.

'The riots concern everybody, I think', he said. 'But I take time to sit and understand the situation. For instance, we've given Transkei independence, yet our taxes support them. The only thing they can do there is grow mealies. You can't make a living on that. I was born there and when the white men still lived there, they used the land for sheep, cattle, pigs — everything. The minute we moved out, it all died. Coons, as soon as they get a couple of pigs, they kill them off and have a party. They can't build up stock like that. We class them as kaffirs because they're not a cultured society. We've got a saying: "You can take the coon out of the bush, but you can't take the bush out of the coon." For instance, you can teach them to sit down at a table to eat, but I guarantee you that every one of them will pick his nose or put his hand in his pants. It's a sort of raw situation.'

People overseas were quick to criticize, Clem said: 'If they were to come here and see the situation, they wouldn't.'

I asked him if he thought there would be a revolution.

'If there's trouble here,' he replied, 'it's nothing that can't be handled. We won't let it get out of hand. I think you had the same problems with Indians. It's the same story here.

'I don't know,' he said reflectively, 'we've built universities for them — Fort Hare and that — and when the riots started they burned down schools and universities. Why? Not very nice.'

'Make no mistake, the revolution has begun'

Fighting on the Border came a lot closer if you had a son approaching military age. And it got really sticky if you were no supporter of the Nationalist regime — what were your sons fighting to preserve? Shirley and David Smith have four sons. The eldest, twins of 17, would enter military service when they finished high school. In 1977, the Smith family was having a difficult time. Because of her sons, Shirley wanted desperately to leave South Africa. David refused to leave.

Shirley is 40, South African born — her mother English-speaking, her father Afrikaans. David, 67, is Scottish. He came to South Africa following the Second World War. Shirley is theatre and television critic for the *Dispatch*. She and her family live on a farm called Cove Woods, located just off the main road to Kidd's Beach and about ten miles from East London.

Turning off at the Cove Woods sign, one travels on a narrow dirt track winding for a mile or so between wattle trees and thorn bushes. Dogs, big and little, rush out — barking madly — until Shirley or one of her children comes out to the rescue.

The house looks English — two stories with a peaked roof and windows of leaded glass. Bougainvillaea climbs white stucco walls and the hedges are hibiscus. Lawns and gardens surround the house and a little distance away are tennis courts and a swimming pool. Evidence of David's love of the 63-acre farm is everywhere. There are plots of roses, groves of macadamia trees, soft fruits and citrus, and a large vegetable garden.

A stable door opens into a comfortable living room filled with overstuffed furniture and fine antiques. A white cat sleeps in a chintz-covered chair by the fireplace. There's an old upright piano, family photos on top. French doors lead to a vine-shaded verandah.

On the walls of a sunny dining room hang framed charters of Round Table chapters, a men's service organization which David introduced in South Africa. The kitchen is a big, old-fashioned room with a coal-burning stove in one corner, plants on the window sills and bowls of fruit on the counters. Children draw at a big wooden table. There are servants working and cats underfoot.

We would stay the night in the guest cottage in the garden. Shirley organized tea. She cut fruit cake and took a tray through to the verandah off the living room. The wooden table was shaded by vines. She found a blossom to show me, butter yellow, shaped like a trumpet and nearly the same size.

After tea, David and Fraser toured the farm while Clay and the Smith twins went to swim in the reservoir. Shirley and I had been friends since my first time in South Africa and had corresponded in between visits. But this would be the first opportunity really to talk since I'd come back. One of the first things I asked her about were her plans for leaving South Africa. She had written that they were going and I half expected her to be gone when we returned.

'The family just didn't move fast enough', Shirley said. 'I finally engineered David into a position where he did go see some agents on selling the farm and one man from South West, who was prepared to pay cash, which is another problem now, was interested — but at the last minute the sale fell through. Since then we just haven't had any bites. After all, who wants to buy a farm during a revolution? And, make no mistake, the revolution has begun.'

David is a retired dentist and though the Smiths obviously live well, apparently there is not a lot of cash available since Shirley had recently sold many of her antiques, much of her china and silver, to get money to resettle. Now it was being used to put the twins through a private boarding school near Kimberley.

But though her plans had bogged down, Shirley was still determined to go. She was prepared to lease their farm or, if necessary, simply walk away from it. She would work overseas. 'Everything is so much closer now', she said. 'I suppose Rhodesia brings it very, very near. It's hanging on with grim determination. They keep on saying they want integration, but every time an interim government is set up, it's rejected. The terrorists are going to knock hell out of them as time goes by, but they're going to hang on in spite of it all.'

Shirley believes that the pattern in Rhodesia will be repeated in South Africa. 'We're equipped to the teeth and every week the television service shows more and more reassurance to white South Africans with one programme after another highlighting the wonder of the boys on the Border. The military images pour forth. I feel they're just preparing us for the *laager* which we are already in.'

Laager is a term often used in South Africa to describe the Afrikaner position. The Boers fought in *laager* form, which meant they pulled their wagons together in a circle; even if there were hordes of blacks outside, they remained in that *laager* and fought to the death.

'I see this *laager* going on and on and on and on', Shirley said. 'Even after a boy has done his military service, he will be expected to go back every year which is going to be an interminable drain on the economy. In other words, our lifestyle here is going to change. It's tougher now than it was two years ago. It's going to get even tougher. White South Africa is going to be bled white.

'And the other thing is that the Border which we are protecting against the Communists is so long, so wide, that God knows how we're going to manage. And if Rhodesia goes, it's going to be even wider. My four sons are in direct line for that combat for the entire length of their prime of life.' That is Shirley's principal reason for leaving — or wanting to leave. There are lesser ones as well.

'The cultural life has already taken a shocking dip', Shirley said. 'We see less of our provincial touring companies. Professional entertainers are coming out less frequently. There's less money around. Our television service operates on a shoestring and is quite appalling culturally. So it will continue because there is not going to be that resurgence of economic growth to pick things up for a long time because the West has turned its back on us, quite rightly, and we're on our own.'

She said she deeply resented being dragged down by a state in which she had no faith, no empathy: 'I feel the psychology of this place is so ghastly. For me it is certainly not compensated by material wealth which I see dwindling anyway, sunshine and the outdoor life and an easy form of existence. No, I don't see this as compensation. These are my feelings about my country right now.'

Shirley, unlike many white South Africans, does not believe the threat is from Communism: 'To my mind,' she said, 'we are fighting the war for black liberation — though we are fighting Communist infiltration because black Africans are determined to have their liberation at all costs and are prepared to use any means — including Cuban Communists. But basically, we are fighting black liberation. And here am I, and my family, who are wanting black liberation, wanting it gradually.' Gradually to Shirley means the easing of apartheid, not one man, one vote. That, she says, would be 'horrific'.

'Quite frankly,' she said, 'I feel I'm caught. I don't know how I'm going to cope. I just don't see how I can allow my children to be sacrificed to maintain this extraordinary white bastion that we have in Southern Africa, based on Nationalist domination, white privilege.'

After David's retirement from private practice, he had joined the government health service and travelled extensively. Since I'd last been on the farm, burglar bars had been added to all the windows on the first floor. Doors had heavy bolts. I asked Shirley if she were afraid when David was away. 'I don't fear death myself,' she replied, 'but I do always think that should there be any kind of attack or entry, I am responsible for the young kids. I lock everything, going through a whole system every night. And I'm careful about it.'

Like all weekends spent with the Smiths, that one was pleasant. Good conversation about theatre and books, people dropping in for tennis or a swim. Excellent food, pleasant walks in the country and along the beach. But there was an undercurrent that was disturbing. Shirley seemed to taunt David. She directed acid comments to him through us or through the children. He looked older, heavier. Tired.

Just before we left Shirley said, 'My sons are on my mind a lot. I think what my feelings would be toward David if one of them should be killed or maimed fighting. How could I not blame David? How could I live with that? That he would not go when I believed we should.'

'Mrs Mohapi, I have bad news ...'

King William's Town is about forty-five minutes' drive from East London. One of the earliest settlements in the Eastern Cape, its homes are old and stately and shaded by tall trees. It's not a big town — perhaps a third the size of East London. At least half a dozen churches line its main street. Very English-looking, they've been built of fieldstone which, over the years, has been blanketed by ivy, though one — a Dutch Reformed church — is stark and geometric. King William's Town looks, on the face of it, an unlikely centre for black consciousness. The answer seems to be that Steve Biko lived here, in its township of Zwelitsha, under terms of his banning.

We had been directed to 15A Leopold Street. This is to the left of the main road, a short street of old-fashioned, modest houses with gables and verandahs and gardens behind low stone walls. Number 15 is in the middle of the last block. Outside, a short, slim young woman with her hair in tightly interwoven braids, talked to a bearded man. She came over and introduced herself as Nohle Mohapi. Her voice was low and pleasant and she smiled often.

Fraser and I went with her into what had once been an Anglican church, owned now by the Christian Institute, a militantly anti-apartheid organization. Several people were inside. The man Nohle had been talking with did not come in and she explained he was banned and under the conditions of his banning order, prohibited from entering the building.

We talked briefly then Nohle suggested the interview be held outside, so we went out and sat in our car, she in the back seat and I in front with the tape recorder on the seat next to me, the microphone resting on the back of the seat facing her. I had no doubt we had left the building because it was bugged.

Nohle had been born in the area, was now living in Zwelitsha with her children, one three, the other a year and a half. She was then 26. In 1973, she had married Mapetla Mohapi.

'I met him at the beach', she said. 'A friend introduced us.' That was in 1971. 'He was quiet,' she said, 'and I liked the quietness.' When they married, Mapetla, who had studied at a black university on a grant from the Ciskei government, was repaying the loan by working for them. He quit after three months.

'He wasn't pleased with their way of treating people, let me put it that way', Nohle said. 'So he decided to work for SASO as the regional secretary.' His office was in the church where we had first spoken to Nohle, and his duties included setting up conferences and student seminars. I asked Nohle if she had been interested in black politics before her marriage to Mapetla.

'No,' she replied, 'I was blank material. He was the one who introduced me to these things. But I did find myself involved, I followed his way.' Mapetla worked for SASO for about a year and a half, until he was detained in October of 1974. Nohle was not surprised when her husband was picked up: 'They were detaining all the SASO people.'

It happened in this way: 'They came to my place in the evening', Nohle said. 'He wasn't in, he was in Durban at the head office of SASO. White security police asked me where he was. I said I didn't know. They told me they already knew he was in Durban. Apparently they phoned Durban and when I called there the following morning, it was to hear that they took him at 4 a.m. So that was that.'

Mapetla remained in prison from 11 October 1974 to March 1975. He told his wife that he was intensively interrogated and beaten. 'I visited him once', she said. 'I saw that he was very lean. He wouldn't tell me anything then because there were two security policemen listening and taking notes.'

When Mapetla was released, someone had replaced him at SASO so he was without work until May when he was hired by the Zimele Trust Fund, an organization which aids families of political prisoners. In July he was re-elected by SASO and worked for two months in Durban. Nohle stayed in King until she found a job in Durban. A day or so before she was to join Mapetla, he was banned and sent back to King.

'I was then becoming more and more involved', Nohle said. 'I didn't mind his being banned, I didn't feel bad really. More especially, I was working, so I could maintain the house and we had a child by then. Mapetla stayed without work for some months and then January, Zimele re-employed him again.' He worked as an administrator for them until July when he was again detained.

It was at this point, I remember, that the interview fell apart. Throughout it, Nohle, while friendly and quite willing to answer my questions, nevertheless responded as if she had said the same things a hundred times. No doubt she had. Security policemen probably asked the same questions.

In an interview a rhythm is established and one gets into it by asking questions initially that the person feels comfortable with. After he is at ease and conversation is flowing, then is the time to ask about personal feelings and responses. We had almost reached this point when Nohle stopped talking. She glanced sideways. I did as well. A white car had stopped alongside. Two men were in it. The one nearest us — and I could have touched him — was black and wore a dark suit. He was writing in a notebook. He looked at me. I became very afraid. It was the only time in South Africa I felt that fear, the same fear I had on the ship in Durban. The feeling that you can't breathe, that you will run away. It was the man's face that frightened me. Something in it — or something not in it. I looked at Nohle. She was apparently calm, smiling slightly. 'The security police', she said and continued talking. The machine recorded her answers but because of my fear, the rhythm was gone. Questions that should have been asked never were.

'When he was re-detained,' Nohle said, 'they came to our place at about 3 a.m.' 'They' were security policemen, among them Captain Schoeman and Warrant Officer Hattingh. While Mapetla dressed, they searched the house taking with them tapes, books and letters.

'They told him to take many things because he was going to stay for some time', Nohle said. 'They were detaining him under Section 6 of the Terrorism Act which meant they could keep him any length of time.'

After they left the Mohapis' house, they searched his offices at Leopold Street, taking files and letters from there. That was the last night that Nohle saw her husband. A month later Captain Hansen of the security police came to tell her Mapetla was dead.

'I was at my place with some friends', Nohle remembered. 'Just before that I got some letters from Mapetla. He was telling me that he was all right, nothing wrong with him. I must keep the kids, look well after them until he comes back because he will come back one day. He doesn't know what the police want from him, such things. I received the letters on the third [of August], then on the fifth, Captain Hansen came to my place and asked for Mrs Mohapi. When I appeared he asked, "Are you Mrs Mohapi?" I said, "I am Mrs Mohapi." He said, "Mrs Mohapi, I have bad news for you. Your husband has committed suicide." '

Nohle said she did not believe it was suicide. 'It was unlike him', she said. 'He used to be against people committing suicide, trying to run away from responsibility, so it was difficult for me to believe that.'

An inquest into Mohapi's death was scheduled and I asked what she thought the findings would be. 'Police being police,' she replied, 'I wouldn't be sure. We are expecting to lose the case, but at least the police will be exposed so I don't mind whether we lose the case.' A few months later, a King William's Town magistrate ruled that nobody could be held responsible for Mohapi's death.

Since her husband's death, Nohle had been working for the BPC. She said she expected to be picked up by the police at any time. 'I've arranged for my kids', she said. 'If anything should happen to me, my mother and mother-in-law will take care of them and the house.'

I remember that I said things seemed really hopeless and why didn't she just leave and live in some other country where she could be free of harassment.

'I hope one day everything will be straight', Nohle replied. 'But it won't be that way until the end. But I believe South Africa will change and I would not leave now because I wish to be here to enjoy it then.'

I did not talk with Steve Biko that day. He would call me at the *Dispatch*, Nohle said. It was several weeks before the call came but there seemed no hurry and there were other people to talk to.

'All the good people are leaving'

In the wake of the Soweto riots, white people were leaving South Africa. Among them were East Londoners. One was Ian Kaye-Eddie, managing director of the *Daily Dispatch*. I talked with him in his office two days before he and his wife and daughter left for Australia. He sat behind a big desk. His secretary brought in tea, then intercepted the telephone calls from her office. With his sharp features, Ian looks English but is not.

'I was born in Rhodesia', he said. 'My grandfather was a pioneer there, one of the first white men. My father decided after the Second World War that Rhodesia wasn't going to last very long and we emigrated to South Africa.'

He grew up in Johannesburg, went to the University of Witwatersrand, qualified as an accountant, then went overseas to London. After a year there, he returned to South Africa and married a fourth generation South African girl. They came to East London on their honeymoon, liked it and eventually settled there.

'I've been here nearly nine years', he said. 'I started out as a secretary and worked my way up to the top. I've been to Harvard, studied under a management course. Travelled quite extensively in America. I have a brother who's an architect in Los Angeles and I visited him. He might have influenced my decision to leave.'

It was a toss-up where they would go — the US or Australia. Emigration would be easier to Australia, they decided. They would go to Perth where they have close friends, also former East Londoners. Australia allows emigrants to enter without a job. 'All they're interested in is your qualifications and they're very short of accountants so the field is wide open', he said. 'Another reason I picked Australia is that there are few people — 13 odd million on a huge continent. They all speak one language which I think is very important in a country to keep it united. There are the aborigines, of course, but they're in a minority. Not that that really worries me, but there isn't a massive race problem in Australia.'

The Kaye-Eddies would take with them the maximum amount of money allowed. In South Africa in 1977, you could leave with a maximum of R30,000 [£18,000] providing assets exceed R60,000 [£36,000] — or half of whatever you have.

When the Kaye-Eddies announced they were leaving, friends were surprised and shocked. 'I'm at the top of the tree with a fantastic job, nice people to work with, nice city, nice environment,' Ian said, 'and here I was throwing it all up at the peak of my career to go someplace else. A lot of my friends were agitated. A lot of them say they wish they had the guts to do the same thing.'

He remembers when his decision was made: 'On September 13 Vorster gave one of his speeches. And I said to my wife that morning, if he indicates he's going to sit down and negotiate by talking to various racial groups and that people, especially the whites, must now adapt, that there must be a change of heart, then I think we'll stay. If he comes on and says, "Well, chaps, I think it's the Communists ...", that sort of thing, we'll go.'

The Prime Minister's speech reiterated National Party tenets. Ian listened, then told his wife they would leave. 'More than ever, I'm convinced they're not prepared to sit down and talk. This year they're spending one thousand million rand on defence. There can only be one reason and that is they're going to fight. And I'm not prepared to fight for a cause I don't believe in. I am in the army. If they called me up, I'd have to go. So, if I'm not prepared to do this, I decided I must pack up and go.

'I also have the philosophy that though Africa is a beautiful country, it's also a tragic country because the blacks have been thrust into the twentieth century. They're trying to catch up, but they never will and the gap is widening. It's like a convoy of trucks. The first truck draws off, the next one, next one, and the last truck is travelling at about 60 miles an hour just to keep up with the first one at 30 miles an hour.

'You're coming in', Ian continued, 'at grade 1 of the Western technological age and, basically, the Africans and the South Africans specifically, are more illiterate in numbers now than they were 40, 50 years ago so we're not winning the war of education.'

During 30 years of Nationalist rule, government money had been spent in the wrong areas, he said. 'For instance, building houses for them — the wrong type of house, soulless, miserable houses. They didn't put money into education and now they're so far behind — they breed prolifically, it's part of their culture — they never will catch up. And we should have also said, "Well, it's going to be majority rule one day" and begun preparing for it. Instead the Nationalists are preparing themselves to hold on to something which they can't actually use or appreciate unless the black man helps them. I'm only here because of the black man and he's only here because of me, because of my skills.'

I asked what he thought about the Afrikaners.

'I suppose I don't know them as well as I should,' he replied, 'and that is one of the problems in South Africa — none of us really knows each other and because we don't know each other, we're frightened. We don't know the blacks. We don't speak their language. When I went to school, I did English and Afrikaans but no Zulu. If I'd learned to speak Zulu, I would understand the black; he'd respect me and I'd respect him more. I have a philosophy that you never understand people or begin to understand them until you speak their language.

'I don't speak Afrikaans now as well as I used to because in East London, one never speaks it, but I was in the army with them, I played rugby with them. I went to an English university but we had Afrikaners there. They're a warm-hearted people. I reckon they've been misguided. If the leader leads them the wrong way, like Dr Verwoerd did, they all follow him. Whether it's a Germanic trait or what, I don't know, but they like strong leaders.' If Vorster had made the decision to talk instead of fight, Kaye-Eddie believes most Nationalists would have accepted it.

As far as his own political beliefs are concerned, he says he is basically very conservative. 'I was never interested in politics at all until I went to university. I must admit that working for the *Dispatch* for the last nine years has made me more liberal. But I'm not really fond of a lot of liberals because I think, based on experience, that most of them talk and do nothing.'

Ian has been involved with the Institute of Race Relations, his wife was chairman of Black Sash. Both have spent time canvassing for the Progressive Party. Now, he said, 'we feel that it's come to the point where our efforts are really useless. The wheel has gone too far. Most white South Africans are apathetic, especially the English-speaking. They never do a damn thing. All they do is sit and moan about the situation and criticize the Afrikaners, but they never do anything — either to help them or to hinder them. They sit and watch which way it's going to go. Lots of them have British passports. There are a tremendous number who are not citizens. They have actually had a tremendous influence in not influencing this government. They haven't voted and now they're going to lose their lives trying to keep the black man from voting. I think the whole situation is ridiculous.'

The preparations, the anticipation of moving, had been difficult for his wife, he said. Their daughter is adopted and their application for another child was again at the top of the list. In Australia they would have to begin the same process again. There were the goodbyes and explanations to get through with friends and family.

His wife had been more emotionally involved in the problems of blacks than he had been, Ian said. As head of the Black Sash Advice Office she knew what they faced. 'She says the problems they had — unemployment, eking out an existence — well, she just feels desperately sorry for them. But she also told me that the problem is so enormous that, in a way, she's relieved she's going.'

I asked what he thought he would miss when he left South Africa, what he had liked about living here.

'I find people generally very friendly, find the home life good — especially in East London', Ian replied. 'A chap can go home for lunch, for instance.' I'd seen him leave occasionally in mid-afternoon carrying his squash racket. 'You get a balance of life in this town', he continued. 'I think Johannesburg is more oriented to western society where the man works his guts out, fights the traffic and never sees his family or is too tired when he gets home to do anything but sit.

'The climate is fabulous and I'd say from a geographic point of view, South Africa is one of the most beautiful countries in the world. Wild life, animal life, vegetation — all these things abound. The variety of life here is unsurpassed. And the colour, we've got black people, brown people, Indians, Greeks, Italians, Afrikaners and English. The challenge, I guess, is to reconcile the human beings to make it a great country.'

Ian believes that if the different racial groups can hammer out a workable settlement in South West Africa, than perhaps South Africa will be encouraged to move in the same direction. But that, he feels, is really a vain hope.

'The way I see it is on the negative side', he said. 'The Russians want much more influence on the distribution of Africa's raw materials, especially Southern Africa's, and I believe they're going to take over Rhodesia. And I don't believe for one minute that America, Britain, or any other Western country, will lift a finger. Whether South Africa will bail Rhodesia out, well, I have my doubts. I think they'll protect whites there — let them run maybe — but I don't think they'll get too involved. They'll just bring the borders back to South Africa and apartheid. The next move will be the collapse of South Africa through internal disruptions, just as we witnessed in Soweto. I reckon there'll be more violence with the children until they get one man, one vote.

'Now, I'm not a coward', Ian said. 'During Sharpeville I was on standby and I was closely involved with rioting in 61, so I've done my stint. I know what it's like to run down the street with an automatic weapon in my arms with the chance of having people in front of me and I have no doubt I would spray bullets into them. Women, children, anyone — it's survival. But it's not a situation I'm going to get myself into again.'

He predicted South Africa would continue its policy of separate development and violence, then change would ensue. Change would spell the end to the Nationalist dream of black homelands. But, he admitted, change is never easy. 'I've found it hard myself', Ian said. 'I've been brought up in this society of apartheid. I don't even notice things like walking into different entrances. But when we had overseas vistors, they said, "You know, you're crazy. You walk into a station — one door here, one door there — then you all mix on the platform." And I don't notice it. Most South Africans don't.' He shook his head: 'All these little irritants and the government hasn't changed them. You go to the beaches and blacks aren't allowed. If we don't allow them to swim on the beaches, how are we going to let them vote? To have a say in the administration, defence, and all that sort of thing — the industry of the country?

'It's amusing to me that whites think they own this country. The blacks were here long ago and, all right, they've accepted us and we should do in like manner.

'I think I'll miss the blacks because I like them. They have tremendous qualities. They are so patient. And they're very tolerant. I've always said they're people who love children. I'm sure that Perth is going to be clean and neat, but the bustle, the laughter of Africans — their high voices as they shout across the street — that I'll miss.'

Blacks are sorry to see them go, he said. Their maid told his wife: 'All the good people are going.' The man who bought their Mercedes told them: 'I hate to see people like you leave. But, don't worry, when it's all over, you can come back and help us out.'

'I've been honest with them', Ian said. 'I tell them it's this present government in power that has made up my mind for me. By choice, I would never, ever leave. If I felt the government was worth fighting for, I would be here. But to fight for the ideology of apartheid is just not for me. We may win a few battles, but we won't win the war ... My friends have said, "Well, how much time do you give South Africa?" And of course, no one knows. They gave Rhodesia 12 months and it's been 12 years. But my own personal view is that unless there are radical changes, it will be 36 months. Then, I reckon, it will be a new ballgame.'

Much of what Ian Kaye-Eddie said reflected my own impressions. For instance, his criticism of white liberals. Some we knew complained by the hour of the Nationalist government yet never challenged it. Some used racism to their own benefit. Many servants in English-speaking homes earned ridiculous wages. The couple who rented us their big house told us how much they thought of their maid, but they paid her £8 a month. We'd seen evidence of vast amounts of money being spent in Transkei and none of it seemed relevant to the needs of the people — nor to the reality of South Africa.

And those miserable block houses in Mdantsane. A half dozen a day were built, year after year after year. Yet each day people escaping the poverty of the country drifted into the township, hoping to find work in East London. Each day many babies were born there. No matter how many houses the government built, there would never be enough.

What Ian would miss in South Africa, I would as well. The land itself — vast, dramatic and empty. The colour and life on the East London streets. What he called the good balance of living.

Shortly after Ian and his family left for Australia, an earlier emigrant returned for a visit. A former Rhodes University professor, he was well known in East London and his family still lived there. In an interview for the paper, he told me what it was like to be there, said it was working out fine, that it had been a good move. But towards the end, he said, 'We are Australians now and glad to be that, but we miss the beauty of South Africa, get sudden yens to be in Grahamstown or travelling along the coast. And we remember the kinds of friendships we could make, black and white. Sometimes we miss the drama of South Africa — the almost knife edge of it.'

In the way that like incidents seem to happen consecutively, we then met another emigrant, a young Indian woman who had gone to live in Scotland. Errol Theron brought her to dinner one evening.

'When you're living here, you're involved'

Apartheid is so basic to South Africa that it came as almost a shock to see something that made you realize life there had not always been so racially defined. The evidence was that of an Indian family, living quietly and uneventfully in Cambridge where Dominee Loubser, Dollie Fourie and hundreds of other Afrikaners also lived.

The two-storey white house with a veranda had been owned by a doctor for many years. He'd brought his bride to it 30 years earlier. They'd raised a daughter and a son there. Since he'd owned the place before the Group Areas Act said that if you were white you lived in a certain district, if black in another, Indian or Coloured in others, he had somehow been allowed to stay. No one could explain why exactly and no one knew of another case. Soon, however, the situation would change. The doctor had recently died, and with him, the right of his family to live in Cambridge. As soon as the proper agency got around to it, his widow would be ordered to sell. Probably within the year.

Like all those of Indian descent, the family is classified as Asian — though Pria, the daughter, adds she is a third generation South African. Pria, 29, had come to dinner with Errol and a few days later we talked in her home in Cambridge. She hadn't been there much during the last five years. Both she and her brother had gone to university in Edinburgh and stayed on. She is a radiologist, he a doctor.

Feelings of repression hadn't sent her away. It was just a simpler thing of liking to live and travel in other places. As far as staying away permanently, Pria doubted it. 'I'm betwixt and between a lot of things', she said. 'I don't want to live in Britain permanently. I'd really like to live here.'

The principal reason is the closeness she feels for her family — not just her mother but a network of relatives. All are very close, she said.

Errol's family was the same — and Peter Mopp's. I'd been in their homes often and people wandered in and out all the time — brothers, cousins, uncles, nieces. One thing apartheid had apparently done, outside of ensuring that people of the same skin colour lived in the same areas, was to develop strong feelings of kinship. A sense of being in it together.

Pria said as much: 'Everything is discussed. Very seldom does one do something entirely on one's own. It doesn't go like that because when you do something, if you fall, everyone around you falls. They share your grief and your joy. Being away, I miss that terribly. Here it is a joint effort all the time.' This is what she misses when she is away. 'I miss family. I miss friends. I miss my way of life.'

She paused, then said, 'I think also — I don't really know how to express it — that growing up in a society that has pressures, in a dynamic society, gives you a better perspective. Generally oppression give you something to strive for. Not that it's right. But I think, in a way, you're better off living here in the heat of it all. When you're here, you're involved. If you stay away, it becomes slighly removed. You tend to forget the little things — like going shopping and having to find a loo. That's a luxury over here. You've got to hang on, the hell with a burst bladder.'

Pria is not involved in any of the anti-apartheid organizations in Great Britain. She said she's simply not interested though she does read about events in South Africa. 'Apartheid,' she said, 'the petty things like not sitting next to whites on a bus, that bothers me not a tiny bit. The only thing that really matters is that we are not able to earn the same.'

In Edinburgh, Pria lives with five black South African students. She is interested in a black doctor, British. Like Errol and Peter, Pria considers herself black. 'I've got loads of friends', she said, 'and I don't, over there, consider them as being black or white — just pals. But on a personal level, I could never, ever, get involved with somebody who wasn't black. I think it's got a lot to do with one's upbringing. Not only one's home environment, but one's situation in life in a country. I just don't feel the same kind of kinship.'

In spite of classifying herself a second-class citizen in South Africa, she says she considers it her country. 'I could never identify with any other country. This is true of all black South Africans, I think.'

It was hard to think of Pria being considered a second-class citizen anywhere. I found her aware, well-educated and an intelligent and warm person.

As she talked of coming back to South Africa to live, the possibilities of this, it was with an awareness that the future might be entirely different to the past. 'I think what is going to happen is an awfully difficult question', she said. 'One would like to believe that it's going to change and probably at some stage the government will be forced into change. How it's going to be and when it's going to be is awfully difficult to say. But change I think is the hope of oppressed people everywhere in the world.

'I would like to think there wouldn't be a violent confrontation', Pria continued. 'But then if I think of the Africans particularly, who have been violated in every possible human way you can think of, it would be very foolish — very difficult — to believe that.'

She looked out the window at the pleasant garden in full bloom of summer, at sunlight diffused by leaves of fine trees, then turned back to say: 'It will be very cold when I go back, you know. I will stand on the street corner, waiting for the bus, and my hands will be cold and my feet will be cold and the wind will chill my ears and then I know I will think, "What the bloody hell am I doing here?" '

'One must be fair'

The Great Trek is a vital part of Afrikaner history, immortalized in legends, museums and monuments. Words orginating from it such as *laager* are in common usage. South Africans with a Voortrekker ancestor speak of him with pride and respect — much as an American would of an ancestor among the pioneers who travelled west in a wagon train. In fact, these expeditions, though half a world apart, were not all that different. The people who were part of them were adventurers, free spirits looking for new lands where there were no restrictions, no laws.

Between 1836 and 1837 thousands of Boers, farmers and their families, left the settled lands of the Cape, travelling in ox carts and covered wagons. Like the pioneers, they fought off native raiders, endured hunger and thirst. These were Afrikaners, seeking to put as much distance as possible between themselves and the British government of the Cape.

Jasper Raats, principal of the Voorpos Afrikaans Primary School, stroked the top of a wooden chest in the dining room of his home. He told how it had travelled on the back of a wagon driven by a great-great-great-grandfather. He led the way to other rooms in the modern suburban house where he lived with his wife and two sons — pointing out other antiques. Outside, a pick-up and a Datsun sedan were parked in the driveway, a camper and a ski-boat beside the garage.

Raats had been in East London about two and a half years. He said he was lucky to have got the job at Voorpos because activities he and his family enjoyed — camping, mountain-climbing, water-skiing — were nearby. He had grown up in the Little Karoo — a vast, treeless, rolling region in the interior. His father had a small farm on the outskirts of a village. 'In most of these Little Karoo towns, people had three or four acres', Raats recalled. 'On the other side of the street is a little town, in the backyard is the farm.'

A fifth generation South African, he is descended from a German soldier brought out in 1756 to homestead land in the Eastern Cape. 'A few families left the ship at Cape Town, illegally,' he explained, 'and they split up into two parts. A few went to South West Africa and a few went over the Hottentot Mountains and that's where my family started.'

Two and a quarter centuries later, some of Raats' immediate family had done the same thing. Two of his brothers emigrated to Canada and married Canadian women. Recently they returned with their wives for a visit. Raats, who has not been outside South Africa, was interested in the women's impressions of his country. 'I said to them', Raats recalled, ' "How is it to be in South Africa?" And we were walking then on the Elephant Track through the forest at Kynsa [an area like the Hogsback along the coast between East London and Cape Town] and one of them told me, "You know, this is something you can't do in Canada. It's so cold and it's a little bit dangerous also." '

Unlike his brothers, Raats has no thought of leaving South Africa. 'I'm very, very happy here', he said. 'I think the most important thing is to live with people who think the same as you do. I really think we've got lovely people in this country. The weather, the nature, these are also reasons I love this country so very dear. And this is the country of my birth. There would be no other place for us to go.'

That afternoon, Raats talked about his school. Generally, he said, he was pleased with his job, how life was going for him at the moment. 'Actually,' he said, 'I'm very happy and I'm a lucky man. My health is good and my kiddies are healthy and my wife and I are happy.'

Did he then have no real problems in his life?

'If I have to tell other,' Raats replied, 'well, sometimes one worries a little about the future of our country.' He doesn't like the pressure on South Africa by the West. 'We've got our policy in this land,' he said, 'and I think the outside world should just leave us and watch us and give us a fair chance to work out our own problems. I'm quite sure we have the ability. We've grown up with our problems. I think there's nobody else able to come and solve them.'

Raats was silent a minute, then said, 'The recent unrest has not been a concern up to this stage, but to be very honest, the last year or so, one feels a little bit worried. I wouldn't say afraid, but one feels a little worried about the future of the Europeans in South Africa.'

The advance of Communism is what concerns him. 'I do see Communism as a threat. When I was a little boy, my father told me: "We are lucky — Angola, Rhodesia and Mozambique — there's sort of a barrier. Communism is not on our border."' Now it is, Raats believes. But he also sees government legislation such as that which barred the ANC and the PAC — 'Communist' organizations — as successful means of keeping the enemy at bay.

Unlike whites in the Eastern Cape who have been raised among blacks, Raats grew up knowing Coloureds who are native to his area. 'In culture and in language', he explained, 'the Coloureds are just as the Europeans. They speak only Afrikaans. In my hometown if you speak English to them, they're completely out.' Raats smiled, 'They've got their own way of saying things, you know. It's like a dialect from Afrikaans. Sometimes it is so amusing the way they say something.'

Coloured culture is identical to Afrikaans, he said. 'They've got the same ways, they go to the same church. They also believe that the seventh day is a day of rest. They play rugby.' He gestured outwards with his hands: 'People growing up together — how could they be different? That was my playmates. They lived on our plot, got their little houses there. Their fathers was working for my father. There were no ill feelings because they were Coloured and I was white.'

Raats shook his head. 'People don't understand this', he said. 'There was always a separation. They go to their houses at evening. I go to mine. But we were very big friends. They like to have this separation. The way we had it, I don't think they were unhappy — not a day. They had their church and their school and their part of town. I think it's a very good thing. I think if you mix them — if it's compulsory — there's going to be a lot of trouble.'

He spoke specifically of racially mixing neighbourhoods. 'There is that part of the Coloured people who have a very high standard of education and of living which will fit in with my community, but there are some of the Coloured people who don't fit in, who wouldn't like to be my next door neighbour. And one must be fair. One can't just say, "This part of the Coloured people can live in a white area." '

This, Raats said, would not square with the Afrikaner's sense of justice. 'I've grown up that there is to be justice to every person we're living with — it doesn't matter if he's black or Coloured or white. All should be treated with respect and there should be justice to all.'

I left Jaspar Raats with very mixed feelings. I'd had the same feeling with other Afrikaners. Raats, like them, seemed a nice person, God-fearing, respectable, responsible, kind-hearted, deeply committed to his country. A total stranger to him, I had been treated courteously. He had, I felt, been open and honest. He spoke earnestly of what he hoped to achieve in education. He must have been a good father and husband.

He, like Dominee Loubser and Dollie Fourie, probably treated blacks all right. Yet there was a total unawareness of their needs and feelings. There was no comprehension of blacks as human beings. Nor, did it seem possible that logic would take them anywhere. The whole situation seemed hopeless and was profoundly depressing.

'The Nationalist Government makes life very comfortable'

Jannie van Gend is an attorney, member of the city council and local chairman of the Progressive Party. His wife Cecily is quiet, loves books and used to be a librarian. Then she managed a shoe store in the Vincent Park Centre. Jannie is her opposite, gregarious, involved in sports. He'd earned his fitness by jogging, first team field hockey for his club and crewing on a friend's sailboat. Jannie is an exception to white political tradition in that he is a liberal of Afrikaans origin. One day we had lunch and he explained how this had come about.

'I guess I've always been interested in politics,' he said, 'though very superficially initially at the University of Stellenbosch [an Afrikaan's university]. There I'd adopted a philosophy that you wouldn't change the government without changing the Afrikaner and I had the idea that one should work within the National Party. But gradually I began to realize that the barrier between liberal thinking and actually being able to break away from the Afrikaner group was too real. As soon as the leaders cracked the whip, even people who felt differently fell into line for the sake of party unity. Our Young Turk movement wasn't strong enough — and didn't show signs of becoming strong enough — to motivate a sufficient number of Afrikaners to change Nationalist policies. Basically, even at university, they stuck to the line of whites, particularly Afrikaners, having total say over their destiny. I then began to realize, look, there's no way this is going to work. I'd better get in on the other side.'

Shortly after moving from Cape Town to East London in 1971, Jannie shifted to the other side. He explained his reasons: 'I just didn't see the white man being able to maintain control over his own affairs by not allowing other people, living with us, to have their share of the democratic say. What in effect the Nationalist Party was trying to do was say that South Africa belongs to whites — that anybody else here is here to earn a living and must exercise his political rights elsewhere.'

Jannie believes that the social reality of apartheid doesn't fit the economic reality and therefore is destined to fail. 'The apartheid dream, I felt, had to come to an end within my lifetime', he said. 'And I felt something strong had to be done about it. To take a different line, to actually accept the reality of black participation in government, power-sharing. And not in separate chambers, but in one chamber because you've got one country. The fiction of separate countries [black homelands] I couldn't see being carried through.'

When Jannie left the National Party, he went all the way, choosing the Progressive Party instead of the United Party.

'I was always very much to the left in political thinking and my ideas', he said, 'were always basically what the Progressive Party ideas were.' For him, it became a question of how to achieve peacefully what he sees as the ultimate destiny of South Africa, black rule — even if this meant he would never be a part of the power structure, or not, as he termed it, in the forseeable future.

He explained the Progressive Party's beliefs: 'Very basically we stand for a completely non-racial society', he said. 'We accept the realities of race, because of our history and because of present government policies and because of human nature. We accept that races do have differences; they have group identities, group differences. In any society these differences are going to result in people going after their group interests and you'll have black power-blocks working against the interests of white, minority blocks working against the interests of Coloured and Indian. And while we believe in an open society and no discrimination on grounds of race, this reality of race we recognize, and believe that any constitution devised for this country must take those realities into account. For that reason, we insist upon a Bill of Rights.

'We also, not because of race but more to retain responsible government in a time of transition, believe in a qualified franchise. Initially, it was property as well as educational qualification, but our policy has changed and we now have only an educational qualification. But we have two voters rolls. One roll would elect 50 per cent of the seats in Parliament on a proportional basis, countrywide, and these would be voted for by the roll where a voter qualifies for franchise on the basis of literacy.' The other half of the seats would be voted for on a constituency basis and voters on this roll would be required to have a minimum of ten years' education.

Voting from either roll would not be qualified racially. 'None of our policies have any bearing on race', Jannie said. 'Every aspect of our policy can be implemented without reference to race. There are no little safeguards that say black, white, Coloured, Indian. Those words don't even appear in our policy.'

He reiterated the basis of Progressive thinking: the qualified franchise. Its purpose was to keep government in responsible hands during the transitional period. Jannie hastened to add that the Progressive Party would also insist on compulsory education being introduced as soon as this became economically feasible. At the time, school was compulsory for whites between the ages of 7 and 16, for Coloureds and Asians between 7 and 15. Blacks were not required to attend school.

Listening to Jannie, I realized that many of the people I knew who had once been enthusiastic Progressive supporters had moved to the left of it. It seemed that the Soweto riots had polarized whites, making them either more conservative or more liberal.

I asked what the chances were that the Progressive Party would replace the National Party.

'It would depend very much on pressures generally and what the effect of pressure is', Jannie replied. 'If pressures cause the Afrikaner to become hardened around present National policy into a *laager* mentality, we will probably not come into power until power is taken from white hands forcibly. If, on the other hand, the effect of pressure would be to cause a real split which could take a large section of the Afrikaner population away from present government thinking, their obvious role would be a link with us.'

Something I'd never understood was the fact that the great decisions of government were often made by cabinet ministers instead of Parliament. I asked Jannie about this.

'A lot of the delegation of power to the ministers has come from the development of emergency powers', he said. 'But, basically, I think it is because there is such a strong government and a relatively ineffective opposition position which, by and large, has really thought the same way as government on matters of state security — at least in the past — and that was when initial steps were taken to give an administrator (which a cabinet minister really is) almost executive powers; where an act of Parliament says he can take decisions which normally would be Parliament's prerogative.

'I think', Jannie continued, 'that the first few times this was done, there was a bit of an outcry from the opposition, but nothing happened and government saw they could do it again and again and again. And basically, everybody thought it was really in the country's interests — certainly in the white man's interests. This just kept going. The PRP [Progressive Reform Party] certainly shouts about it now and the press shouts about it. But even a person like myself, I've seen it so often in the press — detentions, what obviously was a hanging in a police cell — it's like explorations on the moon. I've seen it before. It worries you if you're taxed on the point, but it's part of your everyday life. People shrug their shoulders and say, "What can be done about it?" '

It seemed incredible that bannings, detentions and deaths in prison could go on, that people knew about it and yet nothing was done.

'I suppose most of us don't feel sufficiently threatened ourselves to be provoked into action', Jannie said. 'This is clear in the present reaction of Afrikaners to the government's economic policies. They never reacted to race policies because these didn't hurt them. They said, "Well, the government is looking after us." But in the present economic climate, Afrikaners are beginning to shout at their own government. But until such time as Afrikaners appreciate that the government's policies on race are a threat to their own lives, to their futures and to their children's futures, they're not going to shout about government powers and arbitrary powers. 'The Nationalist government, after all, makes life very comfortable. It makes life secure when a policeman can just nab a guy and put him away — when a minister can, just by decree, ensure that everything is hunky dory for a man's business.'

I asked Jannie what changes he expected in South Africa and how he thought these would come about.

'I hope', he replied, 'that the West will make it sufficiently clear to the South African government that they [the West] will, in fact, have to come in with very real support for the majority of South Africans, blacks, and say, "If we don't support the people that want change in your country, we must lose out because the Eastern Bloc will then support them and we'll be seen as on the other side." I believe it is important that the West keep South Africa. Apart from our mineral resources, I think it is strategically important to have the southern tip of Africa pro-West — not a little white regime but ultimately a country ruled by blacks and one in which, we hope, whites, Indians and Coloureds can continue to play an important part.

'I don't think the West will achieve this if they dilly-dally, give black power the impression that they're not really all that unhappy about what the whites are doing. They certainly won't achieve this if they give any impression of bolstering the whites. I don't think the West can even be negative because the Russians aren't going to be negative or neutral — they're going to grab any opportunity to get the black man on their side. If this reality of the West's position can be brought home to our government, it could have great influence on its future actions.'

Before the end of 1977 the Progressive Reform Party had become the Progressive Federal Party, a name change made to accommodate the left-wing parliamentary members of the United Party who joined it. The UP, long doddering, then died. Since 1948, it had been the official opposition to the National Party and the voice of most English-speaking South Africans. Towards the end, its leadership and its supporters had split into three factions. Initially six of its elected representatives (MPs in the House of Assembly), and one senator joined the Progressive Party.

Remaining UP representatives sought homes in either the South

African Party or the New Republic Party, both organized in 1977. Six MPs became members of the right of centre SAP (South African Party) while nine senators and 24 MPs in the ideological centre of the UP got together in the NRP.

Another development, more surprising than the predictable end of the UP, was the announcement by Prime Minister Vorster that there would be a restructuring of the legislative branch of government. Constitutional changes would provide for joint decision-making at the top level in a council of cabinets made up from cabinets of three separate Parliaments — one for whites, one for Coloureds, one for Asians. When he made this announcement, Vorster specifically excluded blacks from the scheme, reiterating that their road to 'self-determination' lay in homeland independence and self-government.

According to Vorster, each of the new Parliaments would have its own prime minister, cabinet and assembly and exclusive powers to handle all legislation pertaining to its own race group. The council of cabinets would initiate all legislation affecting the three groups and would advise the three Parliaments. The council of cabinets would be chaired by an executive president chosen by an electoral college composed of members of the three Parliaments.

Along with this Vorster announced a general election for November. The proposed new system, as articulated at the executive level, was certain to be rubber-stamped after the election by a Parliament which only the most devout Progressive believed would change in composition.

Trying to sort out Vorster's proposal for racial representation boggled my mind. And in fact, so did the interpretation of Progressive policy as Jannie explained it. Keeping blacks out of South African government required some fancy footwork.

'Where is justice?'

One part of Prime Minister Vorster's plan to develop new, multiracial governing bodies called for dissolving one of the two houses of Parliament — the Senate. One of the 54 men who would then be out of a job would be Senator Geoff O'Connell, appointed in 1974.

O'Connell, 54, is a civil engineer and head of an engineering firm which has offices in a handsomely remodelled, traditional Dutchburgher house on upper Oxford Street. Like Jan van Gend, the Progressive of Afrikaner descent, O'Connell is the political exception, an English-speaking Nationalist. His father, an attorney in a small Eastern Cape town, was a United Party activist, a close personal friend of the UP Prime Minister, Jan Smuts.

O'Connell's interest in politics began following graduation from the University of Cape Town. He went to work for the Department of Bantu Administration. 'In those days, it was the Department of Native Affairs', O'Connell said. 'There I came into contact with the essence of our problem — the black man and the white man in South Africa.' O'Connell paused, his face serious. 'I think you will agree with me that politics in this country has centred around the — ah — you might say, the confrontation between black and white and there could have been no more important department involved in this than the Department of Bantu Administration.' O'Connell said the problem, as it revealed itself to him, was based on 'great numerical disparity' and the 'socioeconomic development of the whites which was comparable to that of whites in other countries while on the other hand, our black people were in the process of developing'.

His concern with the problem 'trapped' him in politics. 'I saw that, in the long run, this would lead to a point where we would have to resolve these differences', he said. 'I saw it clearly at that stage and I believe my sense of the political issues has not changed since then.'

O'Connell helped develop the National Party policy of black homelands. He was convinced that the kind of government that would work best for blacks was a combination of white direction carried to the blacks by tribal chiefs. I reminded him that the majority of South Africa's blacks had moved from the black homelands to the white cities.

'I accept that you are dealing with two different categories of political response', O'Connell replied. 'And I think there is absolutely no doubt that our most pertinent problem is the question of the urban black. And,' he smiled slightly, 'I say problem though I do not say his being is a problem. I say the manner in which he is accommodated within society creates a problem. He has moved from the country into a white society, established himself within the economy, and the situation is that, on the other hand, he has not left that which is his ethnic background. We believe he is still tied, still part of the country from which he has come. But many do not believe that and, somehow, this conflict in philosophy between ours to them and theirs to us is going to be our most important problem to resolve.

'On the other hand,' he continued, 'the question I would put to you is this: does the population growth of a particular community establish a changing right to its part in this world? In other words, if the growth rate of the Chinese increases, do they have different territorial rights? Will we redivide the whole world? Where are these rights, how are these rights defined? If the ratio of white to black in this country is changing continuously, does that mean that the rights of both are to change continuously? There must be a point where, if you are to protect the rights of a minority — or of a majority, for that matter — these rights have to be defined.'

O'Connell sidestepped the question of how white South Africa would accommodate black aspirations. 'I believe that too often we are engrossed with the immediateness of every type of solution', he said. 'I see that there is continuous change, a process of development. A man who has a sense of history must be aware of the necessity of looking into the future and place himself in time in relationship to that. To say that we could simply resolve everything by giving one man, one vote, is patently an over-simplification. I don't think anyone with knowledge of South Africa's wide spectrum of development ... could say that is the answer. But, on the other hand, I would be the last man to say that there may not be, some time in the future, a time when that may be possible.

'What I do say is that the rate of development here does not create any confidence in my mind that this can be achieved in my lifetime. So I would reply that, for the present, let us place our priorities correctly. At present I hope to see the black man evolve as rapidly as possible in the fields of learning and economics.'

What O'Connell was saying reminded me of what an elderly black had once said to me, 'They talk about us sharing in government when they have taught us. They've had 300 years to prepare us and they say we are still not ready. When will that day come?'

I asked O'Connell what he thought his role was in the development of South Africa.

'As a member of the Senate, my present role in this is important', he said. 'A Parliament is essentially, I would say, an electoral body to establish the cabinet and Prime Minister and, having established this, it divests itself of direct particiption. You may say then, that Parliament is a body of people in which the individual has a part to play, has an influence to make, but has no direct political part to play within the limitation of other than his party.

'I think in the discussion he has with his colleagues, in the manner in which he encourages those who are in a position of authority, in the manner in which he discourages them, in his public image outside of Parliament, he is bound to follow the party discipline. Having placed in authority those who will determine and enunciate the policy, he must leave it to them to do so.'

I asked O'Connell what he thought about the new three-tiered cabinet proposed by the Prime Minister. He called it a 'good beginning'. He said he would stay in government and planned to be a candidate for Parliament in November.

There are two kinds of Nationalists — the *verligte*, or enlightened Nationalist, and the *verkrampte*, or hard-liner. The former sees change as unpleasant but inevitable, the latter remains opposed to change. O'Connell defined his own position in this way: 'I flow so naturally though my environment that I believe I'm completely acceptable to Afrikaners as an Afrikaner, to the English as an English-speaking South African — as a *verligte* by the *verligtes*, as a *verkrampte* by the *verkramptes*. But', he asked, 'how important is this? Some issues are really irrelevant. They are ephemeral. Like the wings of butterflies, they drop off. To adopt an attitude on something which is so transient is not of any real significance. What is of significance are the long-term issues, the foundations of which are being laid now. And there one must have a very strong attitude. If this sense of harmony in a community is disturbed, for example, by the intrusion of another community with factors to which your community has not become accustomed, then it would be wrong to tolerate that until such times and circumstances have allowed a different pattern of response to evolve.'

I asked if it was not rare for an English-speaking South African to be a member of the National Party?

'The Afrikaner', he replied, 'is the backbone of the party, but increasingly, the English-speaking South African has sought a new political home. For myself, I don't think I ever sought a new political home. I just saw the situation as it was — along with the solutions and the answers to these problems. The National Party convinced me there was a greater chance of solving them successfully through that party. I saw the National Party as definitely getting to grips with the evolvement of the different communities. They had been able to identify the black man and to create within him a sense of nationalism.

'You know,' he said 'we are no different from people in the society from which you come. I've travelled there and I've found it easy to move among your people. Yet I'm faced with problems which are infinitely different. And I'm subjected to accusations which reach beyond limits even thought of during the Nazi period. And yet, we are, at essence, simple of heart. You and I come from the same stock. Where is justice? Will you not give us the opportunity to evolve progressively?'

I'd been looking forward to meeting O'Connell. It seemed important to find out why a South African of English descent would move into the ranks of that stronghold of Afrikanerdom, the National Party. My anticipation had been heightened by the difficulty in seeing him. O'Connell was rarely in East London — his home was at Port Alfred, further south along the coast. When he was in town, time after time, his male secretary had called to cancel an appointment made weeks before. Getting inside his doors seemed significant.

I wanted to find out for myself what he was like. Roger Omond called O'Connell a fool. Kingsley Kingon had, with irritation, related his conversation with O'Connell over an individual's right to trial. Ruth Belonsky and O'Connell had had a confrontation over the brief desegregation of the city library. But when you weighed their responses, you had to allow for the fact that these reactions were from dedicated anti-Nationalists. However, Ryno King, the National Party organizer in East London who had finally arranged for the interview with O'Connell, had been aggressive in suggesting interviews with other party members instead of O'Connell.

After talking with him, I felt just as negative as the others. I hadn't responded in quite the same way to other Nationalists. Dominee Loubser, Dollie Fourie, the Afrikaner schoolmaster, Jaspar Raats, all were basically nice people. They were warm, open and honest. Their views seemed sincere — and inevitable. It was easy to see why they believed as they did.

The senator seemed put together in another way. He had talked for an hour and a half. It had been impossible to get any feelings from him. Often, numbed by his monotone and dulled by his generalities, my mind wandered.

'We do more for our blacks than any black government'

Under Malcomess, the East London phone book lists six private residences plus Malcomess Toyota, Malcomess Peugeot and Citroen, Malcomess Agricultural Division, Malcomess Limited, Malcomess Leyland and Malcomess House, the latter, just off Oxford Street, a white mansion taking up a large city block. Once the Malcomess family home, it is now an orphanage for white children.

The most visible of the Malcomess clan is John, 45, a ruddy-faced, handsome man with a shock of wavy white hair. His offices are in Barnes Volkswagen which he owns and this is on Oxford Street about a block from the Malcomess Home. I met him in his air-conditioned private office, where he began by talking about his background.

'My great-grandfather on my father's side of the family came out from Germany in the 1860s with Baron von Stutterheim to fight in the Kaffir Wars [nine wars between blacks and white settlers between 1780 and 1880]. That's a dirty word nowadays,' Malcomess said, 'but that's what they were called. He went into business in King William's Town and ended up a very, very wealthy man. About the mid-70s, he moved to East London, married an Irish girl and had eleven children. My grandfather was one of them — a farmer, politician and senator for native affairs under the Smuts government. So I was brought up meeting a lot of the better-educated black people. Later on, I found this very rewarding. I don't look on the African as does the average South African — as being someone who can't rise to great heights.'

Malcomess was educated at St Andrew's College in Grahamstown then went on to university at Oxford in England. There he met and married an English girl and returned to South Africa to join the family business. At that time it consisted of a large automobile dealership and a separate division for import and sales of agricultural machinery, much of it imported. After trying both, Malcomess elected to stay with the automotive side and eventually became managing director of a group of several dealerships and related businesses.

'At the same time', he said, 'the company became public and was quoted on the Johannesburg Stock Exchange. We also did a merger with a plastics and packaging company. I served as managing director for five years and did several trips to the States at this time. I think at that stage, the average dealership in American sold about 600 new units a year, well, we were doing close on 3,000.'

In terms of money, this translates into an annual turnover of approximately £17,000,000. But because of the pressures on a company of that size and the rate of taxation — 'if I got a R2,000 [£1,200] a year increase, it was worth R40 [£24] a month to me' — he chose to resign and buy a dealership of his own.

'It's the best thing I ever did', Malcomess said. 'I'm entirely my own boss. To work for myself means the total profit comes back to me and this is far, far greater than I would have ever earned.'

That was in mid-1973. Shortly afterwards he turned it into a limited partnership which allows him to share responsibility for the business.

'I can now do things I never would have dreamt of doing', he said. 'If somebody phones me up and says, "John, let's go to Mauritius and fish for marlin for a week" — or two weeks or a month — I can just drop everything and go.'

Though his family was politically active, John stayed out of politics until 1976. Before that, he said, 'being in a large company I thought it wise to stay out because politics in this country can become very, very heated. It's not just politics,' he continued, 'to a certain extent, it's racialism between Afrikaners and English. An Afrikaner would much rather do business with an Afrikaner's business and, if he knows that you, as managing director of Malcomess, are an active United Party supporter, this can have a deterrent effect. So I kept right out of it and was totally amazed when it was suggested I stand as a member of the Provincial Council for the United Party.' (Each of the country's four provinces has a Provincial Council. These are concerned with dispensing funds to regional roads, schools, hospitals, etc.)

When he was approached to be a UP candidate, Malcomess was not a signed-up member of the UP, was not even certain whether he wished to support the UP or Progressive Party. He turned down the offer, then spent the next year sorting out his own political ideas.

Ultimately he chose the UP because he believed its policy on federation better than that of the Progressive Party. 'Though I felt both policies would lead ultimately to majority rule,' he said, 'I felt it would happen too soon in terms of the PRP policy — too much of a swift change resulting in a lot of disorder, chaos and instability. I felt the UP policy would lead to the same thing, but it would be in more gradual stages and, as such, would give everybody a chance to settle down with a new thought before the next stage arrived.'

He explained the UP plan for federation — one retained by the New Republic Party which Malcomess joined after the UP folded.

'It's a racial plan initially,' Malcomess said, 'in that you would have federal states that were not geographically defined. They would be federations of people. The whites in the Cape Province, for example, would have their own state house, the Coloureds would have theirs, your Bantu — or blacks — would have theirs. [This plan is like that proposed by Vorster except that he excludes blacks from participating and people are divided on a national basis according to race, rather than on a provincial level]. 'These state houses', Malcomess continued, 'would control education, hospitalization — in fact, as many portfolios as we could reasonably give them concerning their own people. We would, obviously, have to exclude defence, foreign affairs, fiscal policies, possibly police, and these would remain with central government. At the same time, central government would be decentralizing into a number of federal assemblies, one for each group. An estimated 16 of these assemblies [one for each of the four races in each of the four provinces] would, in turn, elect representatives to go to central government.'

Central government would be made up of these representatives and others allotted according to the contribution each racial group made to the national economy. 'The country would have an overall tax', Malcomess explained. 'If the Cape White Federal Assembly, for example, provided 10 per cent of the central government's funds, it would be entitled to 10 per cent of the remaining 100-plus seats. So you would start out with a situation where the bulk of the money, obviously, would be in white hands. They would have the bulk of the seats, giving whites effective control of the central government. At the same time, all apartheid measures would be dispensed with. All discrimination on the statute books would disappear altogether. This would then give blacks a chance to build up their incomes. As they did so, obviously the tax they would pay would increase and, along with it, the number of seats they would hold. Ultimately,' Malcomess said, 'it boils down to those who pay for government, control government.

'I see it very, very simply. My position is that we are going to ultimately have majority rule. I don't know how long it's going to take — what safeguards are going to be involved, but ultimately we will have majority rule.'

Philosophically, he has no problems with this. 'Obviously,' he said, 'one hopes for stability, protection of rights and things of this nature. What worries is that it is either going to be done peacefully or through revolution and bloodshed. I'm quite happy if it will happen peaceably, but I frankly hold the view that if the Nationalists stay in power, it will not happen peaceably. I see no signs of change at all. I think Vorster, over the last eight months, has demonstrated that he is extremely *verkramp*. You know that six months speech? "Give me six months and people will be amazed where South Africa stands." Well, hell, that was two years ago. What happened? Nothing, absolutely nothing.'

Malcomess has no illusions about his own influence on South African policy as a member of the Provincial Council: 'The situation is that when Union was first accomplished in the early part of this century, provincial councils were fairly important. As the years have gone by, under Nationalist governments, these powers have been whittled away. While, in fact, we do still control education, hospitalization and things of this nature, inevitably what happens is that central government will tell Nationalists in the Cape Provinical Council that this is what they want done and it gets done. It's a rubber-stamping operation.'

He also knew that the United Party would never again control the political destiny of South Africa. 'But', he said, 'I am hopeful that the new party which is in the process of being formed [the NRP] will give us a chance of becoming the alternative government. I hope that we'll see change in the next election — a very big swing away from the Nationalists. But', he added, 'one mustn't forget that the voting in this country is a fairly odd system in that it takes 12 to 20,000 people in an urban seat to select a member of Parliament and it can take as little as 8,000 people in a rural seat and your support for the opposition parties is predominantly in your urban areas. So, when you look at the number of seats the Nationalists win in Parliament, compared to opposition seats, it is simply not representative of the number of people who vote.'

Malcomess put this on a 60-40 basis. Currently there were 123 Nationalists in Parliament's House of Assembly, 37 from the UP, 11 Progressives. In fact, when the National Party took over government in 1948, the majority of people voted United Party and it was not until the 1958 elections that the government won more than 50 per cent of the vote.

I asked if, in view of the recent black unrest, he'd considered resettling in another country.

'I have thought about leaving South Africa on lots of occasions, starting right back at Sharpeville in 1960', Malcomess replied. 'But, look, we have a wonderful life here. I'm South African born and bred. On my mother's side we go back to the 1820 settlers. When I was at university in England, I was the proudest man in the world to be a South African. I still think if we can get cooperation from black and white in this country, we could be the greatest country in the southern hemisphere. But I'm not proud of the things that have been happening over the last 20 years.

'Still,' he said reflectively, 'I think things are much better here than most people in the Western world realize. I truthfully believe that the black man in this country is better off than the vast majority of black men in any other place in Africa. I believe we do more for our blacks than any black government does in terms of hospitalization, education and all the rest.'

And on a personal level Malcomess finds South Africa has given him a wealth of choices. 'I play golf a couple of times a week. I'm on the doorstep of the beach — a wonderful, white beach, beautiful sand, lovely surf. Within a few miles of my home I can go shooting, I can go trout fishing, I can go surf fishing, estuary fishing. Tennis courts and swimming pool at home. Servants, obviously. On a Monday, in fact, we have something like four at home — the girl who's been with us for 20 years who's our cook. We have a laundry girl who comes in on Monday and Tuesday. We have a garden boy a couple of days a week and a weed girl twice a week.

'We lead', Malcomess said, 'a very good life'. He paused, then said, 'But I would like to stress that I totally disagree with what happens to the black man in this country — though it isn't as bad as the rest of Africa thinks it is, nor one-tenth as bad as the rest of the world makes it out to be. You know', he said, 'people come here expecting to see blacks chained to the lamp post — walking around with ankle irons. But it's like walking in Detroit to be downtown in East London — with the blacks mingling with whites on the streets, going into all the shops and utilizing all the facilities. The only things they can't use are the white toilets, this sort of thing. But, at the same time, there are a lot of things that are wrong and do need to be changed.'

From the South African Party came still another white viewpoint on change. Thanks to an introduction from Corder Tilney, Bill Deacon, one of its founding members, explained SAP policy. William Deacon, a United Party Member of Parliament since 1969, represented a constituency which included Grahamstown and parts of East London. In January, 1977, Deacon, along with five other MPs, was expelled from the UP for not accepting a leadership decision to dissolve the party and reform it on a broader base.

Subsequently, the UP simply disbanded, its members going on to other parties. The SAP accommodated right-wing members.

Bill Deacon is a tall, distinguished man with silver hair and a clipped moustache. He lives on a farm near Grahamstown that has been in his family for a century.

He outlined SAP's plan for South Africa. Basically, it is a federal concept, structured on a loose federation of separate states, similar to the European Common Market. This would begin with re-education of South African whites to the fact that adaptations would have to be made 'peaceably and in an orderly manner. And this', Deacon explained, 'is how my party differs from the other two opposition parties [the Progressive Federal and New Republic parties]. We are also exceptionally strong on security measures since we believe that South Africa is currently in a state of undeclared war.'

So who was the enemy? Deacon was no more specific than any of the others. Subversion from inside plus unnamed outside powers who provided black dissidents with arms, training and motivation. And, he added, 'certain Western powers, in all innocence, are playing into the hands of Marxists by casting a blind eye to the facts of life in Southern Africa — that our problem is race'.

Unless the West comes in on the side of moderate whites, Deacon believes that Communism will engulf Africa. He says it is essential that Rhodesia and South Africa remain with the West: 'A lot of people talk about the strategic Cape sea route, but I don't think that is the vitally important thing. There are our strategic metals and the power we have to create jobs for the blacks. The white man in Southern Africa may appear to be wrong; he might indeed be an oppressor, but he has the intelligence, the capital and the know-how to create the jobs these people need.

'At this stage', Deacon said, 'there are few blacks who are capable of making that amount of work for black people. If the West lost out in Southern Africa, it would be recolonized by Russian experts — or Chinese experts — whoever wins the ideological struggle — and its great resources would then go to them.'

Deacon's own personal goal is to bring moderates together. 'I'd like', he said, 'to see Afrikaners and English-speaking people work together on finding solutions. And', he added, 'I've no pecuniary interest in this whatsoever. If, in the process of bringing this about, I lose my seat, but know that I've succeeded, then I'll lose happily and go into retirement. I can afford to and I'd love to go farming again.'

Deacon sees South Africa's problems being resolved by a coalition of whites. He did not include blacks. So when it came down to basics, the difference between what O'Connell believed and what Deacon espoused seemed more cosmetic than anything else.

Roger Omond said, 'UP and Nat feelings about blacks are essentially about the same — except that the UP adds, "but let's not be beastly about it". '

'If we are going down, we are going down fighting'

Jan van Gend's counterpart in East London is the National Party organizer, Ryno King. Unlike Jannie, King works at this fulltime. His offices are in a corner suite on the fourth floor of an Afrikaans saving and loan building in the centre of town, across from City Hall and around the corner from the Window Theatre. Pictures of party leaders decorate the walls and through curtains on the bay window you can see the Indian Ocean at the end of Oxford Street.

Kingsley Kingon had suggested I see King; he called him a 'good type'. When King got in, we talked in his office. King's manner is warm, open and sincere. He is obviously dedicated to his country, his party and his job.

King had been a National Party organizer since he graduated from the University of Stellenbosch in 1969, but his interest in politics had begun much earlier.

'I was about nine years of age when I went to boarding school', he said. 'My father wrote in for me for *Die Burger* [the newspaper of the National Party].' At that age, he said, anything was better than studying and he became a 'very keen newspaper reader'.

Of his background, King said, 'Originally, we're from United Party offspring — we're wine farmers about 90 miles from Cape Town. My father was a very keen politician — Nationalist — but my grandfather was a staunch Jan Smuts fan. He left his family twice to go to war with Smuts.'

King followed his father politically. 'I always argued within, as they say, party policy — within the framework of separate development, though,' he added, 'I had many doubts when I was a student. At Stellenbosch, where I studied political philosophy, my professors criticized the government and criticized everything else, and I went through stages where I criticized too. I got into a lot of arguments about this whole thing. I was a staunch Nat, but to the *verlig* side. I remember, we had an argument in the hostel one afternoon that nearly ended in a fist fight. They bet me I won't go to a Nationalist meeting to ask them some questions. They put on some money, so I had to accept. 'That night I went and asked questions and there was hell to pay — they nearly threw me out.'

He tried to remember exactly what he had asked, dismissed these with a wave of his hand: 'It was as far as party policies and discrimination and blacks and the old, atrophied, stories that to be a Nationalist you must discriminate against the non-Europeans. "You can't be a true Nationalist if you don't keep the black man in his place." That kind of thing.'

'Then afterwards, as we walked out of the hall, one of our senior Members of Parliament came to me — I didn't even know him at that stage. He took me by the arm and asked me — what do I do? Said he'd heard about me and heard about my father. Asked some questions: What am I going to do after I finish my exams? I said, "Actually, I think I'll go farming, although I don't feel like it. I'm a bit idealistic at the moment. I feel for something." So he asked me if I would like to join the National Party as an organizer. We went to the hotel after that, had a chat, and I decided that very same evening I'm going to give it a try.' His parents were upset, King remembered, but they've come around and he himself has never looked back.

'I don't think you can have a more interesting job', he said. 'It covers absolutely everything in life — troubles with pensions, domestic problems, troubles with work. But, mostly, they just come and sit and talk. They say, "I feel like voting for the National Party, but we have these troubles"; or, "my daughter's husband left her and she's staying with us. We live on a meagre pension, please can you help us?" And you must listen to this story even if it takes hours.' King will try to direct people to helping agencies, to possible employers and, in all cases, he will try to be a sympathetic listener.

He figures he will last about ten or twelve years. 'I don't think you can keep it up too long', he said. 'You must be full of life. You can never be gloomy, the future of the National Party must shine out of your face. Though possibly it is not always sunshine and roses, you must still be optimistic when people talk to you.'

It seemed logical to think that King might eventually be a candidate for political office. 'Let me explain a little bit', King replied. 'We work with people who don't get paid and if you haven't got the right attitude, they absolutely won't work for the party and you will have to do it all yourself. Actually, you start making friends out of them first and then later on, they work for the party. And if you have these attributes, then people will come to you and ask if you want to stand for office. And if they do that, timing is very important. You must make it out for yourself whether you think you're right or whether you must wait. If they ask you, you go a step higher in politics.'

I asked what is was about the National Party that made him believe it had the right answers for South Africa.

'As far as the party is concerned,' he said, 'I do believe — and that's been all my life and this belief has rather grown in the past few years — that the policy of separate development, separate freedoms for black states, is the only policy that can work in South Africa. I don't believe in a multiracial state. I believe we must give them their freedom in independent states though it will cost us a fortune. We must spend all that is possible to make them stand on their own feet. And with respect, without bloodshed, with as little race friction as possible.

'The white man in South Africa is in a battle for existence, and I don't think many of the white people believe that having the blacks on a common voters' role will ensure their existence, and I don't think you'll get them to believe it. No one can guarantee them that by giving them [blacks] everything they want — by giving them the vote on a plate — that this craving for white blood will stop immediately and we will have a safe future. As I see it, the only way we can have a say in our future is to keep power in the white Parliament and see that the white people are the only people that plan and work out the future of the white man.

'The Progressive Party, for example. It is very easy for them to talk as they do talk, but I think they realize that they can't be much more in South Africa than a mere white head for a black body and that is steering South Africa in a dangerous direction. We must be very careful not to get irresponsible — to do things for quick political gain and in the end bring racial disharmony or create expectations in people that can't be fulfilled.'

But no matter what the future of South Africa is, King is dedicated to it. 'I have never thought about leaving', he said. 'Though we all realize there may be dangerous times ahead, that these are bad times, I just can't see myself out of this country. People say they'll be the last to go, but I believe I will be. I might, if things get worse, think about sending my wife and children out, but I'll stay and fight to the last end. To tell the truth, I think I'll be better to die than to leave South Africa.'

King spoke of the increasing pressures on South Africa. 'We've all come to the realization that South Africa has very few friends left', King said. 'I think that is not always for a nation to the good. Especially for South Africa where we tried, where the government tried, to do everything possible to create goodwill. That's a thing they must be careful of — putting the white man against the wall, telling him that his time has come. South Africans — especially the old stock, the old English immigrants, the old Afrikaner stock — are hard people. They will say, "OK. If we must fight, then the hell with the rest of the world. Why shall we make concessions to the black people? Why shall we make concessions to the Coloureds, to the Indians? If we are going down, we are going down fighting." '

King shook his head: 'I'm afraid this is now something loose among our people. The people are coming to the stage where they say, "Nobody cares about us, so it's time we care only about ourselves." And when they talk about "ourselves", they mean only the white people. All the good will, all the racial harmony will be thrown overboard.

'It will then really be the end, I suppose. Not the fighting end, but still the end. I think that the Western world will get much further with the whites of South Africa if they show a little more consideration for the problems we have. If they can only understand that if they try and help us, they will free us to help the black people very much more.'

'Now you can see how Mapetla died'

Later Fraser and I went back to King William's Town, this time to see Steve Biko. It hadn't been easy to get to him. In spite of restrictions, he was busy. A succession of journalists, photographers and representatives of other governments sought him out. It may have been true, as Prime Minister Vorster said a few months later, that not one black South African in a hundred knew of Bantu Steve Biko. But he was known in London, Washington and the capitals of Europe.

South Africans didn't know of Biko because he was banned as a student, silenced and restricted since then. No speech or remark of his had been allowed to be published in South Africa except for evidence he gave in a court trial in 1976. That was the sole exception.

I had called the BPC offices in King William's Town and asked for an appointment with Biko. Some days later, I got a phone call from Biko. We set up a time. But before going to King, I went back to the library at the *Dispatch* to look at his files. 'You'll see there's a block missing', said the librarian. 'Someone got in here one night and pulled all of the clippings between 1973 and 1976.'

A break-in by security police would have been not only awkward but probably unnecessary. Certainly they had their own file of clippings. It didn't seem reasonable to think someone at the paper would take material which they could use freely. But one tends towards paranoia in South Africa. I remembered an incident concerning an Afrikaner on the paper's staff. He had passed us when we were on our way to King to see Nohle Mohapi. He waved and so did we. Later, in the office, he had stopped: 'Where were you going when I saw you?' he asked. I hesitated, instinctively, then I lied: 'We'd heard about the museum and thought we'd see it.' Nothing he had ever done or said to me would suggest he might be a police informer. Yet he was an Afrikaner. How could I be sure he was not?

From the remaining clippings in Biko's file I learned he had first been banned in 1973 when he was a medical student, and after that restricted to the King William's Town area. The original banning order had been extended in 1975. Biko was the third son in a family of four and was born in 1947. Married, Biko had two children, then six and two.

In August 1976 — shortly after Mapetla Mohapi died in prison — Biko was detained. Thenjiwe Mtintso, a reporter for the *Dispatch* working out of its King William's Town office, was detained at the same time. Biko had been held for 101 days, then sent back to King. According to the published account, Steve, his wife reported, had lost 15 kg in weight. Biko had been held in the maximum security section of Fort Glamorgan Prison in East London, often in solitary confinement, and extensively interrogated.

Three days after his release, Biko had met US Senator Dick Clark at the East London airport.

Then, late in March 1977, Biko, buying cigarettes in a cafe, was arrested by Hattingh and Schoeman — the same security policemen who had arrested Mapetla Mohapi. Biko was again taken to Fort Glamorgan. In court the following day, he was charged with 'defeating the ends of justice'. The state alleged that in January and February of that year, Biko persuaded state witnesses, secondary school students charged with burning their school, to give false evidence.

Biko pleaded not guilty and was allowed out on R500 [£300] bail. This had been paid by a representative of the *Daily Dispatch*.

So it was a few weeks after that when Fraser and I went to King. We parked again in front of the old church at 15A Leopold Street. A tall, broad-shouldered man wearing a plaid shirt was just coming out. 'Hi', he said. 'If you don't mind waiting a few minutes, I was just on my way to get cigarettes.'

He went away, jogging easily. In the middle of the street, the sun picked out the russet tones of his shirt, then the colours darkened again as he disappeared among the trees on the other side. This is the image that remains: a big, healthy, good-looking man, moving comfortably in the sunshine.

When Steve came back, we went into one of the back offices in the old church. He sat behind a desk, relaxed, jovial, easy to talk with.

I asked about taping our conversation. He said it would be better if I didn't. Since I was a journalist, the presence of a tape recorder or notebook would imply a consent to be interviewed and that was prohibited because of his banning order. 'If you'll leave me specific questions, I'll write you a letter answering them', Steve promised.

I asked if that would be safe for him. 'We know what we can do', he replied. 'How to manage our end of it.'

So, as he wished, we spent an hour or so talking.

Biko spoke of the black consciousness movement and its importance to South African blacks — that they learn through it of their value as individuals; of the importance of a new educational system, one developed by blacks and not based on what whites believed best for blacks to know.

Judging from recent reports in the *Dispatch*, the government had begun a new attack against blacks. Many detentions and bannings were being reported. I asked Steve if he thought the black consciousness movement would be allowed to continue.

'I think it will', Steve replied. 'Black consciousness is, first of all, not really an organization. We have no membership cards that Security Police can find in people's pockets. We don't have meetings. What black consciousness actually is, is simply an expression of feelings of South African blacks at this time. For this reason it will survive. You cannot, after all, ban feelings.'

'I also believe', he continued, 'that the government learned its lesson banning the ANC and the PAC. It's a great deal harder to follow an organization's activities when it moves underground. I think the government realizes that it needs contact with moderate blacks and, if it bans us, that contact will be gone. I believe the government will continue to ban individuals though not groups.'

I asked what would happen to the black consciousness movement if he were again jailed.

'If one of us is taken, others will move up and take that place', Steve said.

I remembered my own fears a few weeks before when security policemen watched Nohle and me. 'Aren't you afraid of what they would do to you?'

Steve smiled: 'No. I know these fellows pretty well. It sounds ludicrous, but you could almost call us friends. We've been together so long that I know how many children they have, what their wives' names are.'

It seemed impossible to ever come to terms with that kind of intimidation.

'You can get used to anything', Steve said. 'The way I do, is to tell them the truth no matter what questions they ask. This really confuses them', he said, a broad grin on his face. 'They don't know how to handle it ...'

We went over the procedure involved in the proposed exchange of letters again and then I left. Early in the week that followed, the newspaper reported an administrative clerk from 15 Leopold Street had been detained by three security policemen from Port Elizabeth. I remembered the name. We had talked briefly when we met Nohle. I had said something about the security police who had stopped that day. 'The ones here are not really bad men', she had said. 'It is the ones at Port Elizabeth who are evil ...'

A few weeks went by with no reply from Steve to my letter. I sent a message to him through the BPC offices. Nohle called me back. 'He said he is busy now preparing for the next trial and wonders if you would mind waiting until after that?' she asked.

At 7 p.m. on 4 July, Biko and two other black consciousness leaders were arrested by security police in King for alleged contravention of their banning orders. One was the woman doctor who had established a clinic for blacks at the BPC headquarters in King. She had represented the Mohapi family at the Mohapi post-mortem and was banned immediately after. Under terms of her banning, she was sent to a small township in the Northern Transvaal. The other arrested was Thenjiwe Mtintso. The two had returned to King because they were to testify at the Mohapi inquest. They were arrested at the Biko home in Zwelitsha, the township near King. The arresting officer said the three, because of their banning, could not occupy the same house nor talk with each other. A BPC spokesman said the three had stayed in different rooms and had not spoken with each other. They were jailed overnight in the Kei Road cells where Mohapi had died, then released on conditional bail of R200 [£120] each — paid by the BPC. Dates were set for court appearances.

The inquest into the Mohapi death which had adjourned in March, reopened the following morning, 6 July, at 9 a.m. in King William's Town. One of the witnesses was Thenjiwe Mtintso. She said she had been detained by six policemen on 17 August, 1976, and taken to the Special Branch offices in King. There she was hit several times, punched on the jaw and kicked when she fell. 'I was bleeding through my mouth', she told the court. Later Captain Schoeman arrived. She told him what had happened. He said this was just an introduction.

Later that day, Captain Hansen told her she would be kept at Kei Road and perhaps Mr Mohapi would tell her how he had died. Warrant Officer Hattingh told her she should be careful lest what happened to Mohapi happened to her as well.

She was taken to East London where she was interrogated by Hansen, Hattingh and Schoeman. 'Captain Hansen slapped me and punched me several times', she told the court. 'He had made certain untrue allegations and each time I denied them, he continuously slapped and punched me. He would not let me sit down. I was made to stand in that office for three days and nights without food, drink or toilet facilities.' Later she was taken back to King William's Town where interrogation 'followed very much the same pattern'.

In the second week of September she was taken to Kei Road by Hansen and Hattingh and put into a cell. 'Captain Hansen had a big wet towel with him. He told me to sit on the floor … he put the towel over my head … until it reached my neck. He stood behind me and held me firmly in his thighs so that I could not move backwards and pulled the two ends of the towel tight over and across my neck. When Captain Hansen took the towel away, he said, "Now you can see how Mapetla died."

'I said, "Yes, I can see now." He said, "How can you see now?" and repeated the treatment. The first time I had the towel treatment, I found it hard to breathe. The second time it was worse and I made gurgle noises because I could not breathe properly. The third time, I felt faint and Hattingh said, "I am sure she will speak the truth now." '

Thenjiwe said while in detention, she had not reported the assaults because she feared further assaults.

The attorney for the Mohapi family asked what the Special Branch had questioned her about. She replied: 'Communication with Donald Woods, his relationship with Steve Biko, SASO, my trips to Botswana, boys leaving the country, the BPC, speeches, boyfriends, family, my school life, Fort Hare, strikes, Communism, socialism, communalism, black consciousness, black power, black solidarity, my reporting, Mapetla Mohapi, Steve Biko attending meetings, Transkei independence, and Bantustans.'

She said she had answered all those questions. She told the court she thought she'd been assaulted because the Special Branch believed her to be lying.

The emphasis in the case, however, was not so much on reports by witnesses such as Thenjiwe, but on the alleged suicide note said to have been left by Mohapi and addressed to the Special Branch officer who had detained him, Captain P.A. Schoeman.

The note read:

Death Cell, Kei Road, 5/8/76
Mr. Schoeman. This is just to say good-bye to you. You can carry on interrogating my dead body, perhaps you will get what you want from it.
Your friend, Mapetla.

The barrister for the Mohapi family claimed the note was written in a handwriting quite different to Mr Mohapi's normal writing. He said, 'Our case will be that it is a forgery.' About 200 people packed the old-fashioned courtroom. They included Dr Ramphele and Thenjiwe Mtintso. Earlier on the opening day, both had appeared, briefly, at separate hearings in another courtroom on charges brought under the Suppression of Communism Act. Their conditional bail was extended and their cases postponed to August.

The finding in the Mohapi inquest came on 8 July. Just before it was delivered, the Mohapi family attorney told the judge there was 'an irresistible inference suggesting homicide as the cause of death'. But the magistrate ruled nobody could be held responsible for the death of Mapetla Mohapi. He did not deliver a formal verdict of suicide, but found death due to 'anoxia and suffocation as a result of hanging'.

According to Roger Omond's published account, the crowd filed out, joining hundreds of blacks waiting on the porch of the old stone courthouse. A shout went up: '*Amandla*' (power)! Clenched fists were thrust forward in the international black power salute.

The same day, 8 July, Thami Zani, who after Mohapi's detention, wrote black consciousness articles for the *Dispatch,* was stopped at a police road block, taken to Special Branch offices in King where he was served with a stringent five-year banning order which included house arrest between 6 p.m. and 6 a.m. He would be able to see no one other than members of his immediate family, must report to the police every Monday and must not participate in BPC activities nor enter the premises.

Biko's trial on a charge of obstructing the course of justice began almost immediately. The state alleged that before a sabotage trial in Grahamstown earlier in the year, Biko instructed witnesses to change their evidence; to say they were forced to make false statements to the police, saying they knew nothing about a meeting at a school where it was agreed to damage the school and set fire to it. Because of those false statements, the charge sheet said that the students were found not guilty and discharged. Biko pleaded not guilty to the charges. One of the witnesses for the prosecution was the investigating officer, Warrant Officer Gerhardus Hattingh of the Special Branch in King William's Town.

During cross-examination by Biko's attorney, one of the youths giving evidence against Biko said he had been taken by police to Security Police offices in King where a number of pupils were held for questioning.

'You started hearing screams coming from the offices where the pupils were being questioned and when it came to your turn, were you not filled with fear?' asked the attorney. 'You claim you volunteered to make a statement after being beaten up yourself — was it not that you dared not refuse?'

On 13 July, the magistrate found Biko not guilty on a charge of obstructing the course of justice, also acquitted him on an alternative count of subornation to perjury, saying Biko's evidence was more satisfactory than that of state witnesses.

On the same day, Nohle Mohapi initiated a R48,409 [£29,000] damages claim on behalf of herself, her two children, against the Minister of Justice, Jimmy Kruger. It claimed loss of support, funeral and legal costs in the death of her husband.

On 15 July, Thami Zani was arrested by seven policemen and

redetained in prison. A spokesman for the Security Police said Zani was arrested in his home during a housewarming party attended by friends of the family — thus breaking his banning orders. But visitors said Zani had remained by himself in one of the rooms. This took place a week after he was banned.

Nohle Mohapi was detained on 25 August, after being arrested by Major Hansen (he had been promoted) in King William's Town. She was held under the Terrorism Act.

'All the opportunities came my way'

If you pressed people for their explanation of Don Card, the most usual answer was that he was 'complex'. Someone called him 'your basic mercenary'. People always seemed on the verge of saying something more about Card. It happened so often — that abrupt pause in mid-sentence, confusion, and finally a retreat into generalities.

Card was a mystery figure. A former member of the Special Branch, he is alleged to have been ruthless — a cruel torturer. Young, eager reporters were always trying to gather facts for an expose of Card though one never appeared. One talked of a secret file in the editorial library containing sworn statements by some of Card's victims. Though I looked for such a folder, I never found it. The only one on Card was with reference to him as a city councillor.

Card, in 1977, headed a successful business and was influential on the council. Some said Card changed completely after leaving the Special Branch. Black friends, reluctant to discuss Card at all, managed to suggest he was the same and had just switched sides when he realized that soon it would be blacks, not whites, in control of South Africa.

I first met him in 1972. Donald Woods arranged for me to go to Mdantsane with Card. We were driving on one of the township's narrow dirt roads. An old man walked along the side. Card called him over. They talked in Xhosa. The old man stood next to the car, hat in his hands, head bowed. He was deferential to the point of obsequiousness. Card asked for directions, but that seemed only an excuse to stop — he obviously knew Mdantsane as well as he did East London. As he drove off, Card said he had arrested the man after riots in the early fifties, that he had served a long prison term and only recently had been released. I said something about his politeness. 'He respects me', Card said. 'Blacks I have sent to prison, when they come out, they come to see me.' Card waved his hand towards rows of cinder block houses stretching to the horizon, 'They all know me here ...'

There and other places. Donald Woods heard him discussed in Zambia. Roger Omond met blacks in England who knew him. Though I also heard much about Card, I found him elusive. He was one of the first people I contacted when I began work on this book. Initially, he set up an appointment. But when the day arrived, his secretary called to cancel. Subsequent calls were always intercepted by her. Finally, I just called every day until he agreed to an interview.

Card is managing director of Night Hawk Patrols, a security service owned for some years by the *Daily Dispatch*, sold recently to an international company headquartered in London. Locally it has 800 employees, 750 of them black, and a kennel of Alsatian guard dogs.

Card sat on the other side of an outsized desk. From the beginning, it was a slightly different interview. I'd worried about getting information from him; but he proved to be a non-stop talker. And though he talked of highly emotional situations, he spoke dispassionately, revealing absolutely no emotion himself — either through expression or gesture.

Card is South African by birth; his parents, farmers in the Transkei, are of Scottish and English descent. He grew up among blacks. 'I know them well,' he said, 'know their customs'.

He spoke particularly of stick fighting on Sunday afternoons. Young men from different locations fought ritualistic mock battles. Sometimes these ended with deaths. Card fought with them.

At 18 Card joined the East London police force. He started as a beat patrolman and moved up rapidly. 'Let's say all the opportunities came my way', Card explained. 'I was involved in every big murder, every big robbery case we had in East London. I was successful in those I tackled, let's put it that way. It was a good life and I enjoyed it.'

In 1952, while he was in the CID, Duncan Village erupted. It was a time, Card said, of heightened political talk, of increased ANC activity. In East London a meeting had been scheduled for a church in Duncan Village. The application, made weeks before for the afternoon of 9 November, was in the name of a religious organization, but police, believing it to be a cover for the ANC, brought in reinforcements. At about 3.30 on the day of the meeting, they moved into the township.

Card related the story: 'When they got to the church, they confronted the leaders, said, "You're not having a church meeting, you're having an ANC meeting." When they tried to break it up, blacks started throwing stones from behind houses. A number of policemen were struck and one was hit in the head by a bullet. Police retaliated with batons and, of course, started shooting. With some difficulty, they were able to get out, but by that time, they'd obviously shot quite a few people.'

The violence spread. Initially Card stayed at headquarters taking incoming calls. One came from the Catholic mission in Duncan Village. 'When the police went in to remove the nuns, they all came under attack — stones and, then again, more sten guns.' The mob set fire to the mission and a nearby school, one of three which burned that day.

'During the course of the afternoon, Sister Aidan was on her way to the clinic at the mission. Unfortunately, she had to drive by the spot where they'd had this meeting — this flare-up. Now', Card continued, 'she'd worked day and night with these people, but when she drove in, they stopped her car. They smashed the windscreen, beat her with sticks, stabbed her and then set her car alight. After the car had burnt out, they turned it over, removed her body, cut up most of it and ate her.'

Card stopped and began going through drawers. 'Somewhere in here I have a photograph of what was left of her body — it's shocking. She was a well-built woman, about 240 lbs. I'd say it was about three feet that was left. The arms were removed at the elbows, her legs removed up to the knees. After that I recovered pieces of her body at different places.'

Card brought out a picture which showed a charred lump, unrecognizable as human. Other people had referred to the riots and to the death of Sister Aidan. Not everyone believed that the photograph — which had been widely reprinted — was of her corpse. A black said it was a doctored print whose purpose was to keep anti-black feelings aroused.

Card put it away, saying that it had been an interesting case. 'Although we charged about 16 people, only two were sentenced to death for her murder. You see, there was no proof at what stage she died and you cannot charge a person with murder unless you can prove the victim was, in fact, alive. There was proof that Number One struck her across the forehead with a stick and Number Two actually stabbed her. There was no movement in her body after that. Then numerous people came up and stabbed her, but since there was no proof she was still alive, we could only charge them with mutilating a dead body.

'We questioned them later', Card said, 'and asked, "Well, why did you do it?" They told us they ate her flesh because they wanted her strength.'

Another white man had been killed that day — a Mr Vorster who was in the township selling insurance policies. 'When the mob spotted him', Card said, 'he ran from place to place and they came after him with sticks and eventually beat him to death.'

Rioting continued through the night. Card became involved about 8.30 — first answering a call in a white neighbourhood where a woman had been attacked by blacks who tried to cut out her tongue, going next to a black reformatory under attack. There Card found the place in flames, more fires being set. Later he chanced on the ringleaders and made the key arrests that ended the riots.

A total of 210 died that night. 'I think', Card said, 'that there were approximately 100,000 blacks in Duncan Village. I would say the number of police was about 100 — though, of course, our chappies had sten guns and armoured vehicles whereas the blacks had stones.'

Card went on to talk of other incidents from those years. Though these were personal anecdotes, they were a microcosm of what was occuring then through the country. These were the last days of the PAC and ANC — the last days of any significant black political moves until Steve Biko started the black consciousness movement. Multiracial political parties were banned — among them Alan Paton's Liberal Party. Beleagured Nationalists pushed through ever more repressive legislation and made the first moves towards disenfranchising Coloureds.

'Shortly before the riots in Duncan Village, blacks went on this defiance campaign', Card said. 'They would walk into East London at night — about a thousand of them, all volunteers — and defy the curfew laws. We would arrest and charge them. One of the leaders would pay an admission of guilt, then go back to the townships and collect another mob for the next night.

'Then in 1960,' he continued, 'we had the pass campaign where blacks burnt their passes and reference books. In July of 1962, I was sent to Port Elizabeth to assist with investigations of the first lot of sabotage committed there. We had also started on this big campaign against the ANC who had, at this stage, formed the *Umkhonto we Sizwe*, or Spear of the Nation, group. They were very pro-violence, used little cells of seven to ten people. One of that number would have contact with other cells and so it went, on and on, until it got back to the high command which we proved was directly linked to the Communist Party of South Africa.'

Card paused, leaned back in the leather chair, obviously enjoying this opportunity to reminisce. 'That was an interesting time', he said. 'I enjoyed it. We started off in Port Elizabeth, then came back here to investigate the first acts of sabotage.' Following his successful investigations, Card was sent to Pretoria to solve problems in that area.

'In January of 1963, they arrested the first lot of terrorists crossing the border into Rhodesia. There were nine of them,' he said, 'and there was proof they had committed sabotage here and were still connected to groups working here. Eventually, I got the whole story — how they trained in Ethiopia, planned to come back and organize people for the revolution here. I gave evidence at the trial in Pretoria and thereafter, I was in their bad books. Letters were written calling for my execution and there were attempts on my life.'

After the Pretoria trials, Card continued investigations of ANC activities in East London and at the University of Fort Hare. 'Then PAC stuck its neck out', he said. 'They were plotting to attack whites throughout South Africa. Leaders were operating from Maseru in Lesotho and whatever was decided there had to be sent by post to local leaders. We knew a lot of people were being sent out to learn to make petrol bombs, hand grenades — things like that — but we hadn't been able to learn the date they planned to strike. Fortunately, police searched a woman riding a bus near the Lesotho border and found 70 to 75 letters written in code: "The rivers are full and at this stage you are not to cross because it is dangerous." In other words, "Hang fire. We're not going to do anything now. There are problems." '

Meanwhile, there had been isolated incidents — among these the killing of several whites near the Transkei border. PAC members were responsible, Card said. 'They had taken action before the set day. From the letters, we knew the leaders. We picked them up and finally, from them, got the information that D Day would be April 8th.

'I had an informer who was directly involved, so that was fortunate', Card said. 'We knew where they were going to gather in East London and the time. We got together with the police to work out a plan of action. My approach was that the area was so vast and so overgrown that we might miss them, and the only way to solve this thing was to go there and have a look.

'We had been told they would meet at a big tree on the banks of a stream between Duncan Village and Amalinda [a suburb near Cambridge]. It had been raining for three weeks and wherever you looked, there was water. It was bright moonlight. We hadn't ever used walkie-talkies before, but we borrowed some from the railway. We set up a post on a farm at the top of the hill in Amalinda. We would call the man there and tell him what was going on and he would use their telephone to call into headquarters. About a hundred policemen had been told to report for duty that night.

'I went in first with three Europeans and my black CID boy', Card continued. 'We painted ourselves black — bought a big pot of vaseline and a big packet of charcoal. I had an old hat on my head, brown gloves. Whatever was sticking out was smeared with vaseline and carbon.

'We went to a shop in Amalinda and I sent my CID chap in to call for the owner of the shop whom I knew. I was sitting in the back of the car. When he came out, I said to him, "Please, if there are any messages coming through here which are urgent, phone the police station as soon as possible." ' Card smiled: 'You should have seen his face. His words to me afterwards were, "You know, I recognized your voice, but I couldn't make out which black man you were."

'We crept into the location — Amalinda is on one side. We went in about half past six, quarter to seven. Time went by and there was nobody going to the spot by the big tree. Then, about quarter to nine, the chappie on the farm, who could see where we were on the side of the hill said, "I'm looking through a telescope at the moment and there's a movement above you." He said, "I'm not sure exactly where you are." I said, "I'll shine my torch in your direction." I flickered the torch. He said, "Yes, I can see you, but be careful. Above you there's movement."

'There were a lot of paths that went down to the stream so we then tried to move back amongst the trees, but we couldn't get back far enough. There were two little bushes and I crept between them. I could hear people walking. There was a big bush hanging out and I took my binoculars and was looking at this bush to see who would come around. Five did, walking not four paces from us. How they didn't see us, I still don't know. I recognized most of them. Some were carrying knives, some revolvers, some axes. Altogether we counted 78, coming by groups of four or five or six.'

Card smiled again, 'I didn't know how to operate a walkie-talkie and every now and then this chappie on the farm would say, "What's going on now?" And these people were coming by us every few minutes and I couldn't find where to switch it off. I didn't know how to keep it quiet, so after awhile, I just sat on it.

'We had to go down and cross the stream to get back to the other side, so when the last lot walked down, we slipped in behind them and followed them across the stream. They turned right towards an open area known as the Big Tree. As we turned with them, my CID boy lost his nerve. There were now about 20 of them with us and I had to hold his mouth because he was just making sounds — he couldn't even talk. We then passed another three on the way out. They had a torch but we were able to duck and get out of the light and then we went up to the farm to collect the other chappie. He phoned the police and told them to meet us.'

Card directed a hundred policemen into the bush. 'When we got there, the officer in charge said, "Are you sure they're at that spot known as the Big Tree?" I said, "Well, I'm not sure, but they've gone in that direction." He said, "Well, I'd rather be sure. I'd hate for them to tackle us from behind." I said, "We'll go take a look." I said to one of the chappies who had painted black and been with me earlier on, "Look, you come with me." We crept around, down the one stream and up another one and these people were all on the banks, about 300 of them, by the big tree.

'I'd come into their view so I just sat down amongst them. I waited awhile and then pretended I had to urinate and sneaked away. At that stage they were busy putting people into groups of ten: "You're going to go to the East London Police Station"; "You're going to attack the Cambridge Police Station." We sneaked away to join our crowd — the chappie with me fell in the stream, I had to pull him out.'

Police moved in to surround the group at the big tree. 'But there were spies and the next thing we knew, shots were fired. Our people retaliated with sten guns and everybody ran. I crossed the stream to catch a few and while I was crawling up the embankment, one of my men shot at me with a sten gun — he didn't know I was a white man and I'd forgotten about the charcoal. I screamed so loud I'm sure they heard me in East London.

'I ran through the bush', Card continued, 'and it was terribly muddy. I sank from nine inches to a foot in the muck each step. There were a whole lot of them on the other side — running — and I fired at two of them. One of them dropped but his friend stabbed me with a panga.' Not seriously injured and furious that he had missed one, Card rushed towards another group.

'Over the walkie-talkie I heard the officer calling me, "Donald come back. Donald come back." I just switched it off.'

Card found no more people but collected haversacks filled with food, first-aid kits and personal gear. 'It was going to be a case of attack a white area and go back to the bush. Attack and go back to the bush. In any case,' he said with satisfaction, 'they weren't used. It was all broken up that night.' Later Card tracked down the leader and a top aide who were hiding out in mountains near the Hogsback. At the trial, the judge publicly commended Card, said he and those with him had saved the city.

Other violent incidents followed. Then, after a wave of arrests in the early sixties, things, Card said, became very quiet. 'Quiet on the surface,' he added, 'but people released from Robben Island have told me that one day, when the time is right, they have been told they would again be at liberty to take action — might even be called upon by certain organizations to assist.'

In 1963, Card had transferred to the Special Branch. After seven years he quit. 'It wasn't the life for me', he said. 'What ever happens you look at it in the wrong light. If a chap said he was anti-this or anti-that, he was definitely a Communist.'

It was the way people thought then, Card explained. I asked if Communists were behind the riots and sabotage of the 50s and 60s, if they were still South Africa's biggest threat. In some instances of earlier trouble Card thought they definitely had been involved. 'But', he continued, 'I've spoken to blacks who are educated and they say, "What difference does it make? If the Communists take over, we'd be better recognized than we are at the moment, so it's not going to worry us if they do." This is the approach. These people are not communistic in their thinking, but they are not satisfied with what is going on and Communism breeds where there is ill feeling.'

I asked about how he got his job at Night Hawk Patrols. He said that Donald Woods, knowing he wanted to get out of the Special Branch, suggested that the *Daily Dispatch* purchase the business if Card would manage it. In 1970, Card took it over. Then the firm had a turnover of about £2,000 per month. Under Card it has grown to £37,000.

In 1972, the editor backed his friend in his successful bid for City Council. Now Card is chairman of the powerful Action Committee which pre-screens issues for the council and makes recommendations as to their disposition.

Later, someone who was talking about Card spoke about the death sentence on him. Actually there were two — one by PAC because Card had made the first arrests of its members and another by the ANC after Card's testimony in court against some of them.

Another man has similar fears of black retaliation. He is Gordon Qumza, a black himself and a reporter at the *Dispatch*. Qumza had been arrested for alleged ANC activities at about the same time as Leslie Xinwa. After being held in jail for six months, he came to trial under the Suppression of Communism Act. Unlike Leslie, Gordon was found not guilty and released.

One day, in the office, Gordon talked about the problems of the country as these related to him. In a short while he believed blacks would take over following a bloody revolution. 'I know I may not live to see the freedom', he said. 'You see, what worries me most is that we had this Mdantsane Township Council of which I was the mayor for two consecutive years. I know for a fact that some of these hardened black politicians, especially those now abroad, do not like the idea of people taking part in these government institutions. They would feel I betrayed the cause. Some of us will not come out alive.'

'I woke up to hear five shots'

To go further than the lobby of the *Daily Dispatch*, it's necessary to sign in, then be announced by a guard. He doesn't dress like a guard, but that's what he is. Other guards, from Don Card's Night Hawk Patrols, were on night duty at the editor's house. Arrangements for protection were made after an incident at the Woods' house in August 1976. Wendy Woods told me the story.

'Donald was away when somebody phoned up. A guy said to me, "Is that Wendy Woods?" I said yes. He said, "Are you alone?" I said yes. I knew that he knew I was alone and besides, I wanted to know what he was going to say. He said, "I'll see you later." I phoned a friend along the street who phoned the police, then I phoned our unofficial bodyguard, Don Card. He came and the police came. It was now about half past eleven.

'I told them the story. The police went off — there was very little they could do. Don Card said, "Don't worry. It's a nut case. He's had his kick now, he won't come back." We saw him off then. But my 14-year-old daughter had heard this whole thing and as we said goodbye to him, I took a look at her face. She was terrified and I thought, no, I'm going to phone someone to come and stay here. I called a reporter from the *Dispatch* and he came.

'We eventually went to bed and at about 4 o'clock I woke up to hear five shots. Very close. Like a fool, I didn't go down, but I was scared to go out. I heard a lorry or van accelerating away very fast.

'I went down the next morning', Wendy continued, 'and the reporter's car was covered with black spray paint with a hammer and sickle on it and the wall just outside our garage had, "Biko. Commie HQ" and an arrow pointing towards the house. On the other wall, a big beautifully done hammer and sickle. The shots went into the front gate. One had gone through the wood. We found the odd shells and they were very small. We gave them to the police but they've never caught whoever it was.'

Wendy has an idea of who was responsible. 'I would think it would be someone who'd been listening to our phone. Our phone is unlisted for the very reason we'd been getting threatening phone calls. That evening I had phoned my mother and told her Donald was in Durban giving a speech. Then Donald phoned and it was only about an hour after that I got the call.' It is generally believed that phones are tapped by the Special Branch. Also that they are bugged to pick up conversation within a house. Any information of a confidential nature is always discussed outside. 'Shall we go for a walk in the garden?' is the usual introduction to this kind of conversation.

Wendy gets anonymous calls frequently, most often on Thursday afternoons, in South Africa the maid's day off. She told of one such call: 'I was out, but my sister-in-law was there and she answered the phone. A male voice said, "Is that Wendy Woods?" She said, "No, it isn't." And he said, "Are you alone?" She said, "Yes, I'm alone." He said, "Aren't you scared?" She said, "No, I'm not scared." He said, "Do you know who's speaking?" She said, "Yes, I do know." And he put the phone down. Since then they often just phone and then there's silence.

'I was scared at night for quite a long time after the attack on our house, but it was obviously a political act. It was by someone who knew of our association with Steve Biko and was upset by this. It had the effect on both Donald and me of making even more solidarity with people like Biko rather than the reverse.'

Because of Donald's views, he has had many threats on his life since he became editor. 'The first time I became really aware of any actual nastiness,' Wendy said, 'I opened a letter in our postbox at home. It was a typed letter and purported to be from a black — at least the name signed was an African name. I can't remember too well, but it said something like, "Mr Liberal Editor Woods thinks he is a friend of the blacks, but actually blacks hate him." He said they were going to come and attack his family, would take his children and gouge their eyes out. I showed it to Donald. It upset me, it really did. It unnerved me. He admitted he'd been getting these letters at the *Dispatch* and hadn't told me.'

I asked Wendy if she'd been interested in politics before she met Donald. 'I didn't have a clue,' she replied, 'but you learn quickly. Everything here is so interesting you can't help but become interested. Politics here throws up all the concepts ... What about socialism? What about capitalism? What about integration? What sort of a struggle is it — is it a class struggle, a race struggle? You go into that and have conversations and it's lovely. I love that side of our life. I'm not involved in all of this in the sense that I'm doing anything, but I think it helps Donald to do what he has to do, to say the things he needs to say, to know that there's a wife who backs him up, who isn't upset about the thought he might go to jail — who doesn't discourage him from sticking his neck out. It doesn't worry me and I think that's quite nice for him.'

Wendy told of Donald's court appearance where he faced a prison sentence for withholding names of informants and when she first learned of the situation. 'I'd been away and he met me at the airport. He had just been interviewed by the Special Branch and he was nervously stimulated by that. I thought, "God, it's this close." For the first time prison was close to us. I'd always thought of this as a problem blacks have.

'Actually, just the fact that you've got a white skin is frightening at this stage. But you simply don't think about it. You do what you have to do or enjoy doing. Nobody can give anybody any guarantees in this country — there'll be no fairy tale ending — and you just put it out of your mind after that.'

What does Wendy think might happen? 'I can't see the Nats giving in. I get the feeling that they won't give an inch because their whiteness is threatened. They really do believe that God wants them to be white. And so, one day, it will be taken from them — God knows how. Violently perhaps, I don't know about that.

'It's like living at the bottom of a volcano and knowing. Seeing the fumes and everything and then you just don't do anything about it. Human nature is the most fantastic thing. When you read about people dying in detention and shocking, gut issues that people in America and England have forgotten about because it happened there hundreds of years ago but is happening here now, then, if you're interested in something like teaching music, it does seem a little irrelevant.

'You know, I've got to start practising a Bach prelude and a Beethoven sonata and it seems a little mad. But then not everybody is as lucky as Donald. He's in the right kind of job. But people have just got to go about doing what they're able to do ...'

'I see myself as a perpetual warner'

The *Daily Dispatch*, circulation 33,000, is the major newspaper in an area bounded, on the Indian Ocean, by Durban and Port Elizabeth and inland, by the borders of the Orange Free State.

From Monday to Saturday, at about 1.30 a.m., vans and trucks line up to get the first of two editions — country, and an hour or so later, city — off the presses. These are delivered to 500 agents in every centre of consequence in an 112,000 square kilometre area, arriving at many homes well before breakfast.

Founded in 1872, the *Dispatch* is an independent newspaper run by a seven-man board of directors made up of editorial, works, advertising and accounting executives. One of their responsibilities is annually to disperse two-thirds of the paper's profits to local charities, according to the terms of the Crewe Trust, set up by Sir Charles Crewe, owner of the paper in the 1920s and 1930s.

Donald Woods, as editor, was responsible for the political tone of the paper, though at that point in his tenure, editors under him were able to reflect the editor's anti-Nationalist, anti-apartheid views, leaving Donald free for behind the scenes manipulations in related policies on a national and local level.

The *Dispatch* is highly controversial in the community and so is Woods. His anti-government stance is detested and scorned by conservative whites; he is a hero to many blacks.

A native of the Border area, Donald was born on a remote trading station in the Elliotdale district in what is now independent Transkei. From the age of six, he attended boarding schools, first in Umtata, about 60 miles from his home, then in East London and Kimberley in the Transvaal. After graduation, he studied law at the University of Cape Town.

'The childhood in the Transkei is very interesting', Donald said. 'All my playmates were black tribes' children. I remember their names very clearly and the games we used to play. Funny, you know my reading — like most kids — was American comic books. And the odd mixture of these two cultures — you would see four or five loinclothed black children taking part in a cowboys and Indians thing that they wouldn't have had a clue as to origin.

'One great memory that sticks in my mind is when the Second World War broke out. Every single adult I knew was suddenly in uniform — every single one, I can't think of one who wasn't. It's been calculated, and checked by me, that in the Second World War among armed forces of every country, there was no higher volunteer rate than the white Transkeians.

'It was an interesting time', he continued. 'You know, there is a lot of feeling against Britain among Nationalists so you had half the whites wanting to fight Hitler and the other half not wanting to. Therefore, the government couldn't conscript. They said only volunteers. Then the Nationalists insisted on a law limiting service in the South African Army to fighting within the borders of South Africa and it required a special oath by a soldier if he was to be sent outside. They then had added to their uniform a narrow red stripe on the shoulder. This became infuriating, sort of a red flag to a bull, to Nationalists because it signified those who were most against Hitler. I know we, as kids, had uniforms — like kids have cowboy outfits — and all of ours had the red flash on them.'

On his father's side, Donald's ancestors came to South Africa in 1820 from Cornwall; his mother's people emigrated from Ireland during one of the potato famines. In South Africa they became traders. 'I would describe my parents as extremely conservative people with all the normal prejudices', Donald said. 'I grew up with these influences. I reckon until I was about 22, I would have described myself as highly racist, highly conservative. I remember horrifying people by telling them the true story of my first lecturer in Roman Law — a great friend of mind today. Early that first year at Cape Town, he was asking questions round the class on the race issue and he said, "You, Woods. You're from Transkei. What is the answer to the race question?"

'I said, quite solemnly, "You know, the only answer is to shoot all the kaffirs." This man was horrified and as I grew to admire him very much, the thought that he had been horrified made some sort of impression on me — at least it began to shake my firm conviction that my racial views were right.

'At about the same time, there was quite a campaign in the Catholic Church against the injustice of race discrimination. This, along with the study of Roman Law and the principles of perfect justice — the Institutes of Justinian — all had an effect on me. Finally, we had a visiting student in our law class who was an American negro. I remember noticing his accent was American. It just seemed to click in my mind that it is environment, not colour, that counts. The combination of all of these things changed my view entirely on the race question.'

After university, Woods was articled to an attorney for five years. During that time, he decided this was not the kind of work he wanted to do for the rest of his life. 'I don't think I measured up to it', he said. 'I didn't have a tidy enough mind. Attorneys have to keep a whole lot of files going from day to day. Well, I messed up at least two divorces that I recall, through forgetting what the return date in Supreme Court was. My mind was not orderly enough to keep track of all these details.

'On the day I finished my 365th day of my fifth year of legal articles, I got into my car at 4.30 in the afternoon and drove 150 miles to East London to be a journalist. What had happened was during the last two years of my articles, I had spent a hell of a lot of time doing things that had nothing to do with law.

'I had done a lot of political organization from about the age of 20, had been listening to parliamentary debates when I was supposed to be attending lectures. I didn't like any of the parties we had here but a new party was formed in 1954 and I joined it. It was called the Federal Party. The part of it that attracted me was its qualified franchise policy. It was non-racial and a federal structure of government. Eventually it assumed overtones of jingoism, Union Jack waving and extreme English chauvinism so it faded on those grounds but, in a sense, it was the precursor of the present Progressive Party.

'I became known, through the pages of the *Daily Dispatch*, as a sort of political agitator. I used to write letters to the newspaper condemning just about everything I saw. One day I had to call on the editor. While I was talking with him, I said, "How can I become a journalist?" He said, "We happen to have a vacancy and judging by the letters you write, you'd do well at it. We'll try you out."

'I got my trial and then I got the job.' He started as a junior reporter in 1957 and within three months had taken leave to contest an election for Parliament in East London for the Federal Party. The editor released me and said if I lost I could come back because, in fact, the views I was propounding coincided with the policy of the newspaper — which was one of the reasons I liked it.'

I asked if the *Dispatch* had always followed liberal lines.

'It hasn't always', Donald replied. 'For instance, if you read back, you'll find there are surprisingly liberal editorials in some directions but very racist in others and I think, according to the standards of 1872, it was not terribly radical at all. Later on it went through a very jingoistic phase when anything British was fine.

'Only in the last 15 years or so did it acquire a South African editor. In those days most of the leading journalists in South Africa were British so they tended to apply British standards. But the *Dispatch* was liberal in many directions under my predecessors and, I think, in my time, I've moved left even since I was appointed 12 years ago.

'Anyway, this election was a bit of a disaster. I got clobbered and came back to the staff. After a year, I decided I should get further experience overseas because, having come into journalism later than most, I had to do something to catch up in pay. I worked on Fleet Street in London, in Canada and in Cardiff in Wales and I also got one very nice assignment from the London *Daily Herald* which was to go to Little Rock, Arkansas, and compare segregation with apartheid.'

What he observed in the US south was a greater personal hatred between races in the sense that racist whites there spoke and acted with a viciousness he had never seen even among Afrikaner Nationalists. 'There have been atrocities in this country but nothing like the lynchings that took place in the south. I don't really know why this difference should have existed,' Donald said, 'but it was evident to me.

'The other thing I found was the central government of the US whittling away at the racism of the south and therefore there was a sort of inevitability about the end of it, whereas here there is more a sense of the central government backing the racists — entrenching racism.'

That first trip to the US was in 1960. He went back seven years later to find 'incredible changes'. All discriminatory signs were down and attitudes were different. 'The same people I'd spoken to who had said they would never compromise, had now accepted the legalities

of the situation even though they were not entirely happy with it.'
Woods is convinced the end of apartheid would be accepted by South
African whites in the same manner.

'During these years I was also exposed to two kinds of democracy',
Woods continued. 'First of all, having grown up in South Africa, I'd
never lived in a democratic society. I didn't know what it felt like to
live in one. I had a year or two in England, then across to America,
and I found it was not only stimulating, but, I think, inspiring in a
way that you tend to think more broadly and you tend to feel more
free. You tend to talk more about things which I think mankind
should be concerned with instead of here where your issues are so
basic and the wrong things are so obviously wrong that you are
functioning at a very basic level all the time. You aren't getting to the
refinements of any form of progress in human life. You're still trying
to chip away at the crude injustices. That was one big difference. I
also revelled in the feeling of a society that's got freedom of speech.
Freedom of speech in the sense that no one is surprised or shocked if
you write or speak strongly about anything — though they may
disagree.

'But, somehow, I felt that I wouldn't by choice live in England or
America, much as I admired and liked these societies. Maybe it was
sentimentality I felt — the old saying that "home is where the cause
is", but I preferred the climate, the look of things here, even the
food.'

When he returned to South Africa, friends tried to persuade him
to work at one of the larger papers but his interest was in the
Dispatch and the part of the country he knew. 'I liked the
newspaper's forthright approach to things and also I had no
ambitions as a journalist to be anything more than a good subeditor
and rewrite man who, on the side, would produce novels and plays.

'I lived two happy years of bachelorhood here, visiting every
nightclub I could — and there were quite a few in those days, good
ones too — playing a lot of golf and writing articles. So it was quite a
surprise to me one day to be called into the editor's office and told
that the board of directors had decided to groom me as his successor.
I hadn't given it a thought and if I had given it a thought, I would
have assumed there were so many senior chaps in the game, this
would have been an absurdity.'

Woods was appointed editor in February, 1965. 'I remember
thinking,' he said, 'if I can last three years — just survive for three
years — well, I'll at least feel I've said enough. So after 12 years, I feel
I'm living very much on overdraft.'

Those 12 years have seen Woods in court on some ten occasions.

'Most of my cases have been civil ones — defamation', he said. 'You know, this country, if the right wing wants to discredit one, they call one a Communist. I've had about four or five cases based on that one and won them all. Some were government officials, some pro-government politicians. And there have been a couple of criminal cases, prosecutions for publishing certain things — for refusing to disclose names. I don't like it myself because it sort of intrudes on the even tenor of one's life. I'd like to get out and play more golf and these things distract one.'

Basically, it has been Donald's political views that have got him into trouble: 'I believe the only sensible and just dispensation to work for here is a non-racial society,' he said, 'but one which, in practical terms, means that blacks will rule this country because most South Africans are black and will then constitute a majority, both of voters and cabinet members.

'I also believe that central to black thinking — and there is a lot of justice in it — is that not only political rights must be apportioned fairly, but there must be some pretty drastic rearrangement of the economic fruits of living in South Africa because they're coming in having had terrible obstacles, handicaps, and merely giving them the vote isn't going to solve their whole problem. We whites have had a very long, unfair, start on them — not only in political rights but in wealth. I think we're just going to have to get ready to rearrange, maybe through extremely heavy taxation, some way to restore to blacks a lot of what has been exploited out of them.'

The *Daily Dispatch* is the forum from which Woods propounded these ideas. When I first read the *Dispatch,* Donald used humour frequently to make his points. In 1976 and 1977, his style had changed.

'I believed, up until now,' he said, 'that humour was an effective weapon in the struggle against racism and for reconciliation, but I'm very much afraid that we have entered an era where it's almost misplaced. Political satire is a luxury permitted to a normal society and we are now such an abnormal society that to use political satire is almost frivolous.

'If you look at how the majority of blacks feel, there's just very little that's funny in the situation. So the political satire phase of my career is pretty well over. I really see myself now as a perpetual warner, warning the government, warning whites. If you don't warn them as seriously as you can, you get the feeling they're not going to take much heed. I'm not saying they take much heed right now, but at least there's more chance if you're serious about it.'

Outside the paper, Woods also chips away at apartheid: 'I've

worked to desegregate cricket and chess and at the moment I'm
working on rugby because I believe that in South Africa sport is of
tremendous importance. First of all, because most South Africans
are crazy about sport; secondly, because as happened in the
American South, sport proved a most effective bridge between the
races — a reconciler. Sport has got tremendous potential for
breaking down prejudice. I believe that a chap rooting in the
grandstands for a team which consists of several races, is going to
identify with them as people. He'll tend to stop thinking of them as
pigmentational groups. That's why I'm so interested in the sport
reforms, but it's an uphill battle because for every success, you get a
failure.

'In the realm of cricket and chess now things have gone well but
the key sport in this country is rugby. We're working against the
clock to get some advances in this by the next season.'

However, the odds are against desegregating rugby according to
Woods. 'The chances are the government will feel it has to move to
the right because, at the moment, it is on a very rightward move. It
seems to be obsessed with keeping its right-wingers in the fold. This is
very dangerous to us all and it's a perceptible move. Vorster, for
instance, is strictly confining black rights to the Bantustans which are
rejected by most blacks. There's just no hint of compromise on this. I
really think Vorster's become slightly unbalanced on the racial issue.
I think he is seeing himself increasingly as a sort of Afrikaner folk
hero. I think he has opted for this role rather than that of statesman.'

Donald's personal feelings about Afrikaners are mixed: 'I'm
frequently touched and moved by the things that I like in Afrikaners.
I hate that phrase — Some of my best friends are Afrikaners — but it
happens to be true. If you stereotype them to the extent that you can
— they tend to be extremely warm-hearted in their personal
relationships and cold in their impersonal relationships. They make
wonderful friends if they know you well.

'The great tragedy of this country is that if the Afrikaner could
meet every black man, I have no doubt at all that in a very short time
there'd be no race problem. The fact of the matter is, at the
moment, the Afrikaner holds the political power and is able to
harden his heart. I'm talking about the Nationalist Afrikaner now.
He is able to do this because basically he knows so few of them. He's
terribly isolated and sees them always as a threat.

'But my experience with Afrikaners has been that once the initial
reserves break down, they're extremely warm people. They have
produced many of our best painters and writers. They've got

tremendous leadership qualities. I just think it is a tragedy that this group seems so bent on obsession with indentity that it looks like it might destroy that very identity.'

He sees English-speaking South Africans — again in stereotype — as somewhat different. 'They seem to have less backbone. Less of a readiness to stand up for what they believe in. But this is a deceptive thing — I think they are very typically Anglo-Saxon in that they don't easily get excited about things. I think they have decent values buried deep down below the superficialities of daily life. They do have deep, almost vestigial attachments to civil liberty and the principles of civil liberty, but they've been dealing with business matters for too long, become so obsessed with their businesses, they have tended to drop out of political things through feelings of hopelessness — the Afrikaners have a monopoly of power anyway. But the English institutions have been very good here. That would be the universities, churches, the newspapers, the youth groups.'

Of his friendship with Steve Biko, Woods said: 'I came to know him by repute, through reading his writings when he was a medical student at Natal University. He is one of the founders of the black consciousness movement and the South African Students Organization whose first acts were to turn against white liberals in an attempt to build up their own self-confidence. To build among blacks a feeling of "we're on our own". I condemned this very strongly. I said this was racism of its own kind, an inverted racism, and for several years I wrote very strong editorials against the black consciousness movement and against SASO and, of course, by inference against Steve Biko. He was banned. I'd never met him. Several people who knew us both kept saying, "You two should meet." And eventually I did go to meet him, grew to be very friendly with him and impressed by him. I still don't fully accept all his views, but I'm impressed by most of them. He's actually a great man in many ways. If he is not murdered or doesn't die in the next couple of decades, I think he will certainly lead this country.'

On the subject of South Africa's future, Donald predicted that the government would deal increasingly harshly with political dissenters, both black and white. 'I then see further rights, maybe isolated rights, taken away', he said. 'I see increased activity on our borders through insurgency. I see increased resentment in the Western world against us and I see all these pressures building up to a massive confrontation which the government will not be able to win. I think they will initially fight it. I don't see them bending from these pressures. They will fight and then I think they will crack.

'I think the future government in this country is almost certainly going to be run by today's young blacks who have pretty radical ideas on redistribution of wealth and a sort of Third World view. This is my opinion right now.

'I hope this future government will not be extremist. The chances are it will be. The chances are that feelings of vengeance will have gone so far that the whole situation will be pretty impossible — certainly for whites. But I'm a perpetual optimist. I keep seeing in all these situations a potential for moderating influences and for compromise — not on basic principles, but on methods for handling human relations.

'I think it is nonsense that the Afrikaner can't be beaten. If we're talking on military terms, it's never been tested. Secondly, I don't think the conflict is going to be basically a military one. I dread the coming of a sort of IRA urban terrorism and conventional military tactics have no effect on this sort of thing.

'I think the present situation will go on for about four years, but then, that's a guess. You'll find very few South Africans prepared to mention numbers of years because over the last few decades, Africa generally and South Africa particularly, has proved to be an impossible sort of place in which to make predictions. We've got a habit of upsetting predictions, of drawing out time scales, concertina-ing them. Well, I stick out my neck and say four years.'

I asked Donald if he had fears for his safety.

'I don't have a sense of grave and immediate danger,' he replied, 'but if I really stop to think about it, I do have fears for my safety. I've received literally hundreds of threats and I think many of them were intended seriously. Only twice has anything happened, anything overt, like something being thrown at the house or fired at it. On two occasions I've experienced some physical threat, like at least being beaten up if not killed. I don't think I'm under any special threat from day to day. I think occasionally when things are very sensitive, like after the assassination of Dr Verwoerd, one is in danger from the crank elements who might think they are doing the country a favour by bumping one off. And the truth of it is that many opponents of this country have actually died in circumstances which are highly suspicious.' Donald believes threats on his life have come from whites who are supporters of the government, 'especially the nutty fringes'.

But for several reasons, he had not considered leaving South Africa. 'First,' he said, 'I feel peculiarly equipped to function in this country — whether successfully or not is beside the point. Secondly, I feel a genuine attachment to it and the people, all the people. Thirdly, I just like the climate and the sport. I like the vibes, apart from the political ones. Lastly, although I've enjoyed visiting other countries, I've never had the deep feeling that I could become a citizen.

'But when I talk of not leaving the country, I do think I have a cut-off point here. That is if by the time my eldest son reaches military age where he's got to go into the army, if this situation is not resolved by then, if the alternative to my leaving is my son having to fight to uphold apartheid, then I would leave. This means they'd better sort it out in five years or else. What I'm saying is rather than bring my kids up to be soldiers for apartheid, I would have to leave until it was over. But', he added, 'I would certainly not give up involvement in the struggle that is going on here.'

Of his own personal hopes and ambitions, Donald said, 'I'd really like to have more time to concentrate on music which I'm very interested in. I'd like to do more leisurely writing and I'd like to travel more, but there isn't a great chance of any of these things happening. I'd also like more leisure to play things like golf and tennis.

'I think beyond anything else, my own personal goal would be to try to reconcile the races in this country — to use whatever talents I've been given, both for the languages of this country and dealing with people, to bring about reconciliation and a more sane society.'

Extracts from 'Daily Dispatch' reports between 23 and 30 August 1977

KING WILLIAM'S TOWN — The arrest and detention of Mr Steve Biko and Mr Peter Jones was confirmed yesterday. The head of the Security Police in Port Elizabeth, Col. Goosen, refused to give details ...

The two men were arrested in Grahamstown...

23 August 1977

JOHANNESBURG — Police broke up a Black People's Convention meeting in Soweto and detained 25 people ... They were held four hours while particulars including names and addresses were taken down ...

24 August 1977

EAST LONDON — Special Branch detectives detained four students here in early morning raids ... Their parents said they had been told they were being held under the Internal Security Act ...

25 August 1977

CAPE TOWN — 'As small as she is, South Africa will say: "So far and no further — do your damndest" — if the world did not stop discriminating against her', Prime Minister John Vorster warned last night ...

The warning was greeted by a rousing, standing ovation by the more than 2,000 people who attended the public meeting ...

25 August 1977

EAST LONDON — Six people were detained in Special Branch swoops yesterday, including the wife of Terrorism detainee, Mapetla Mohapi, who died in detention ...

Arrests were made by the head of the Special Branch in King, Major Hansen ... Mrs Mohapi is being held under the Terrorism Act ...

26 August 1977

EAST LONDON — Police arrested 42 students in Mdantsane yesterday as they moved to break up a meeting of 600 students ...

30 August 1977

On 27 August 1977, Fraser got a two-paragraph letter from the Department of Immigration stating that its selection board was 'not prepared to authorize the issue of a permit for permanent residence in your case. The Board is an autonomous statutory body which does not have to give reasons for its decisions.'

A covering letter said he must be out of the country by 7 September 1977. Intermediaries obtained a delay until the end of September on the basis that a booking had been made — up to the time of the letter, tentative, but then confirmed — on a ship leaving South Africa in the third week in September. Clay had flown home a few weeks earlier.

'We will stand singlehanded against the rest of the world'

One of the roads in Vincent ends abruptly at the top of a bluff running parallel to the sea. A single house is on the right. The view is one of the best in a city which, because of hills and sea, has a thousand prime vantage points. You can from there see green, rounded hills, their outlines softened by tree tops, their bases lost in deep narrow valleys that will eventually open on to sandy beaches. Red tile roofs poke up from green hillsides and the Nahoon River is an occasional glint of silver. At the horizon a cloud bank hangs above the Mozambique current where ships travel.

But none of this can be seen from the house — actually estate would be a better word — because it is surrounded by a concrete wall, eight or ten feet high. Even from the upper stories the view would be hidden since the area around the house is heavily forested. I waited at the end of the driveway for someone to open the gates. Through the wrought iron scrollwork, I saw a formal Roman-style swimming pool, a fountain, gardens and lawns.

Dr H.A. Veen lives there. He is a dental surgeon and it was his name Dominee Loubser printed on a slip of paper many weeks before. It was he who came down the walk to take away two barking dogs and then open the gate.

We went into the library. He asked why I wanted to see him. I explained about the book, that the Dominee had said he had interesting theories about South Africa and its future. Dr Veen considered this, then wanted assurance that what he said would not be used in the *Dispatch*. He sat in a straight-backed chair, a tall, thin, austere man. His speech was guttural, heavily accented with Afrikaans.

'We feel', he said, 'that South Africa is going to play a most important part in the world's history. In the past people didn't realize the importance of South Africa because they couldn't place it according to the Old Testament. But now, we've found two chapters that strongly indicate we will play a very important part beyond the rivers of Ethiopia. Certain prophecies were made about this. Also that our name would go low in history, but eventually would be high in history.'

He explained these things were not known to the rest of the world because their religions had failed properly to interpret the Bible:

'The whole of the Old Testament is on how to bring order to this world — "Thy will be done on earth as it is in Heaven." The Bible gives us, in the third chapter of Genesis, the three big personalities', he said. 'It speaks about the woman and the man and the seed of the serpent. Once you understand, then you realize that the seed of the serpent has to deal with the Satanic side and there's a conspiracy between descendants of the woman and the serpent.'

It was difficult to follow him and the more he talked, the less he allowed interruptions for questions. Later, back home, I listened again and again to the tape. What Dr Veen believed was that the descendants of Adam were God's chosen people — the lost tribe of Israel — and these were the whites who live in Southern Africa 'beyond the rivers of Ethiopia'. White people who populate the rest of the world are descendants of Eve, blacks descendants of the serpent.

'There are several cycles that finish in this decade', he said. 'It would seem now, the way things are shaping south of the Zambezi — that would be Rhodesia and South Africa — the forces that want to overthrow us are coming up fine and on the very date the Bible says. The threat is that the rest of the world will try to destroy the people of Israel and we will be in such a precarious position that the Day of Judgement will coincide with this. Because if God does not intercede, we would be wiped off the face of the earth.'

Dr Veen paused to search for a particular passage and I asked how he came to understand the Bible in the way that he did.

'In 1935,' he replied, 'I went overseas to study at Edinburgh University. On the ship going over, I met up with an educated person and he said, "Now, how long are you going to be overseas?" I said, "About five years." He said, "Well, you may be able to make it. As near as I can make out, a second world war will start about 1940."

'You know,' Dr Veen continued, 'people say things like that and you forget about it. But somehow that stuck in my mind — this chap was educated. I've always had an inquiring mind and it interested me how he could work it out. I knew one thing and that was he did it from the Bible. So I said to myself, "How could someone knowing the Bible come so close?" And I started studying. And it's all there, but it's like putting a jigsaw puzzle together.'

He returned to the future of his country: 'The heat', he said, 'is going to be put on Southern Africa very soon. And we will then stand singlehanded against the rest of the world until divine intervention takes place and we are saved. It will be a battle of white against non-white. The battle will spread and then we will become aware of our ancestory and know who we are and the rest of the world will know us too.'

'Well, that is a dream of the future'

Six of us sat around our table after dinner. It was a kind of good-bye party. Patricia Powrie had a story to tell. Patricia always picks up hitchhikers on her way to and from the Hogsback and East London because, she says, it makes the trip seem less long, but this time, the dirt road down the mountain had been deserted. 'Well,' she said, 'I didn't see anyone until I got to Fort Hare. I stopped at the stop street in Alice and it is just around that corner that I normally pick up passengers. There are nurses or lecturers or Fort Hare students trying to get home for the weekend. They're a good type on that corner.

'On this occasion I saw this group of men. No women there. And there was a lot of luggage and I thought, "Oh, my godfathers, I can't give them all a lift." But they came round to the side of the car and they said, "Where are you going?" And I said, "To East London." And they said, "We're not going that far, but we are going to about a mile beyond Middledrift." And I said, "Well, all right, I'll take you there."

'Then I looked and saw there were four of them and, you know, my car is very small. They had record players, gramophones and big plastic bags and what looked like a big walking stick poking out of one of these big bags. I said, "You'd better be careful about that. You might poke your friend in the head." He said, "No, I'll be very careful."

'They got in the car, three in the back — I normally take two — and one in the front. They said, "Can't we put our things in the back?" I said, "I've got a whole lot of my own things there and I wouldn't like them to be squashed. I'm sorry, but you'll have to put your luggage on your lap."

'As I looked in the rear-view mirror, I could see one man, his suitcase was up to his chin, but he was perfectly happy. Then, the man next to me, well he was smooth. I don't say he was smooth in the wrong sense of the word, but I mean he was easy to talk to. I said, "Couldn't you take something at your feet?" He said, "No, they'll manage it at the back."

'I said, "Well, see you don't get a crack in the neck." He said, "No, that'll be all right." He had a big parcel on his lap and off we went. I thought, "My poor little car. Those tyres ..." But actually it helped the car to hold the road because it was very windy.

'They had come up from East London to visit their family in what they call the Amatola Basin. They pointed to a range of mountains in the distance. "Do you see those two mountains in the middle? That is where we live."

'Then they said, "You know, this is our lucky day." And I said, "Well, how is it your lucky day?"

'They said, "We got a lift from Amatola Basin in a police van. And when they brought us to Alice, they didn't charge us anything. So that was our first bit of luck. Then we're waiting at Fort Hare and you come along. That's our second piece of luck."

'I said, "I'm very glad I came just then."

'As we were driving along, I said, "You know, I'm not a very good driver, but I'll get you there." And they all laughed. And this one chap said, "All old people drive well."

'I said, "Not all old people. Some of them are very fierce." He said, "Yes, but it is their children who bugger up the cars. The old people look after them."

'Then he said, "I'd like to buy this car." I said, "Well, I'm not really thinking of selling it yet." He said, "When it's buggered up, will you let me know? Will it be about June?" I said, "I can't say. It's still perfectly good."

'We drove on a little way and he said, "You know, I've been talking to these men in the back. I know you can't understand, but what we've been saying is that it is not often that a white woman stops and gives four black men a lift. Will you give me your full name and address?" I said, "Whatever for?" He said, "Well, I'd like to write a letter to the *Daily Dispatch* and tell them." I said, "No, please don't. You've said it."

'Later this man next to me said, "You know, things are getting better." I said, "Do you mean we're becoming more multiracial?" He said, "Yes, I think so." He said he thought prejudices were disappearing slightly. He said, "I don't see why we can't all live together because those who don't want to mix, needn't mix, but those who want to come together will come together." And I said, "Well, that is a dream of the future and I hope it is realized." And then their turning came and I stopped and they walked on up their road and I drove on to East London.'

'I have to go away'

A week before we were to leave, Fraser and I sat and ate breakfast by the kitchen window. In the back yard, Elsie, our once-a-week 'weed lady', dug in the dirt under the avocado tree. The labrador pup tossed around a dried frond from the banana tree by the fence. Tryfyna, our three-times-a-week servant, would show up about 8.15.

I checked my list. Fraser and I didn't talk much. I didn't know what he was feeling, but I was tired and depressed. Fraser said he would wait for Tryfyna who would be on the 8 o'clock train from Mdantsane.

'OK then, see you at the office.'

I walked under drooping narrow leaves and red bristles of the bottle brush tree and out the gate. Around the corner, a lizard darted across the dirt path and disappeared under weeds. Across the road from our garden, a man mortared bricks around the flower beds in front of Jannie and Cecily's house. Sun glinted off the leaded panes in the bay window next to the drive. Further along, the Belonskys' old dog sniffed around the base of a kaffirboom tree, pushing shrivelled orange blossoms out of the way with his nose. New green shoots showed along the tree's umbrella rib branches. The kaffirbooms had been in full bloom when we arrived in South Africa a little over a year before.

'Go home, Patches', I said.

A few blocks on, a black woman stopped in front of me.

'I want odd jobs', she said. She was old and wore no shoes. 'Do you know of anyone who needs a garden girl?'

'No, I'm sorry.'

She smiled. 'That's all right.'

When I turned on to the main street, I could see the sea beyond signs and buildings in the distance. There was no wind yet and the sky was blue and cloudless.

At the museum, the curator unlocked the double front doors, then came down the walk.

'When do you go?' he asked.

'Next week', I said.

'Will you be sorry?'

'Yes.'

'Perhaps you'll come back', he said.

Johnson and his dogs went past and I caught up with them at the corner. The people Johnson works for have three generations of Scotties and Johnson has walked them all. An hour and a half in the morning. An hour and a half late in the afternoon.

'I probably won't see you again', I said. 'I have to go away.'

'You'll come back', he said. 'You'll see, it won't be long.' Other times when I had left, I felt I would return. This time I didn't believe I would.

As I got closer to downtown, I wondered if there would be anything seen or sensed to suggest that day was different. At the Southernwood station, a train pulled by a steam engine agleam with polished brass, started up, blasting a cloud of white around people crossing the overpass, then chuffed slowly away.

At the corner a bicycle leaned against a tree. In the cardboard box tied to the handlebars were morning papers. The man alongside waited for a nod from one of the cars. A rusty metal frame, propped up by the wheel, held the day's poster. Blue letters on white: 'Death of Steve Biko.'

I had known since the day before. Leaving the shipping office, I'd met a reporter. He told me. First word to the paper had been phoned in from the Biko family in King William's Town. Bits and pieces came later by telex. Surprisingly, no one in the office talked much about it. Beyond the fact of Steve's death — someone we all believed to be indestructible — what could be said? Sometime in the afternoon, the Minister of Justice, Jimmy Kruger, confirmed the death.

As I walked that next morning, the day when the paper carried the news, I saw the front page of the *Daily Dispatch* through the window of a parked car. The driver held it open to read the classified pages.

'People won't really care that Biko is dead. Not the men on the street', Fraser had said. 'They're used to deaths in prison. Until that happens to whites, they're not going to get excited.'

After work the day before we'd gone by the Belonsky house, had a drink with Bernie and stayed on for dinner with him and the kids.

Ruth was in Durban for a conference on black housing. We talked about Steve's death. What was happening in the country. What might happen.

'I'm convinced now', said Bernie. 'I must get my family out as soon as I can.' He said he had great concern for the safety of Donald Woods.

About 11 p.m., Fraser and I had gathered our things, then stood awhile longer on the porch with Bernie. Rain had come during the early evening, and water dripped from vines on the lattice overhead.

'There must be other places in the world where if you get together of an evening, you'd talk of something besides bloody politics', Bernie said. 'I sometimes dream of having conversations about music or golf or art. Think that maybe I'd talk a little about architecture. Here, whatever we begin talking about, it always turns into politics ...'

The following morning two men on the corner by the bank talked quietly, their faces serious. 'This is too much', I heard one say. Was it Biko's death they talked about?'

On the editorial floor, that morning's paper had already been added to the open binders on the counter in the back near my office. That day's issue didn't really look like a newspaper because the entire top of the page was a drawing, in colour, by the staff cartoonist. It was of Biko's face and above that was the headline: 'Biko dies in detention.'

The bottom half of the page was filled with an account of the known facts: 'Security Police yesterday informed Mrs A.N. Biko that her 30-year-old son Steve, leader of the Black Peoples' Convention and the black consciousness movement of South Africa had died in detention ...

'Yesterday afternoon the Minister of Justice, Mr J.T. Kruger, issued the following statement: "Mr Bantu Stephen Biko, previously attached to SASO and the BPC, had been restricted to the magisterial district of King William's Town.

"Mr Biko and a Coloured man [Peter Jones, BPC chairman] were arrested at a road block near Grahamstown on August 11 after information had been received that Mr Biko was travelling between Cape Town and King William's Town.

"He was arrested in connection with activities related to the riots in Port Elizabeth, *inter alia* for the drafting and distribution of pamphlets which incited arson and violence.

"He was detained in Walmer Police Station in Port Elizabeth. Since September 5, Mr Biko refused his meals and threatened a hunger strike, but he was, however, regularly supplied with meals and water which he refused to partake of.

"The district surgeon was called in on September 7, after Mr Biko appeared to be unwell. The doctor certified that he could not find anything wrong with him.

"On September 8, the police arranged that Mr Biko be examined again by the district surgeon as well as the chief district surgeon and, because they could diagnose no physical problem, they recommended that Mr Biko be sent to the prison hospital for intensive examination.

"A specialist examined him on the same day. On September 9, Mr Biko was examined again by a doctor who kept him for observation. On September 11, Mr Biko was removed from the prison hospital to Walmer Police Station on the recommendation of the district surgeon.

"By Sunday Mr Biko had still not eaten and appeared to be unwell. After consultation with the district surgeon it was decided to transfer him to Pretoria. He was taken to Pretoria the same night.

"On September 12, Mr Biko was again examined and medically treated by the district surgeon in Pretoria. He died the same night ..." '

In the week that followed, news of Biko — the man, his family, the circumstances of his death and official reaction to it from inside and outside the country — dominated the news pages of the *Daily Dispatch*.

Anonymous letters arrived. One of them included a copy of the Wednesday portrait of Biko. A hammer and sickle had been inked in on the forehead. Others said, 'Good riddance' and, 'We're going to get you next, Mr Communist Editor.' Many people didn't bother writing. They just picked up their phones and dialed the *Dispatch*, spouting abuse and threats to whoever picked up the phone.

I met Donald outside his office. He said that although he was used to anonymous threats, the letters and calls now arriving seemed to have more purpose.

On day the *Dispatch* printed a call for a judicial inquiry into the death alongside the Minister of Justice's statement at the Transvaal National Party Congress in Pretoria. 'I am not glad and I am not sorry about Mr Biko', said Mr Kruger. 'He leaves me cold. I can say nothing to you. I shall also be sorry if I die. (Laughter.)'

The BPC issued a statement: 'Mr Biko and other black political martyrs have not died in vain ... we vow to continue from where they were forced to leave off and carry the struggle to its logical conclusion ...' More BPC members were detained. Mr Kruger announced Biko had been fed intravenously before he died.

In the little town of Alice, police arrested 1,200 students at the University of Fort Hare during a memorial service on campus and charged them with contravening the Riotous Assemblies Act.

Donald Woods flew to Cape Town where he talked to a gathering of 1,000 white students at the University of Cape Town. 'This is the big one', he told them. 'The one they cannot get away with. The one they cannot explain away.' Donald's wife, Wendy, drove to Grahamstown and talked of Biko at a memorial service held by students and staff at Rhodes University.

I worked Saturday morning and Gordon Qumza came in looking harried. His brother and sister-in-law had driven up from Port Elizabeth to try to locate their son, who was among those arrested at Fort Hare earlier in the week.

'They've put the students in jails all over the country', Gordon said. 'We finally traced my nephew to Fort Glamorgan. But when we went there, they would not let us see him. They finally said they would let me in, but to tell you the truth, I was frightened. If I went in, perhaps they would not let me out. Once you've been in prison, they do not forget you.'

Mr Kruger said over national television that he had never suggested at any state that Mr Biko had starved himself to death.

Donald got back to East London on Friday. We saw him and Wendy at the Omonds on Saturday night. Donald had driven to King William's Town earlier in the day. Steve's body had been returned to King for burial. Security police had taken him to a mortuary designated by the state, but BPC members had moved the body to another mortuary. A reporter from the *Dispatch* had taken pictures of the body and these showed a massive swelling across the forehead. Donald wanted to see for himself. 'It was funny', he said. 'When I got ready to leave my house it occurred to me it probably wasn't wise to go anyplace by myself anymore. It's the first time I've ever thought that.' He called Jan van Gend who drove to King with him.

Roger asked about the condition of Biko's body.

Donald explained the size and area of the swelling then said, 'It was such a strange experience. I went in. There was no one there to stop me, no guards at the door. When I said I wanted to see Steve, an attendant took me into a room that had metal boxes in it. They were like filing cabinets. He went over to one of these and pulled it out, as you would a drawer, except it was a body covered with a sheet.

'He asked me if I wanted him to take off the sheet and I said yes. When he pulled the sheet back, I felt as if I were looking at a stranger. What kept it from being unbearable was that it didn't look anything like Steve. It was the face of a man who had been murdered, a man I didn't know. The eyes were wide open and the lips pulled back over the teeth in a grotesque grimace. I didn't want to look, but on the other hand I knew I had to. That it was important to observe him clinically so that I could describe the differences in him at the inquest.'

The first suggestions of brain injuries were reported a week after Biko's death and were quoted in the South African press from US television news sources.

Early the next week Donald flew to Durban to address a meeting there and in East London, members of the Black Sash organized an all-day vigil at the Methodist Church downtown. I was asked to take an hour of the day.

I got to the church a few minutes before 12. 'Do I relieve you?' I asked a woman holding a plain green wreath outside the door of the church. 'I believe you're inside', she replied.

I went into the church. A woman sat by herself along one of the aisle pews. She held a lighted candle. We talked for a moment, she gave me the candle and left. There was organ music and I could see the grey head of the organist bobbing up and down behind the wood panels across an arched nave. An old woman, thin and stooped, paddled through a door at the side and climbed steps near the organ. She disappeared somewhere back there, popping her head out from time to time to peer at me.

As the hour went on, people started filing in. A noon service called 'Prayers for South Africa' was also scheduled but unrelated to the Black Sash vigil. Pews in front gradually filled with white-haired women who whispered to each other. Out of the corner of my eye, I could see whites and a few blacks taking seats towards the back. I dabbed at wax dripping on my leg and waited for the woman who was to replace me.

The organist began in earnest and after that the minister took his place at the front of the church.

'May I sit next to you?' I looked up at a small, neat man in a grey suit and then slid along the seat to make room for him. He sat close to me. 'I am a member of the church council,' he whispered, 'and I must ask that you blow out that candle'.

I was astonished. 'Why?'

'The council did not approve the burning of candles. We told the Black Sash it could use the church providing there were no candles.'

I was too surprised to reply.

'I must insist you blow out that candle', he said.

'We will begin with Hymn 884', announced the minister.

'You must extinguish that candle', the man next to me said. People were turning their heads to look at us. I blew out the flame.

'Would you like to share my hymnbook?' the man asked.

I shook my head.

When the hymn ended, the minister began: 'Let us bow our heads in prayer for this country and its leaders ...'

Epilogue

In the months since these interviews, I have followed as closely as possible — and of course, at a great distance — developments in South Africa.

These began almost as soon as we left the ship with 'Black Wednesday'. On 19 October 1977, the South African Government banned 18 organizations, three publications and six whites. At the same time, dozens of blacks were detained, without trial, under the Internal Security Act.

In the months following, one by one, the scandals that have become known as 'Muldergate' unfolded, revealing misuse of public funds accompanied by cover-ups at the highest levels of government. When the smoke had cleared, four of the country's most powerful leaders were in disgrace. Gone now is Cabinet Minister Dr C.P. Mulder who lent his name to the whole affair. Former Prime Minister B.J. Vorster resigned the premiership allegedly for health reasons, became State President (a largely ceremonial post) and then left that position, apparently at the insistence of his successor as Prime Minister, P.W. Botha. General Hendrik van den Bergh, head of BOSS, is in retirement. J.T. Kruger, who as Minister of Justice signed the 19 October banning and detention orders, was kicked upstairs to become President of the Senate.

After 'Muldergate' the news from South Africa was quite different. There were signs of a less rigid leadership, reports that apartheid was being relaxed by a Nationalist Government under Prime Minister P.W. Botha.

Henceforth, he said, blacks would have trade-union rights; more white land would be incorporated into the black homelands. Multiracial sport was being encouraged, more restaurants had been opened to all races. The Prime Minister even indicated that the Immorality and Mixed Marriages Acts, those foundations of apartheid, would be 'reviewed'.

Though the Western world may have applauded his words, not all of his white countrymen did. By-elections in 1979 showed the ranks of those voting for the extreme right-wing Herstigte Nasionale Party swollen by fiercely loyal whites who believe that not only their prosperity but their very survival depends upon apartheid.

And what, in fact, has really changed? For instance, what of unions for black workers? By the end of 1979 black unions were still unregistered, a condition that gives them no legal protection against employers and makes it difficult to collect dues. White lands given to the Bantustans have increased these areas by only 1 per cent — giving the black homelands 14 per cent of a country where blacks outnumber whites by seven to one.

It appears possible that the Immorality Act and the laws prohibiting mixed marriage may be scrapped. Further desegregation of hotels and restuarants, particularly in the highly visible urban areas, can be expected. Probably sport will be more open than in the past though this will have built-in deterrents since toilets as well as bars of sport clubs will probably continue to be available only to whites and the sociability that accompanies sports is important to South Africans.

What effect will all of this have on the basic structure of apartheid? Virtually none. There are the public statements by Prime Minister Botha. Cabinet Minister Piet Koornhof made a well-reported trek to Soweto to dine with a black family: the Western world, wishing change, perceives change. But the reality of apartheid persists and as long as it is practised there will never be equality.

Internally there are strong indicators that the future of South Africa will be a troubled one. Blacks continue to press for a share of South Africa though, in the aftermath of the 1976 riots in Soweto, the death of Steve Biko and the Black Wednesday bannings and detentions, they have regrouped.

The black consciousness movement is surfacing again under a different name. Its leaders espouse the same values and goals as did Steve Biko, focusing on black identity, self-reliance and solidarity and by choice removing themselves from any alliance with whites, even radical whites. There is the Soweto Civic Association which aims at promoting municipal self-help, demanding autonomy in the townships and massive funding through government grants.

Another direction is being taken by Chief Gatsha Buthelezi's Inkatha. Based in Natal, it had, by the end of 1979, enlisted some 280,000 members. Its leaders are purported to be ready to cooperate with existing councils and assemblies to improve the status of blacks. In addition there are the first stirrings of the black labour unions.

In the meantime black nationalist guerillas are gunning down black South African policemen who, they say, represent white rule and who are sell-outs to the black cause. These are the groups 'outside'. The alternative direction for blacks is seen in the homeland governments, the community councils and management committees — work within the white system.

In South Africa, the question of which group, black or white, will ultimately hold power, and by what means, is the final irreducible issue.

The most authoritative source on the prospect of voting rights for all South Africans is certainly the Prime Minister. In his public utterances Botha has indicated his government will ease apartheid measures, but in a moment of candour — and spontaneous anger — he told a group of Coloured and Indian leaders, 'One man one vote is out in this country. That is, never.'

This is the news that comes from newspapers, television and magazine articles. Through letters, relayed information and telephone calls comes the more personal information concerning the changes in the lives of the people introduced in the preceding pages.

On 2 December 1977, an inquest verdict — after 14 days of testimony — cleared security police of criminal responsibility in the death of Steve Biko. (An autopsy had attributed Biko's death to extreme brain damage).

In mid-1979, Shun Chetty, lawyer for Biko and for his family at the inquest and for other black dissidents, a South African of Indian descent, fled South Africa to seek political asylum in Great Britain. In July 1979, the South African government paid Biko's family £39,000 and said it considered the inquiry into his death closed.

Two days before the verdict in the Biko inquest, white South Africans had gone to the polls, given Prime Minister John Vorster a landslide victory. The National Party won 134 of the 164 contested house seats. The new official opposition in Parliament, the Progressive Federal Party, won 17 seats.

On 19 October 1977, at Jan Smuts International Airport in Johannesburg, security police served a five-year banning order on Donald Woods as he boarded a plan for the US where he was scheduled to speak at an Anglo-American Institute conference. Two and a half months later, Woods, in disguise, escaped to Lesotho after hitchhiking 300 miles to the border. Wendy and their five children, travelling separately, met him in Maseru. There he told the press, 'The Nationalist Government made it impossible for me to continue to function as a journalist and critic of its policies and I was no longer prepared to remain silent while they continued doing the things they were doing and saying the things they were saying.' Wendy said, 'Donald declared himself unbanned.'

Woods and his family now live in London.

Mary Omond: left South Africa, April 1978, to live in London; now a copy-editor for Penguin Books.

BPC, BCP, SASO: banned since 19 October 1977.

Leslie Xinwa: resigned from the *Daily Dispatch* in 1979; worked for Goodyear Tyres in Uitenhage as a public relations officer, resigned in 1980 because he felt exploited as a black and returned to the *Dispatch* as a senior news reporter.

David and Mary Saunders: their life seems unchanged.

Corder and Suria Tilney: have had an addition to their family, a son, Gordon Dean. Otherwise things are the same.

W/O Hattingh: retired to Alice.

Alan Paton: 'I remember the interview but I'm afraid I cannot remember what I said ... it is highly improbable that my views would have changed fundamentally, but it is on the other hand possible that my predictions about the future would have changed.'

East London Branch of Black Sash: executive committee asked for the resignation of a prominent member after it was proved to their satisfaction that she acted as an informer for the Special Branch.

Kingsley Kingon: 'Family and work are still the same — and I still think the same way.'

Prince Ngxolwana: died late 1977 after an asthma attack.

Trudi Thomas: is training clinical nursing sisters at Mdantsane Hospital under funding by Ciskei Government.

Mr Gozongo: director at Khayalethemba.

C.A. Gouws: left Khayalethemba, 1978, now caretaker at an Afrikaans high school in East London.

Anne Coppinger: her husband emigrated to Canada mid-October 1979; she followed in 1980.

Errol Theron: chairman of Window Theatre.

Roger Omond: emigrated to England, April 1978; foreign subeditor on the *Guardian*, London.

Dominee J.H. Loubser: 'Life is going well, thank you.'

Ruth and Bernie Belonsky: emigrated to the US, June 1979. Living in Los Angeles area. A public swimming pool in the Coloured section of East London was named for her.

Cyril Mjo: still leader of Harmony Set, now sells insurance. His wife has lost her job.

Zola Mjo: four years left to serve on Robben Island.

Peter Mopp: resigned as chairman of the Coloured Management Committee in August 1979. In a statement to the *Daily Dispatch* he said he could no longer allow himself to be part of a system that aided and abetted his perpetual subjugation to a position of authority. 'The mood of the Coloured people is ugly. They are hungry, homeless and desparate and they have been left without an effective voice. I realize the struggle to gain redress is through meaningful dialogue, but this dialogue is only permissible as long as it does not disturb the *status quo* ...'

Dollie Fourie: her husband, Louis, has had heart trouble. They are happy in their new and larger house in the same area. Vera is still with them and 'wouldn't change for anyone'.

Amelia: before they left South Africa, the Belonskys bought her a house in Mdantsane. She is looking for another job.

Clem Green: whereabouts unknown.

Shirley Smith: sold Cove Woods, emigrated to England with four of her five children. David Smith remained in East London, and in late 1979, Shirley and the children returned. Both twins are now in the army.

Thenjiwe Mtinstso: released from prison where she had been detained under the Internal Security Act (Section 10) in December of 1978, fled the country early in 1979 and is now living in Lesotho.

Thami Zani: arrested under the Terrorism Act on 24 August 1977; released early 1979, escaped to Lesotho in spring of 1979.

Peter Jones: released from prison 13 February 1979, immediately served with a five-year banning order under the Internal Security Act. Married a social worker and is living near Cape Town.

Christian Institute: banned 19 October 1977.

Nohle Mohapi: arrested 24 August 1977, released 9 August 1978, redetained on 11 September 1978, then banned.

Captain Schoeman: transferred from East London, Special Branch; now in the CID.

Major Hansen: also transferred and whereabouts unknown.

Ian Kaye-Eddie: living and working (as Director of St John's Ambulance Unit) in Perth, Australia.

Pria: married the doctor in Edinburgh she had been dating and they are living there. Her mother still lives in Cambridge, East London.

Jasper Raats: still principal at Voorpos. 'All as usual.'

Jan and Cecily van Gend: moved to Cape Town, 1979.

Geoff O'Connell: now living permanently in Cape Town where his consulting engineering firm has offices.

John Malcomess: Elected MP for the New Republic Party. Resigned 1980 saying he felt out of step with the party over its refusal to consider future power-sharing with blacks outside the homelands, and also because NRP leaders ceased negotiations with the Progressive Federal Party towards a united opposition. Now MP for the PFP.

William Deacon: defeated 1977 election; Town Clerk in small holiday resort of Bushman's River Mouth south of East London.

Ryno King: defeated in a bid for Parliament; transferred to National Party headquarters in Cape Town; elected 1979 to Cape Provincial Council.

Dr Mamphela Ramphele: banned to Tzaneen, small community in the Northern Transvaal where she has established a clinic for black residents. After Biko's death she bore his son. The child's Xhosa name means 'little plant that will survive'.

Don Card: Mayor of East London.

Dr H.A. Veen: retired to Knysna, December 1978.

Noel and Patricia Powrie: still residents of the Hogsback.

Tryfyna: doing odd jobs.

Gordon Qumza: 'Life goes on the same ...'

A year after our return, Clay joined the US Marine Corps. Fraser works for Hughes Helicopters in Los Angeles and we live in a small beach community nearby.

My own life is quite different. I did not go back to newspapers and it seems unlikely I ever will. As Roger Omond said, news that concerns journalists in the Western world just doesn't seem as important as the gut-level issues of South Africa — though in spite of conscientious reporting, that situation seems as unsolveable as ever.

When I first came back, I often had the feeling that someone was behind me, had slipped into the room when my back was turned, and I locked doors where before I had not. This still happens though not as frequently now.

In my head, I still live a good part of every day in South Africa. Quite irrationally, I wish we had not left and regret and resent the decision to return. We could have tried to appeal the government order against permanent residency for Fraser though East London would probably be very different now that the Omonds, the Woods, the Belonskys and others are gone. We see them all from time to time and it is clear we all are haunted by South Africa — its tragedy as well as its beauty. For me, and I sense for them as well, no other commitment will ever be as compelling.

Since South Africa, life for those of us who have left is not the same. For those who remain, there is a tragic and terrifying sameness.

ANGOLA

ZAMBIA

ZIMBABWE

NAMIBIA
SOUTH WEST AFRICA

MOZAMBIQUE

BOTSWANA

SWAZI-
LAND

JOHANNESBURG

SOUTH AFRICA

LESOTHO

DURBAN

TRANSKEI

KING WILLIAM'S TOWN

GRAHAMSTOWN

EAST LONDON

CAPE TOWN

PORT ELIZABETH

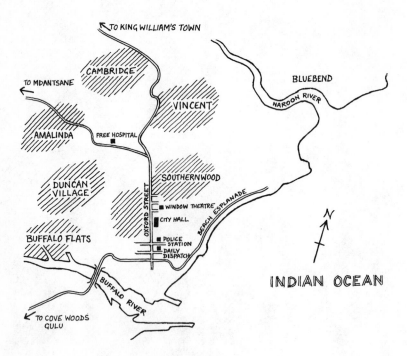

TO KING WILLIAM'S TOWN

CAMBRIDGE

BLUEBEND

TO MDANTSANE

VINCENT

NAROON RIVER

AMALINDA

FREE HOSPITAL

SOUTHERNWOOD

DUNCAN
VILLAGE

BEACH ESPLANADE

OXFORD STREET

WINDOW THEATRE

CITY HALL

N

BUFFALO FLATS

POLICE
STATION

DAILY
DISPATCH

BUFFALO RIVER

INDIAN OCEAN

TO COVE WOODS
GULU